Beginning PostgreSQL on the Cloud

Simplifying Database as a Service on Cloud Platforms

Baji Shaik

Avinash Vallarapu

Apress®

Beginning PostgreSQL on the Cloud

Baji Shaik
Hyderabad, Andhra Pradesh, India

Avinash Vallarapu
Hyderabad, Andhra Pradesh, India

ISBN-13 (pbk): 978-1-4842-3446-4
https://doi.org/10.1007/978-1-4842-3447-1

ISBN-13 (electronic): 978-1-4842-3447-1

Library of Congress Control Number: 2018937882

Managing Director, Apress Media LLC: Welmoed Spahr
Acquisitions Editor: Nikhil Karkal
Development Editor: Matthew Moodie
Coordinating Editor: Divya Modi

Cover designed by eStudioCalamar.

Cover image by Freepik (www.freepik.com)

Distributed to the book trade worldwide by Springer Science+Business Media New York, 233 Spring Street, 6th Floor, New York, NY 10013. Phone 1-800-SPRINGER, fax (201) 348-4505, e-mail orders-ny@springer-sbm.com, or visit www.springeronline.com. Apress Media, LLC is a California LLC and the sole member (owner) is Springer Science + Business Media Finance Inc (SSBM Finance Inc). SSBM Finance Inc is a **Delaware** corporation.

For information on translations, please e-mail rights@apress.com, or visit http://www.apress.com/rights-permissions.

Apress titles may be purchased in bulk for academic, corporate, or promotional use. eBook versions and licenses are also available for most titles. For more information, reference our Print and eBook Bulk Sales web page at http://www.apress.com/bulk-sales.

Any source code or other supplementary material referenced by the author in this book is available to readers on GitHub via the book's product page, located at www.apress.com/978-1-4842-3446-4. For more detailed information, please visit http://www.apress.com/source-code.

Printed on acid-free paper

"Dedicated to our be-loved parents and family"

Table of Contents

About the Authors...xiii

About the Technical Reviewer xv

Acknowledgments...xvii

Introduction xix

Chapter 1: Introduction to Databases in the Cloud...............................1

What Is Database as a Service?...1

    Who Should Use DBaaS?..2

    What Database Platform Does an Organization Need? 3

Features of DBaaS 7

    Provisioning...7

    Administration 9

    Monitoring 10

    High Availability 10

    Scalability...11

    Security 11

Cloud Versus On-Premise Computing 12

    The Pros and Cons of Cloud and On-Premise Computing....................12

Should You Move Your Databases to the Cloud?......................................14

Cloud Vendors Available for PostgreSQL 15

    Amazon...16

    Rackspace 18

    Google Cloud 19

    Microsoft Azure 21

IaaS 23

Migrating to the Cloud 24

    Before Migrating to the Cloud 25

    Planning Your Infrastructure on the Cloud 26

    Tools and Extensions 29

Summary 31

Chapter 2: PostgreSQL Architecture 33

Key Features of PostgreSQL 33

PostgreSQL Architecture 37

Components of Shared Memory 38

    Shared Buffers 39

    WAL Buffers 39

    Temp Buffers 39

    CLOG (Commit LOG) Buffers 39

    Lock Space 39

    Other Memory Areas 40

Utility Processes 40

Directory Structure 42

Installation 44

    Source Installation 44

    Binary Installation 47

    RPM Installation 48

    Installers for Windows and Mac 49

Setting Environment Variables 49

Getting Started with PostgreSQL 50

Configuration Parameters 53

    Connection Settings 54

Security and Authentication Settings 55

Memory Settings 55

Query Planner Settings..56

Write Ahead Log Settings 56

Where to Log 57

When to Log...58

What to Log 59

Background Writer Settings..60

Vacuum Cost Settings..60

Autovacuum Settings...61

Summary...61

Chapter 3: Amazon Cloud **63**

Amazon Cloud or Amazon Web Services...63

AWS Regions and Availability Zones...63

Getting Started with AWS 64

Creating an AWS Account...65

Choosing an AWS Service 68

RDS...68

EC2 79

Summary...105

Chapter 4: Rackspace Cloud...**107**

Managed Hosting 107

Creating a Dedicated Server...111

Creating a Virtual Server 117

Connecting to the Virtual Machine and Installing PostgreSQL 121

Cloud Block Storage..124

Summary...132

Chapter 5: Google Cloud 133

Getting Started with GCP 133

What Is a GCP Project? 133

Project Quota 134

Creating a Project Using the Console 135

Deleting a Project 136

Types of Google Cloud Platforms 137

Compute Engine 137

Google Cloud Storage 151

Cloud SQL 153

Summary 167

Chapter 6: Azure Cloud 169

Virtual Machines 169

Virtual Machine Creation 172

Connecting to Virtual Machines 184

Installing PostgreSQL on a Virtual Machine 185

Dealing with Storage 188

Azure Database for PostgreSQL 189

Advantages of Azure Database 189

Azure Database for PostgreSQL Service Creation 190

Summary 197

Chapter 7: Security on the Cloud 199

Security on Amazon Cloud 199

Identity and Access Management 199

Create a User Using AWS IAM 201

Restricting Access to an RDS or an EC2 Instance 206

Rackspace Cloud Security 212

    Securing the Rackspace Account...212

    Securing the Dedicated Cloud Server of Rackspace 218

Security for the Google Cloud 219

    Control Access to the Compute Engine..220

    Restricting Compute Engine VM Instances......................................226

    Managing SSH Keys 226

Microsoft Azure Security..227

    Security for VM Machines...228

    Security for SQL Database..232

Summary..234

Chapter 8: Backups on the Cloud 235

Backups on the AWS Cloud..235

    Backing Up an RDS Instance 236

    Restore an AWS RDS Instance from Backup 237

    Backup of an EC2 Instance..239

    Performing Backups on an EC2 Instance 243

    Restore Your Backup to an EC2 Instance..244

Backups on Rackspace Cloud..245

Backups to Google Cloud 250

    Backups Using the Snapshot Option 250

    Back Up Your Files Using Storage 254

    Back Up Your Cloud SQL for PostgreSQL 258

Backups to Microsoft Azure 259

    Virtual Machines..260

    Storage 264

    Azure Database for PostgreSQL 269

Summary..269

Chapter 9: Replication and High Availability on the Cloud 271

The Purpose of Replication and High Availability...271

Replication and High Availability in AWS...274

    Read Replicas for RDS...274

    High Availability for EC2...278

Replication and High Availability of Rackspace Cloud 281

Replication and High Availability of Google Cloud Instances 282

    Configure an Instance for High Availability..283

    How Failover Works..285

    Read Replicas...286

Replication and High Availability of Azure Services..288

    Azure Database for PostgreSQL 288

    Virtual Machines..289

Summary...291

Chapter 10: Encryption on the Cloud 293

Encryption for Amazon Cloud Servers 294

    Enable Encryption for an RDS Instance..297

    Encryption on an Amazon EC2 Instance...299

Encryption for Rackspace Cloud Servers...301

Encryption for Google Cloud Instances 303

    Encrypting Cloud Storage...304

    Cloud SQL Encryption 304

Encryption for Azure Cloud Services...305

Summary...308

Chapter 11: Connection Pooling on the Cloud 309

Connection Pooling 309

    What Is Forking?...310

    Understanding Why Process Creation Is Costly 311

    What Is Connection Pooling and How Can It Help?.........................311

PgBouncer...312

    Session Pooling 313

    Transaction Pooling 313

    Statement Pooling 314

    When Should You Think About a PgBouncer?.................................314

    Installing PgBouncer..316

    How Does PgBouncer Work? 327

    High Availability While Using PgBouncer 327

Connection Pooling on AWS 328

Connection Pooling for Rackspace Cloud Servers 330

Connection Pooling for Google Cloud Instances..................................330

Connection Pooling for Azure Cloud Instances 332

Summary...334

Chapter 12: Monitoring Cloud Databases 335

Monitoring with Amazon Cloud 335

    Monitoring an RDS or an EC2 Instance..336

    AWS CloudWatch Dashboard 345

    Create a Customized Dashboard for an EC2 Instance 346

Monitoring for Rackspace Cloud Servers..349

Monitoring Google Cloud Instances 354

    Monitoring Your Project Activities..354

Monitoring VM Instances 357

Monitoring PostgreSQL Instances 358

Monitoring Azure Cloud Instances 361

Virtual Machines...362

Azure Database for PostgreSQL 369

Summary..372

Index...373

About the Authors

Baji Shaik is a database administrator and developer, working as a senior database consultant at OpenSCG, Hyderabad, India. He was introduced to databases in 2011 and over the years, has worked with Oracle, PostgreSQL, and Greenplum. He has a wide range of expertise and experience in SQL/NoSQL databases and has developed many successful database solutions addressing challenging business requirements. He has been working with a database service in Predix cloud from GE, where he continuously supports databases in automation and helps in developing features, fixing and testing defects of the service. Baji has organized a number of PostgreSQL meet-ups and maintains his own technical blog at bajis-postgres.blogspot.in, where he likes to share his knowledge with the community. He co-authored *PostgreSQL Development Essentials,* released in September 2016.

 **Avinash Vallarapu** works as a database architect/trainer for one of PostgreSQL's parent companies—OpenSCG. He has over 11 years of experience in various database technologies such as Oracle, PostgreSQL, MySQL, MariaDB, and MongoDB and is an avid Python developer. He is also an author of pgPulse that enables features like AWR and Snapshotting on PostgreSQL 9.2 and above. He has been a speaker at a number of PostgreSQL conferences and meet-ups and holds expertise in migrations from Oracle to PostgreSQL and cloud deployments of PostgreSQL. He holds vast experience in performing architectural health checks of PostgreSQL and MySQL environments for customers across the globe. Apart from being an expert with databases, Avinash has won several hackathons. His interest toward simplifying complex issues using automation makes him a unique addition to the Open Source community.

About the Technical Reviewer

 **Jobin Augustine** is an industry expert in database systems, with more than 16 years of experience. He has technical expertise in handling the planning, development, and set up of large infrastructure setups and is an expert in consolidation environments. His experience is with a variety of database systems, including PostgreSQL, Oracle, MySQL, PostgreSQL, SQL Server, and MongoDB. He developed award-winning tools and automations ranging from plugins, scripts, and self-service portals for DBAs and developers (DevOps), DBA tools, and more. He is a contributor to various Open Source projects and an advocate of Open Source. Jobin is among the top bloggers in the Postgres community. He also regularly presents at meet-ups and Postgres conferences.

Acknowledgments

From Baji Shaik: I have many people to thank, as without them, this book would not have been possible. Thanks to Apress Media for believing in this book and providing us this opportunity. Thanks to Sanchita Mandal for referring us to this book. Thanks to Avinash Vallarapu for being a wonderful co-author. Thanks to Nikhil Karkal and Divya Modi for working with us and giving us extended time in busy schedules. Thanks to my Guru, Dinesh Kumar. Thanks to Jobin Augustine for reviewing the book. And thanks to my loving parents—Lalu Saheb Shaik and Nasar Bee—because of them, I am who I am today.

From Avinash Vallarapu: A special thanks to Apress Media for believing in me and giving me the great opportunity to write this book. Nikhil Karkal and Divya Modi from Apress have been very helpful in making the process very seamless for the authors. I want to thank Baji for collaborating with me and introducing me as an author. I want to thank my wife Samhitha Garudadri for all her support during the days of writing this book. Thanks to my dad, Srinivas Vallarapu, and mom, Padmavathi, for all the encouragement. The technical discussions I had with my wife and my brother Rajesh Vallarapu helped me a lot while writing this book. Many thanks to my guru, Jobin Augustine, who also reviewed this book.

Introduction

Gone are the days where we had to use our own data centers to create our database infrastructure. We have seen a lot of progress in the cloud computing arena. We can now peacefully deploy our databases or applications on the cloud and avoid the cost and pain of managing the infrastructure. Likewise, most organizations have special projects in place to migrate their proprietary license databases to Open Source databases like PostgreSQL. Most such organizations consider it the right time to migrate to a PostgreSQL database deployed on the cloud, because doing so can save them money and effort. Thus, we knew it was time to write a book that helps users understand the advantages and limitations of all the existing cloud vendors available for deploying PostgreSQL on their platforms.

This book contains the details about the major vendors available to deploy a PostgreSQL database on the cloud. It starts with an introduction to DBaaS and IaaS and a brief description of the criteria considered by organizations when deploying databases as a service. We talk about the major concerns and issues you might come across while deploying databases on the cloud. We included steps and procedures involved in migrating from on-premise to the cloud. As this book is mainly written to address the process of deploying a PostgreSQL database on the cloud, we include a detailed architecture of PostgreSQL in one of the chapters. The architecture of PostgreSQL should help you understand most of the parameters that are needed to better tune your PostgreSQL environment.

The main part of the book is a beginner's guide to deploying
PostgreSQL as a service on Amazon Web Services, Microsoft Azure,
the Google cloud platform, and the Rackspace cloud platform. You will
read an introduction to the services offered by each of these vendors for
PostgreSQL, along with the steps to create your first PostgreSQL instance
in a production environment. This book focuses on helping novice
PostgreSQL users deploy a production PostgreSQL database as a service on
any of these cloud vendors.

The book covers major aspects of this process—such as security, high
availability, encryption, replication, monitoring, and connection pooling.
All these topics are discussed about every cloud vendor, along with the
services each of these vendors offers to satisfy the requirements.

CHAPTER 1

Introduction to Databases in the Cloud

This chapter is an overview of databases as a service (DBaaS) and their benefits. We also talk about the key things to be considered when choosing a service provider, including how to implement it on PostgreSQL using popular cloud vendors. The chapter also discusses the pros and cons of on-premise and cloud databases. We discuss all the cloud vendors available for PostgreSQL and explain how PostgreSQL is different from the other databases in the cloud.

What Is Database as a Service?

DBaaS is a service that delivers a powerful on-demand database platform to provide an efficient way to satisfy all the needs of an organization. DBaaS enables DBAs to deliver database functionality as a service to their customers. This service eliminates the need to deploy, manage, and maintain on-premise hardware and software on a database or on a software stack, in the case of IaaS. It allows businesses to concentrate more on the application without worrying about the complexities of database administration and management.

© Baji Shaik, Avinash Vallarapu 2018
B. Shaik and A. Vallarapu, *Beginning PostgreSQL on the Cloud*,
https://doi.org/10.1007/978-1-4842-3447-1_1

DBaaS can simplify the deployment of your development and testing environments during the software development and testing phases. Maintaining a production environment with a failover mechanism and load balancing adds overhead to any organization. DBaaS can help you meet these requirements through self-service portals that manage load balancing and failover.

DBaaS helps deliver production and non-production database services with an architecture that is designed for elasticity and resource pooling. DBaaS also enables businesses to effectively use their resources for everyday DBA work. By consuming DBaaS, you can easily avoid the costs and possible delays in setting up and maintaining an infrastructure. This enables applications to be deployed to the database with no CapEx for hardware and software, and only OpEx for the database service. Most of the tools and automations are embedded as services by several cloud vendors.

The elasticity of DaaS services helps you avoid investing in capacity and resources in advance. DBaaS enables you upgrade resources and capacity as needed in the future through on-demand and self-provisioning portals. Monitoring solutions are nearly free for managing the logical infrastructure maintained as a service. DBaaS also avoids costs associated with maintaining the infrastructure and training in-house expertise. Having more visibility to the performance and diagnostic data helps you upgrade or downsize the service and thus have rightsized resources. Metrics collected through various solutions by the vendors are helpful in forecasting the business. DBaaS also brings improved availability through several monitoring solutions and high availability solutions implemented by the vendors.

Who Should Use DBaaS?

DBaaS has no limitation on the type of business and the size or volume of the business it can serve well. There are a number of companies using DBaaS that manage several thousands of transactions per second and have terabytes of data. Start-up companies as well as multinational companies use DBaaS as their choice of database platform. DBaaS has been the right choice for numerous small and medium sized businesses.

What Database Platform Does an Organization Need?

Organizations need a platform that achieves the following requirements:

- A secured database
- Fast performance
- Reliable, redundant, and durable
- Geographically distributed and independent
- No single point of failures
- Can be integrated into their existing systems
- Help globally distributed teams and collaborate

Let's discuss these needs in detail.

Secured Database Environment

DBaaS helps protect databases against data theft, confidentiality, integrity, and unauthorized or unintended activity, and misuse by hackers or unauthorized users. DBaaS enables you to configure a database environment that avoids leakage or disclose of personal or confidential data. This is an important aspect in maintaining a secure database.

DBaaS helps administrators create users with limited or the appropriate set of roles and privileges so that no resource is overallocated with more destructive privileges. One of the important aspects of maintaining a secured database environment is encryption. Businesses consider it as a must to encrypt the data in motion and data at rest.

3

DBaaS helps businesses achieve this through various solutions, such as Secure Socket Layer (SSL) communication and encrypted storage volumes. Practical implementation of these features is discussed in the forthcoming chapters.

Fast-Performing Database

How can I make my database perform better? This is one of the concerns raised by businesses while subscribing to DBaaS. Consider the database software—PostgreSQL. PostgreSQL requires several sets of important parameters to be tuned in advance to achieve a fast performing database. Parameters such as `shared_buffers`, `work_mem`, and `autovacuum` settings should be tuned in advance during the provisioning stage.

DBaaS provided by most vendors simplifies this requirement by tuning these settings automatically during the provisioning stage. Vendors use several algorithms based on existing instances and several benchmarks done by experts. This allows administrators or developers to self-provision an instance without worrying about tuning the database parameters. DBaaS vendors allow users to choose a disk that performs better starting from a raw hard disk to SSD and better.

Reliable, Redundant, Durable Database

Database reliability is a serious concern. PostgreSQL, or any database software solution for that matter, is often deployed on hardware. It is the hardware that can cause reliability issues. For example, faulty RAM or a bad hard disk can result in reliability issues, as they can bring down a database or cause performance issues and downtime. Such issues are avoided in an infrastructure by continuous monitoring by DBAs or admins. The only applicable solution in such situations is to purchase new hardware.

DBaaS and deployments on the cloud take care of this issue by eliminating the need to monitor the hardware and avoid the efforts and cost involved in replacing faulty hardware. Vendors provide efficient ways to back up databases, create replication instances, and back up transaction logs for databases deployed on the cloud.

For a production database, one of the important challenges is being able to recover a database to a certain point in time during disasters. Vendors that provide DBaaS take care of this requirement and make it easy for users. It is a UI and requires a few clicks to perform PITR during disasters, which makes it more redundant and durable.

Geographically Distributed and Independent

Gone are the days when infrastructures were designed for vertical scaling. New generation techniques involve horizontal scaling and horizontal computing. What does horizontal scaling mean for database systems? It is all about slicing and dicing data across multiple machines horizontally to scale out.

When your users are distributed across the world globally and the applications are being accessed by users from various locations and countries, you must build infrastructures in several distributed regions. Building such environments is expensive but can be simplified by using the services provided by cloud vendors. DBaaS allows users to deploy their databases across several regions. Most vendors provide the infrastructure on various locations distributed globally. Users or businesses can choose several database services distributed across various regions with ease.

No Single Point of Failures

In the vast topology involved in an infrastructure that consists of a web application or an application connecting to a database, there are lot of infrastructure components that can have single point of failures. For example, a router, a switch, a database server, a hard disk, RAM, or an application server can all cause failures or downtime.

Several cloud vendors enable users to configure environments that prevent single point of failures by providing sufficient redundancy/backup mechanisms. These systems are generally called *high availability features*. DBaaS provides APIs and options on the dashboard that help to configure database high availability.

Integrated into Existing Systems

Cloud vendors make it easy for developers and database admins to integrate their applications or environments into databases deployed using DBaaS. Most cloud vendors provide a way to deploy the DBaaS with no modifications needed on the application environment. Developers can just use the appropriate database drivers, which enable them to talk to the databases and perform their routine tasks. Moving from a database deployed on commodity hardware to a database on the cloud is no longer a tedious task. The options available for migrating and the steps involved in migrating to DBaaS are discussed in further chapters.

Help Distributed Teams Work and Collaborate More Efficiently

Developers, admins, businesses, and testing teams work from various locations across the world. It is important to collaborate with other team members and continue structured and incremental code development. These development and testing teams should be able to deploy their code changes and test cases on development databases and revert to changes at different points in time. Most cloud vendors enable users to create snapshots of their databases. It is easy to create databases using these snapshots. This obviates the time and effort needed to involve a DBA.

Features of DBaaS

There are always feature-related questions about using DBaaS:

- How secured is the service?

- What level of availability does the vendor provide?

- Is it scalable?

DBaaS delivers a powerful on-demand database platform that provides an efficient way to satisfy all the needs of an organization. These features are covered in the following sections.

Provisioning

DBaaS provided by most cloud vendors enables easy provisioning mechanisms to its users like DBAs and developers.

Users are provided with on-demand provisioning and self-service portals or mechanisms that enable user friendly and rapid provisioning. Organizations can spend days provisioning a database server.

Provisioning involves the following:

- Allocating a server with the CPU, memory, and disks requested.

- Installing an operating system.

- Adding hard disks as requested.

- Partitioning the disks.

- Installing database software and any additionally requested software.

- Configuring the database instance.

- Managing host based access control.

- Managing encryption of hard disks.

- Distributing the data directory and the transaction logs to multiple hard disks.

- Creating users with appropriate sets of privileges.

All these stages can be automated using DBaaS.

DBaaS allows users to create a database service with the appropriate number of CPUs, RAM, and hard disks in the first phase. Hardware resources can be limited to each customer and can be upgradable on demand. If the user wants to modify the server capacity to satisfy the growing transactions in the business, it is very easy to upgrade or downgrade the server resources on demand through dashboards.

Self-service portals enable users to create database services on the fly. You cannot choose the underlying operating system of the DBaaS. If you are particular about the operating system, you must choose IaaS.

For example, you get an option to choose your own operating system while building an EC2 instance in Amazon but not an RDS instance.

You would be able to increase the disk space and the type of storage while choosing your DBaaS. Most vendors support on-demand upgrades to storage capacity, which in turn gives you more IOPS. But you may not be able to partition the disks or select physically partitioned disks to balance the IO across multiple disks while using a DBaaS.

While choosing the database type, you can select a supported version of the database software and any extensions that help you look into the diagnostic data or PostgreSQL. Many cloud vendors do provide APIs for automated provisioning/DevOps style of orchestration of DBaaS. They provide APIs for monitoring and managing services. A few cloud vendors also provide dashboards that help you look into the underlying CPU, memory utilizations, disk IO, replication lag, and a lot more for free. DBaaS has a few limitations and thus customers will choose an instance or a virtual server if their requirements are not met.

The following list describes a few of the features that may not be available with DBaaS and could be a great concern while using DBaaS.

- Choosing multiple disks to redirect logs, transaction logs, and data files. Separation of storage volumes is common practice to decrease the IO bottlenecks and improve the performance of the database.

- If you have a concern with the disk IO due to the previous limitation, you may need to purchase more disk space to get more IO.

- Additional storage space, which is not be usable by the database, cannot be used for any other purpose such as storing HTML files or backups.

- You do not get a choice to install most of the Open Source extensions available while using DBaaS. In a way, you are at the mercy of the cloud vendor to provide extensions.

- You cannot create tablespaces while using DBaaS. It is common practice to create tablespaces that span on different storage volumes to improve the performance of a database. You might want to create partitions of frequently accessed transactional tables and redirect them to multiple tablespaces.

Administration

As a user, you may not want to deal with sophisticated platforms that require a lot of knowledge to implement DBaaS or an infrastructure on the cloud. Gone are the days when you implemented a database using numerous manual steps. Users like to view the performance data and the diagnostic data, including the methods to monitor this, in a few clicks.

Every well-known cloud vendor provides several APIs that not only help when provisioning a database environment but also give users several features to enable monitoring and alerting in a few clicks. Vendors provide several dashboards that help users view all the performance data for diagnostics in single page or multi-page views. Most everyday DBA activities include database cloning and database refreshes to enable functional and performance testing. Simplified cloning procedures help users perform database refreshes and cloning and are just a few clicks away. Hence, the time consumed in refreshing a development, testing, QA, and performance environments can be avoided by several APIs and options for refreshing.

Several maintenance operations can be configured automatically without an impact on the application or on the users connected to the database while using DBaaS.

Monitoring

Most of the monitoring tools used with database environments require great effort from the DBAs in terms of setup and configuration. An admin has to build the monitoring server to configure monitoring for all his database environments and manage the monitoring server. If the monitoring server goes down, there is nothing that can continue monitoring a database environment. With DBaaS, you get several monitoring and alerting mechanisms. This saves you time and allows you to build an efficient monitoring system, as most of the monitoring checks are derived from the most frequent customer requests.

High Availability

An important question raised by many users and businesses is whether a DBaaS solution enables options for high availability.

This is one of the important ways to avoid downtime and loss during disasters. DBaaS does indeed provide several high availability features in the case of disasters.

Most customers look for options that provide seamless failovers during disaster recoveries. In fact, it may not be the DBaaS, but the cloud vendors, that allow us to configure load balancers and set up several other features that make a system highly available automatically and seamlessly.

Scalability

The issue of scalability is raised by many customers who build their data warehouses and critical transactions systems on the cloud using DBaaS. The massive growth of data is a very big issue. Several petabytes of data are generated every day. In such a world, where we see several millions of transactions in a few critical transaction systems and several terabytes of data in a few data warehouse environments, scalability is a burning need. This same concern is likely raised for DBaaS. However, cloud vendors who provide DBaaS are well equipped with the features that enable scalability. You can still continue to partition your database tables and perform archiving as usual. We have all the possibilities to incrementally add hardware with new requirements but not anytime earlier and not in a hurry. Most cloud vendors provide load balancers that allow you to distribute your transactions across multiple database services.

Security

The database technology has advanced to the level where access management can be considered at the cluster/instance and server levels, as well as the database level. The user is created inside the database and has to be assigned the required roles and privileges to connect and perform actions on the database. This advanced to the host-based authentication techniques on Open Source databases such as PostgreSQL

11

and MySQL. It has also been advanced to the firewall and network level rules to allow users to connect to a database. Most vendors (like Amazon) enable organizations to design their infrastructure that meet SOX, HIPAA, PCI, and several security compliances. That is the reason behind several financial and secured data driven companies choosing DBaaS.

Cloud vendors allow users to configure firewall policies and encrypt data in motion and data at rest.

Cloud Versus On-Premise Computing

On-premise computing is the type of computing in which all the computing resources are accessed and managed by or from the premises. Overall costs are incurred by the premise that owns it; this translates to diminished returns in the long run.

In cloud computing, the pool of resources is accessed online. It is a usage on-demand service and is perceived as a utility—you pay as you go.

The Pros and Cons of Cloud and On-Premise Computing

Let's look at each approach in turn.

On the Cloud Pros and Cons

- Databases can be deployed on the cloud using two types of services. They are DBaaS and IaaS. While using DBaaS, you have no choice of choosing your operating system, for a few vendors. However, when you subscribe to an IaaS, you can install and configure an OS and tools or the software of your choice on the database server.

- No manpower is needed to manage your hardware. No extra cost is involved to replace hardware faults and no insurance or warranty cost is paid for your hardware.

- It's easy to setup with a quick registration with the cloud vendor for the time and the resources you use. This makes it easily affordable.

- Most of the software updates, especially for the DBaaS, are managed by completely the vendor.

- These may incur security breaches or man in the middle attacks if they're not configured properly. You should be aware of how to secure your database on the cloud.

- There may be a vendor lock-in, as DBaaS are more vendor specific.

- You may be limited to the list of services you can use.

- Any damage or outage at the cloud vendor may make you helpless. You need to wait until the vendor gets a fix.

- Monitoring can be enabled and managed by the cloud vendor for you. You do not have to configure or set up your own monitoring solutions on your infrastructure.

On-Premise Pros and Cons

- You are free to install any software you want. Software licensing costs are managed by you and your team.

- You need to manage your hardware, which may involve additional manpower.

13

- To achieve disaster recovery capabilities, you may have to build the same hardware in a different data center.

- You need to manage your software updates or hardware break fixes, which may involve more time during emergencies.

- You have complete control over your data and have an estimate of time to fix an issue during a disaster.

- You may have to manage your data backups and recovery.

- You have to enable your own monitoring tools and that may involve additional costs.

Should You Move Your Databases to the Cloud?

Should your company move your data and infrastructure to the cloud or keep it on-premises?

Current IT organizations talk about three pain points.

- They need to save on cost.

- They need to improve the developer's productivity in a cost-effective way.

- They need to retain the skillset that they already have.

In the long run, cloud computing is cost effective compared to the on-premises approach. It reduces the overall capital expenditure while maximizing efficiency and productivity. Let's compare the cost models next.

On-premises cost model:

- Initial investment for procurement of hardware and software for a projected/anticipated load.

- Scaling up requires investing more on hardware and other data center infrastructure.

- Hardware refresh and upgrade investments at the end of life.

- Software licenses.

Cloud-based cost model:

- Subscription based (pay what you use).

- No hardware related costs.

- No dedicated software licenses fees.

Cloud Vendors Available for PostgreSQL

There are several vendors in the market who provide database services on the cloud. This book includes descriptions of solutions provided by a carefully selected vendor who are well-known in the market for PostgreSQL on the cloud.

Here is the list of vendors we discuss in future chapters.

- Amazon (Chapter 3)

- Rackspace (Chapter 4)

- Google Cloud (Chapter 5)

- Microsoft Azure (Chapter 6)

We talk about each vendor briefly in the following sections.

Amazon

Amazon Web Services, also known as AWS, is a well-known cloud hosting platform that provides services to several databases.

AWS is growing at a rapid pace. The Amazon public cloud is chosen as the best platform for deploying several applications and databases on the cloud and it is the largest cloud computing platform on the market. Amazon offers thousands of services, which makes means it provides more than 90% of the services of all the other cloud services combined.

AWS is distributed across 16 geographic regions and is expected to grow five more regions in North America, Europe, and Asia. To overcome the major challenges of such an infrastructure, such as reliability and durability, AWS provides 44 availability zones. Customers are allowed to build multiple availability zones and that means customers can build highly available database environments.

Amazon supports two major platforms on which PostgreSQL can be deployed.

- Amazon Relational Database Service (Amazon RDS)

- Amazon Elastic Compute Cloud (Amazon EC2)

Amazon RDS

Amazon RDS is a well-known and widely implemented DBaaS solution for PostgreSQL. This is especially built to make the deployments and setup of PostgreSQL as a DBaaS platform faster and easier. Amazon RDS is one such solution and it allows customers to scale their databases on demand.

PostgreSQL service on Amazon, which is known as Amazon RDS, makes PostgreSQL deployments easy to set up and scale in the cloud. You can deploy PostgreSQL deployments, which are scalable and resizable, cheaply and on-demand. The AWS RDS Console helps administrators and developers operate and manage their cloud platforms with many features.

- Provisioning the database service including software installation

- Seamless software upgrades and patches

- Enable replication or high availability for PostgreSQL with a few clicks

- Cost-efficient and on-demand resizable hardware capacity

- AWS Cloud Watch dashboard that stores the diagnostic data for analysis of the RDS instance

Amazon RDS instances restrict access to the operating system. Once provisioned, a user cannot manage the operating system and is limited to managing their instance through the available options on the dashboard. PostgreSQL does have several extensions that need to be installed or compiled to use them effectively. RDS restricts access to the OS and the limited number of extensions that it supports means fewer options for users.

Amazon EC2

Amazon EC2 instance is the best choice for those users who want to go beyond the limitations of an RDS instance. IOPS in RDS are provisioned and depend on the storage chosen. Users are required to purchase more storage to get more IOPS. Storage purchased additionally cannot be used for any other purpose by the users. However, such limitations can be ignored in the case of an EC2. Customers can use the additional storage to store application-related data or backups. Users have the option to install any extension and software as needed on an EC2 instance. A few of the features that are provided to the users on the console may not be available to the EC2 users.

Amazon Cloud is well-known for satisfying several compliances needed for a secured cloud hosting environment. Most customers get a performance hit while implementing security features such as encryption paying a huge expense. However, customers have a wide number of features they can use to encrypt and secure the data in motion and data at rest with a small or seamless performance hit. Amazon is also known for its network security, which enables users to configure firewalls and inbound/outbound rules for every RDS or EC2 instance. Security and encryption are further discussed in Chapter 3.

Rackspace

Rackspace is a managed cloud computing company that operates their data centers across the globe. As you know, every cloud has to be managed by someone. Rackspace offers services like managed hosts, managed cloud, and application services with fanatical support. It provides public, private, hybrid and multi-cloud solutions under managed cloud services. The platforms that Rackspace supports for these are services are:

- Dedicated servers

- VMware

- Amazon Web Services

- Google Cloud Platform

- Microsoft

- OpenStack

- Pivotal Cloud Foundry

Rackspace offers fully managed dedicated servers and physical firewall configurations. You can look at the detailed dedicated configurations that Rackspace can deploy at https://www.rackspace.com/dedicated-servers.

For the AWS platform, it provides ongoing architecture design, security, migration, and recurring optimization. Rackspace is the first premier managed services partner for Google Cloud Platform and it provides ongoing optimization and fanatical support for GCP.

You can run PostgreSQL on Rackspace in two ways—via the Managed Cloud and via the Private Cloud. More details on Managed Cloud are found at https://www.rackspace.com/cloud and more details on Private Cloud can be found at https://www.rackspace.com/cloud/private.

You can compare pricing details at https://www.rackspace.com/openstack/public/pricing.

Google Cloud

Google, a well-known search engine platform, has come with their innovative thoughts to build a cloud platform that suits databases like PostgreSQL. As with other vendors, Google includes a lot of features especially related to security that are very important to any enterprise. On their cloud platform, Google promises to keep the same security model that has been implemented on its applications like Gmail, Google Search, and other applications. On top of its excellent approach to network security and the default SSL-like policies, Google data centers are physically featured with a layered security model. Google builds its hardware, networking, and the software stack while keeping security in mind.

Google introduced transparent maintenance for Google Compute Engine in December 2013. Since then, most of the software updates, hardware break-fixes, and other issues don't require downtime to the database or applications. This is addressed by one of their innovative features known as *Live Migration*. This features allows Google to address the following issues with no impact to its customers.

- Regular infrastructure maintenance and upgrades

- Network and power grid maintenance in the data centers

- Bricked memory, disk drives, and machines

- Host OS and BIOS upgrades

- Security-related updates, with the need to respond quickly

- System configuration changes, including changing the size of the host root partition, for storage of the host image and packages

If you want to try the Google Cloud, check out the price calculator, which helps you build and understand the cost of spinning up your VM: https://cloud.google.com/products/calculator/.

Google currently has a hard limit of up to 64 vCPUs as a maximum number you can select for your virtual machine. This also includes a CAP of 6.5GB of memory per vCPU. gcloud compute is the command-line tool and it has a lot of options for managing your Google Compute Engines on top of its Compute Engine API.

Google Cloud platform services are currently available in 12 regions and 36 zones in locations across North America, Europe, and Asia.

Here is a list of regions where GCP has a presence.

- Oregon

- Iowa

- N Virginia

- S Carolina

- London

- Belgium

- Frankfurt

- Sao Paulo

- Tokyo

- Taiwan

- Singapore

- Sydney

It is also building new regions in Los Angeles and Montreal.

Every region consists of at least one or more zones. High availability is a major concern for any business. Google allows its customers to build their database infrastructures in multi-zones to allow failovers during disasters. Google provides features such as load balancing for the customers who want to redirect some of their read traffic to disaster recovery sites.

Google provides APIs, command-line tools, and a friendly dashboard to all its customers to manage their virtual machines.

Microsoft Azure

Microsoft, a well-known multinational technology company that is best known for its software products such as Microsoft Office, introduced its cloud platform in October, 2008. It is an emerging cloud platforms that could become a great competitor to AWS. Azure provides a wide range of cloud services related to compute, analytics, storage, and networking.

Azure is scattered across 36 regions around the world, almost equivalent to the number of regions provided by Amazon. Azure also provides DBaaS for PostgreSQL Open Source databases, called Azure

Database for PostgreSQL. Users can create a PostgreSQL database in minutes, just a few clicks away on its self-service portals, which are truly user-friendly.

Azure provides the following features to attract customers with its data security model.

- Multi-factor authentication

- Encryption of data in motion and data at rest

- Support for encryption mechanisms such as SSL/TLS, IPsec, and AES

- Key vault service

- Identity and Access Management

Azure offers 57 compliance offerings to help users comply with their national, regional, and industry-specific requirements governing the collection and use of individual data.

If you want to choose an Azure Cloud but are not sure if your compliance requirement is met, use the following URL to validate.

`https://www.microsoft.com/en-us/trustcenter/compliance/complianceofferings`

Azure allows you to select from 20 cores to 10,000 cores per subscription. You can increase the cores or your quota using the self-service dashboards given by Azure upon subscription.

This pricing calculator helps you calculate the cost of your subscription: `https://azure.microsoft.com/en-us/pricing/calculator/`

Azure Database for PostgreSQL is a fully managed database service that helps users deploy apps with ease. This service has built-in high availability with no additional costs for extra configuration and replication.

Features like Automatic Backup help users achieve point-in-time-recovery up to 35 days. CPUs and IOPS are provisioned for this service upon prediction and subscription.

Microsoft is expected to launch a premium service for Azure Database for PostgreSQL shortly.

IaaS

IaaS is one of the services offered by cloud vendors along with DBaaS. IaaS stands for Infrastructure as a Service. Cloud vendors provide consoles through which users can self-provision and start a virtual machine/server on the cloud. These machines are managed by the vendors and do not require users to perform any hardware fixes or maintenance.

For example, Amazon provides EC2, S3, and several other services that come under IaaS. Google provides Google Compute Engine. Likewise, Microsoft Azure and Rackspace provide virtual machines on the cloud.

Several large and small/medium-sized business organizations build their own infrastructure at several locations. Building multiple locations enables them to improve performance and decrease latency to their globally distributed customers and helps them achieve high availability. If one data center is down, another standby site can take its role.

Consider, for example, an organization that has been globally distributed over 40 locations across the globe. Considering the latency between regions, it is almost impossible to build individual data centers at all the regions. This could be a burning need for all the organizations planning to have their business expanded all across the world.

Cloud vendors consider this fact very seriously. They build their data centers across several regions across the globe. Most cloud vendors expand their services to almost every continent. They have set up high availability zones within every region with several milliseconds of latency.

Large organizations simply subscribe to the service and the vendors manage their infrastructure.

Physical hardware used by vendors to provide IaaS may not be dedicated to an organization, unless requested. You may have to explicitly request a dedicated server for your organization. This way, you let all the cloud virtual machines be hosted on the same physical server. We need to consider the fact that not all cloud vendors take this approach. However, it may not be a burning need for all organizations. You may subscribe to an IaaS that's hosted on a physical server shared by several other organizations. This makes it even cheaper for users to subscribe to an IaaS. To get more customers and revenue, cloud vendors continue to expand their data centers across the globe. This is why we see a notification of a new region being added almost every time we log in to a vendor's website.

We have already discussed the features of DBaaS such as provisioning, monitoring, high availability, scalability, and security. These same features are considered major features of IaaS offered by cloud vendors.

Migrating to the Cloud

In the previous sections, you read an introduction to DBaaS and IaaS on the cloud. We also discussed a few of the vendors that have a great customer base subscribing to their cloud solutions. You have learned in detail about DBaaS and IaaS.

This section explains what is involved in moving to a DBaaS or an IaaS. Consider these situations that could make you think about migrating to the cloud.

- Huge cost involved in maintaining the infrastructure and the disaster recovery sites.

- Huge licensing costs involved in purchasing the software licenses.

- Regular/periodic maintenance and man hours involved in hardware fixes and upgrades.

- Issues with scalability.

- Cost involved in monitoring the infrastructure and achieving more 9s of availability.

- Options to have the instances up when needed and terminate them to avoid cost involved when not needed.

As discussed, migrating to the cloud provides a lot of benefits in terms of cost and availability. Your organization can thus concentrate on improving their business more than managing their infrastructure and tuning it for better performance.

Before Migrating to the Cloud

Let's say you have a PostgreSQL production database cluster hosted at your own data center (on-premise). You might have already thought about high availability while using your PostgreSQL environment and built one or more slaves for high availability. You may have also installed or configured tools that help you achieve automatic failover and seamless application failover at your site.

Most organizations plan to replicate their existing architecture on the cloud and have their architecture design tuned at later stages. A few organizations may plan to redesign their architecture while moving to the cloud, by learning from current issues. For example, you may not have a load balancer in your existing architecture. A load balancer can redirect your application reads (such as reporting queries) to master and slave PostgreSQL instances using a round robin or least connection count algorithm. Likewise, a load balancer can also be used for automatic failover, by letting a failover service calling the load balancer API redirect

25

all the new connections to the promoted slave (the current master that was previously a slave). This is just a basic example.

Cloud vendors offer you several services that enable you to achieve load balancing, high availability, etc. Hence, you may want to redesign your existing environment on-premises by making the most of the services offered on the cloud. Be sure to understand the existing pain points in your database infrastructure design, be aware of the services that could help you overcome the existing issues, and create a test environment using the new architecture design.

Planning Your Infrastructure on the Cloud

Most organizations follow several approaches when migrating their PostgreSQL databases to the cloud. The following approaches are all legitimate, depending on your needs:

1. Subscribe to the same number of CPUs, the same amount of RAM, and the same volume of disks as your existing PostgreSQL database on-premise.

2. Subscribe to bigger hardware needs than your existing environments, as it is a lot cheaper, or with an assumption that the performance can go down on the cloud.

3. Learn from your existing database usage metrics and plan hardware efficiently on the cloud.

4. Along with the point 3, test the performance metrics by generating almost double the peak application traffic on the hardware created on the cloud, as a phase of performance testing. If performance testing does not show fruitful results, upgrade the hardware as needed.

You may follow any of these approaches, but it is always important to fine tune your database server and rightsize it by learning from its usage metrics over time.

After learning from several such migration experiences, here is how I recommend you start your migrations to the cloud. Let's divide this migration into two types.

- Moving from other databases like Oracle to PostgreSQL on the cloud.

- Moving from PostgreSQL on-premises to the cloud.

In this book, we are concentrating on beginning PostgreSQL on the cloud, not migration from other databases to PostgreSQL, which means we only discuss the second point, assuming that we have an existing Postgres database on-premises or on bare metal.

Consider these points before moving to the cloud:

1. Understand the database peak transaction time/hour/minute of the day and peak transaction day of the week and peak week of the month of an year.

2. Take a snapshot of the OS metrics using a tool like sar. The ability to draw a pattern using the history data drives you toward choosing the perfect server specifications for your database on the cloud.

3. Compare the load averages of a certain period and see if the load has been increasing with database growth or over a period of time.

4. Check if the CPU, memory, and IO utilizations are increasing gradually or staying under-utilized even at the peak transaction times.

5. Enable snapshotting tools on the PostgreSQL database and look at the database traffic during the peak utilization times of the server resources.

6. Fix any contention issues caused by the application logic. Identify such locking SQLs or application logic using snapshotting solutions.

7. If the existing database server on-premise has a pattern of increasing server resource utilizations, estimate a server architecture that could accommodate that transaction load for an year. As you know already, you can scale up the resources such as CPU, RAM, or disk space and IOPS.

8. Note if there are any historic tables or tables with lots of historic data not being used by the application. Such data can be safely archived to avoid SQLs scanning the data blocks containing older data. If you find it difficult to archive such data at this point, enable opportunities for partitioning on the DB server being created on the cloud. PostgreSQL allows you to enable partitioning on your tables seamlessly.

9. When you create your database service on the cloud, be sure to create all the extensions that help you deep dive into performance data and tune your database to an optimal level.

10. As discussed, have at least one slave for high availability and use the services such as connection pooler or load balancers to effectively use your slaves for reads or reporting queries. Connection pooling is discussed in Chapter 11.

Tools and Extensions

These tools and extensions can help you rightsize your PostgreSQL server on the cloud. Rightsizing in this chapter refers to choosing the server or DB resources that suit your database traffic efficiently. You may have already deployed your PostgreSQL DB on the cloud, or you may be planning to do so in the future. Let's say that you chose an instance type that you feel is not rightsized. Here are the methods and tools that could help you efficiently rightsize your PostgreSQL on the cloud.

- `sar`: Can be used to snapshot your Linux server resource utilizations.

- `pgPulse`: A snapshotting tool that helps PostgreSQL gather and store its history. Oracle-like databases have a feature that enables you to see the activity in the database at a certain point in time. This helps you be more predictive than reactive while managing PostgreSQL databases. Unlike with other databases, this tool allows you to capture historic information in a remote centralized database. Thus, you can avoid huge write IO on the production database where the data is being collected.

- This tool helps you query the historic data and understand the SQLs that have performed bad, tables/indexes accessed, locks acquired, etc., on the PostgreSQL database at a certain time. See `https:// bitbucket.org/avinash_vallarapu/pgpulse`.

29

- Here's a list of extensions to be created on the
  PostgreSQL database on the cloud:

  a. `pg_stat_statements`: Historic data for SQLs
     that have hit the DB server with their total
     resource utilizations and average execution
     times.

  b. `pg_buffercache`: List of tables in the shared
     buffers (PostgreSQL memory area) along with
     the amount of memory used by them.

  c. `pgstattuples`: Amount of bloat/fragmentation
     in a table.

  d. `pg_repack`: Tool used to perform online table
     maintenance.

Using all these tools, you can look into the following metrics to decide
whether you have rightsized your PostgreSQL database:

- **CPU usage trend:** The percentage of CPU being used
  and the maximum CPU used at any given time.

- **Memory usage:** Amount of memory that is always
  free in the server. If you never have any free memory,
  including the cache, you need to have more RAM
  allocated to your instance. Or there is a culprit in the
  database that could be hanging all the server memory.

- **IO queue depth and IO wait:** This indicates how many
  processes are waiting for IO and the amount of time
  they waited to get IO.

- **Temp usage:** More usage of `temp` indicates that your
  application is badly designed or that your server's
  memory is not at an acceptable size.

To conclude, you need to plan the future scope while deploying a database on the cloud and have all the tools and extensions in place that could enable you to efficiently tune your PostgreSQL instance. Having a rightsized PostgreSQL instance on the cloud is more efficient and cost-effective.

Summary

This chapter covered what database as a service is and who should think about using it. It also covered the perfect business need and explained the differences between on-premise databases and cloud databases. This chapter explained the major cloud vendors for PostgreSQL service in brief, as well as the security features and limitations of each vendor. The next chapter covers the basic architecture of PostgreSQL, including installation, configuration, and limitations. It provides some basic commands to get started with PostgreSQL.

CHAPTER 2

PostgreSQL Architecture

In this chapter, we are going to cover the architecture of PostgreSQL. This includes how it is designed, its limitations, and how to install it. We explain each component in the architecture. We talk about different installation procedures and getting started with commands to work with PostgreSQL. We also talk about the basic parameters.

PostgreSQL is the world's most advanced Open Source database. It is designed for extensibility and customization. It has ANSI/ISO compliant SQL support (strongly conforms to the ANSI-SQL:2008 standard specification). It has been actively developed for more than 25 years. It is well-known for its portability, reliability, scalability, and security.

Key Features of PostgreSQL

It's portable:

- PostgreSQL is written in ANSI C. As we all know, C is a very powerful and widely used language. Despite the prevalence of higher-level languages, C continues to empower the world.

- PostgreSQL is POSIX complaint and supports Windows, Linux, Mac OS/X, and major UNIX platforms.

© Baji Shaik, Avinash Vallarapu 2018
B. Shaik and A. Vallarapu, *Beginning PostgreSQL on the Cloud*,
https://doi.org/10.1007/978-1-4842-3447-1_2

It's reliable:

- PostgreSQL is ACID compliant. So need to worry about the atomicity, consistency, isolation, and durability of your databases.

- PostgreSQL supports transactions. Transactions bundle multiple steps into a single, all-or-nothing, operation. If you see a failed statement in a transaction, that transaction would be rolled back.

- PostgreSQL supports savepoints. You can create savepoints within a transaction and roll back to that point when needed.

- PostgreSQL uses write ahead logging for crash recoveries and point in time recoveries of the databases.

It's scalable:

- PostgreSQL uses multi-version concurrency control, which protects the transactions from viewing inconsistent data.

- PostgreSQL supports table partitioning, which is used to improve the performance of the database in case of large tables.

- PostgreSQL supports tablespaces to store some data into other filesystems to save I/O.

It's secure:

- PostgreSQL employs host-based access control. You can specify the clients allowed for your database.

- PostgreSQL provides object-level permissions, which can secure objects from other users.

- PostgreSQL supports logging for more visibility on the database on what is happening and supports SSL for more security.

It's available:

- PostgreSQL supports replication of data, which is useful for load balancing.

- PostgreSQL supports high availability using streaming replication in disaster scenarios.

It's advanced:

- PostgreSQL supports full text search for searching documents through queries.

- PostgreSQL supports triggers and functions like other databases.

- PostgreSQL supports custom procedural languages such as PL/pgSQL, PL/Perl, PL/TCL, PL/PHP, etc.

- PostgreSQL supports hot-backup and point-in-time recovery and it supports write ahead logging.

- PostgreSQL supports warm standby/hot standby/ streaming replication and logical replication for load balancing and high availability.

PostgreSQL maintains data consistency internally using Multi-Version Concurrency Control (MVCC). While querying a database, each transaction sees a snapshot of data (a database version) as it was some time ago. It prevents transactions from viewing inconsistent data and provides transaction isolation in concurrent transactions. Readers do not block writers and writers do not block readers.

PostgreSQL has a Write Ahead Logging (WAL) mechanism, which does the following:

- Makes a record of each insert/update/delete before it actually takes place.

- System does not consider data safe until the log is written to disk.

- Provides recovery in case of system crash or failure.

- Similar to Oracle REDO logs (no separate undo).

PostgreSQL has some limitations, which are generally defined by operating system limits, compile-time parameters, and data type usage. Here are some of its limitations:

- Maximum database size is unlimited.

- Maximum table size is 32TB.

- Maximum row size is 1.6TB.

- Maximum field size is 1GB.

- Maximum rows per table is unlimited.

- Maximum columns per table is 250 - 1600 depending on the column types.

- Maximum indexes per table is unlimited.

Visit this link for more information: `https://www.postgresql.org/about/`.

The PostgreSQL community keeps adding new features, which are for bigger databases for integrating with other Big Data systems. PostgreSQL is a reasonable choice for big data analytics, because of its development features. For example, PostgreSQL 9.5 includes BRIN indexes, faster sorts, cube/rollup/grouping sets, FDWS, tablesamples, etc. These features ensure that PostgreSQL continues to have a strong role in the rapidly growing Open Source Big Data marketplace.

PostgreSQL Architecture

PostgreSQL utilizes a multi-process architecture, which is where one process is created per session.

It has three types of processes—primary (postmaster), per-connection backend process, and utility (maintenance processes). Each process is explained in detail in the following sections.

A typical PostgreSQL architecture is shown in Figure 2-1.

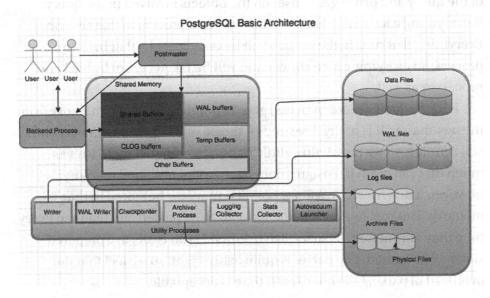

Figure 2-1. *PostgreSQL basic architecture*

When you start PostgreSQL, the postmaster starts first. The postmaster is a supervisory process and its responsibility is to start up and shut down the database, handle connection requests, and spawn other necessary backend processes. When you start the database, the postmaster is started first and it:

1. Allocates the shared memory.

2. Starts the utility processes.

3. Starts semaphores (a semaphore is a label that
    indicates the status of the process).

4. Accepts connections and spins off a backend for
    each new connection.

As soon as the postmaster receives the connection, it creates a backend
process that does an authentication check as part of the parsing process
(checking the query syntactically and symmetrically—which is syntax
of the query and privileges of user on the objects involved in the query).
If everything goes well, it attaches that backend process to that session.
Everything that runs in the session will be taken care by that backend
process. So everything for a connection will be taken care of by backend
processes as well.

Each backend (server process) gets its pointers to shared memory from
the postmaster. It is pretty disastrous if the postmaster dies with backends
still running, so we have it do as little as possible, so that there isn't as
much that can crash it. Postgres does have a pool of shared memory;
however, it does not have a library or dictionary cache stored in that
memory. This means that statements need to be parsed and planned every
time they are entered. If parse/plan overhead is an issue, use prepared
statements instead. The parser is quite lightweight, so we feel that the
overhead of parsing the query each time is acceptable.

Components of Shared Memory

PostgreSQL has shared memory that can be used by all sessions of the
database. Each component of shared memory is explained in the following
sections.

Shared Buffers

The biggest chunk of shared memory is the shared_buffers. When pages from a table or index are read from the OS, they are read into shared_buffers, and the backends reference the pages and their contents right there in the shared memory. An exception are temporary tables, where (since only the creating backend can reference the temp table) data is accessed in the temp_buffer space as much as possible. temp_buffer is separate. It is not in shared memory. It's faster to access process-local memory like that because you don't need to worry about pinning or locking the data, since you are not sharing it.

WAL Buffers

These are for buffering data to be written to the WAL files.

Temp Buffers

These are buffers created from temp tables.

CLOG (Commit LOG) Buffers

PostgreSQL holds the status of each ongoing transaction in buffers, which are called *CLOG buffers*. If there are any crashes or improper shutdowns of the database, these buffers will be used to determine the transaction status during the recovery.

Lock Space

Memory structures in shared memory are generally protected by "lightweight" locks, which are in shared memory. Tables are protected by "heavyweight" locks, which are also in shared memory (and themselves protected by lightweight locks). Of course, lightweight locks are protected by spinlocks.

39

Other Memory Areas

Other buffers are probably mostly SLRU buffers besides CLOG (which was the first user of the SLRU system). SLRU is good for data where you mostly want to use recently accessed data and you are done with it relatively quickly.

The opposite of shared memory is process-local memory—only the one process that allocates it can access it. Each SLRU system has a separate subdirectory. Shared memory is memory that all of the backend server processes can directly access. To prevent chaos, access to shared memory must follow some rules, which tends to make it a little slower, like locking areas of memory a process will be using. Process-local memory is allocated by one backend server process, and the other backend server processes can't see it or use it, so it's faster to access and there are no worries about another process trashing it while you're using it.

Utility Processes

With a default configuration, we can see the postmaster, the checkpointer process, the writer process, the WAL writer process, the autovacuum launcher process, and the stats collector process. You will see more processes running if you turn on archiving or streaming replication. You might also get a process for writing the server log, depending on the configuration. As their names say:

- The WRITER process is responsible for writing the dirty buffers to data files.

- The CHECKPOINTER process is for checkpoint. This process is responsible for creating safe points as a checkpoint record in current WAL from which a recovery can begin; the background writer tries to keep some pages available for re-use so that processes running queries don't need to wait for page writes in order to have free spots to use in shared buffers. Both the checkpointer and writer processes write to the same files; however, the checkpointer writes all data that was dirty as of a certain time (the start of the checkpoint) regardless of how often it was used since the data was dirtied, whereas the background writer writes data that hasn't been used recently, regardless of when it was first dirtied. Neither knows nor cares whether the data being written was committed, rolled back, or is still in progress.

- The WAL WRITER process is for writing the dirty buffers in WAL buffers to WAL files.

- The AUTOVACUUM launcher process launches autovacuum when required (depends on your autovacuum settings in PostgreSQL configuration file).

- The STATS COLLECTOR process collects the statistics of objects in the database required by Optimizer to improve the performance.

- The LOGGING COLLECTOR is responsible for writing database messages into database log files. According to the level set in the configuration file, it writes into log files.

- The ARCHIVER process is responsible for copying files from the pg_xlog location to the archive location.

Directory Structure

All the data needed for a database cluster is stored in the cluster's data directory, commonly referred to as PGDATA. See Figure 2-2.

- Each table/relation/index in PostgreSQL gets a database file that can be extended to 1GB. So file-per-table, file-per-index.

- Each tablespace is a directory under the PGDATA/ pg_tblspc.

- Each database that uses that tablespace gets a subdirectory under PGDATA/pg_tblspc.

- Each relation using that tablespace/database combination gets one or more files, in 1GB chunks.

- Additional files used to hold auxiliary information (free space map, visibility map) look like 12345_fsm, 12345_vm.

- Each file name is a number that's called an Object ID (OID).

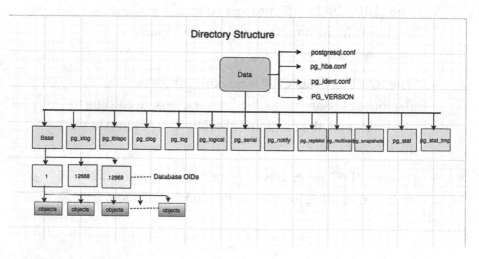

Figure 2-2. *PostgreSQL directory structure*

You can get a detailed description at https://www.postgresql.org/docs/current/static/storage-file-layout.html.

The catalog cache is information from the system tables, which describes the tables, indexes, views, etc. in the database. If you had to re-read that from the system tables each time, it would be slow. Even shared memory would be clumsy for that, so each backend process has its own cache of system catalog data for fast lookup.

When anything changes, all backends are sent a signal to update or reload their cache data. When pages are read or written, they go through the OS cache, which is not directly under PostgreSQL control. The optimizer needs to keep track of a lot of information while it parses and plans a query, which is why that is shown. A plan has execution nodes, some of which may need to use memory. That is where work_mem comes in—a sort or hash table (as examples) will try not to exceed work_mem *for that node*. It is significant that one query might use quite a few nodes, which each allocate memory up to work_mem. But since most queries are simpler and might not use any work_mem allocations, people often do their calculations based on an expected maximum of one allocation per backend (i.e., per connection). But that could be off by quite a bit if all connections are running queries with five nodes allocating memory.

It is worth noting that if there is enough RAM on the machine to have a good-sized OS cache, a PostgreSQL page read will often just be a copy from OS cache to pg shared_buffers, and a page write will often just be a copy from pg shared_buffers to the OS cache. The fsync of tables is the part of the checkpoint process when they are actually written from the OS to the storage system. But even there a server may have a battery-backed RAM cache, so the OS write to storage is often just a copy in RAM. That is, unless there is so much writing that the RAID controller's cache fills, at which point writes suddenly become hundreds of times slower than they were.

Other interesting dynamics are pg will try to minimize disk writes by hanging onto dirty buffers (ones that have logically been updated) before writing them to the OS. But buffers may need to be written so they can be freed so that a new read or write has a buffer to use. If a request to read a page or write to a new buffer can't find an idle page, the query might need to write a buffer dirtied by some other backend before it can do its read (or whatever). The background writer can help with this. It tries to watch how fast new pages are being requested and write dirty pages at a rate that will stay ahead of demand.

Installation

Before you use PostgreSQL you need to install it, of course. You can install PostgreSQL in four ways.

- Source installation
- Binary installation
- RPM installation
- One-click installer

As PostgreSQL is Open Source, the source code is available on the postgresql.org website. We are going to cover each installation in detail in the following sections.

Source Installation

Source installation is nothing but compiling the source code of PostgreSQL. Here are the high-level steps that you should follow to install from source.

The following steps use PostgreSQL version 9.6.2 as the example, but nearly the same steps are applicable to the other versions.

1. Download the PostgreSQL source from here:

    ```
    https://ftp.postgresql.org/pub/source/
    v9.6.2/postgresql-9.6.2.tar.bz2
    ```

2. Unzip the downloaded file:

```
unzip postgresql-9.6.2.tar.bz2
```

3. Go inside the directory created by unzip of Step 2
    and run the configure command as follows:

```
cd postgresql-9.6.2
./configure
```

A simple configure installs in the default location,
which is /usr/local/pgsql. If you want to install
it in a different location, use the prefix option to
configure it.

```
--prefix=/location/to/install/
Configure basically looks at your machine
for dependency libraries necessary for
PostgreSQL. It reports if your machine
is missing any. You can install missing
libraries first and then re-run the
configure command. So basically, it prepares
your machine for installation.
```

4. Once the compilation is done, you can use make and
    make install to complete the installation.

```
make -j 8 && make install
```

-j is for parallel jobs. Define this value based
on your CPU cores, which can be utilized for the
compilation job.

45

5. Once the installation is done, create a data directory where data can be stored. You need to create the postgres user to own that data directory.

Each instance of PostgreSQL is referred to as a "cluster". This means an instance can have multiple databases. Don't get confused with a cluster of server nodes. Each data directory contains all the data and configuration files of one instance. So each instance can be referred to in two ways:

- Location of the data directory

- Port number

A single server can have many installations and you can create multiple clusters using initdb.

Here are the commands that need to be executed to create a user, create data directory, and initialize that data directory:

```
adduser postgres
mkdir /usr/local/pgsql/data
chown postgres /usr/local/pgsql/data
su - postgres
/usr/local/pgsql/bin/initdb -D /usr/local/
pgsql/data
```

Note that /usr/local/pgsql/data is the data directory. initdb is the binary to initialize a new data directory.

6. You need to start the data directory to connect the database. pg_ctl is the binary to start/stop a PostgreSQL data directory.

```
/usr/local/pgsql/bin/pg_ctl -D /usr/local/
pgsql/data start
```

Details of basic requirements, installation procedure, post-installation steps, and supported platforms are found at https://www.postgresql.org/docs/current/static/installation.html.

Binary Installation

This installation is nothing but downloading already compiled binaries (from source installation) from different repositories maintained by communities and PostgreSQL support vendors.

Binary installation expects the server to satisfy all the dependencies. However, most of the package managers are smart enough to detect the required dependencies and install them if required.

Some of the notable binary repositories are as follows:

- https://www.postgresql.org/ftp/binary/

- https://yum.postgresql.org/

- https://www.postgresql.org/download/linux/ubuntu/

There are portable/relocatable binaries also, such as what BigSQL package manager offers at https://www.openscg.com/bigsql/package-manager/.

RPM Installation

PostgreSQL maintains a repository where you can see all versions of PostgreSQL at `https://yum.postgresql.org/rpmchart.php`

RHEL, CentOS, Oracle Enterprise Linux, and Scientific Linux are currently supported by the PostgreSQL yum repository. Only current versions of Fedora are supported due to the shorter support cycle, so Fedora is not recommended for server deployments.

1. Install the repository RPM:

   ```
   yum install https://download.postgresql.org/
   pub/repos/yum/9.6/redhat/rhel-7-x86_64/pgdg-
   redhat96-9.6-3.noarch.rpm
   ```

2. Install the client packages:

   ```
   yum install postgresql96
   ```

3. Optionally install the server packages:

   ```
   yum install postgresql96-server
   ```

4. Optionally initialize the database and enable automatic start:

   ```
   /usr/pgsql-9.6/bin/postgresql96-setup initdb
   ```

   ```
   systemctl enable postgresql-9.6
   ```

   ```
   systemctl start postgresql-9.6
   ```

5. Post-installation.

Automatic restart or auto-initialization of the data directory is not enabled for Red Hat family distributions due to some policies. You need to perform the following steps manually to complete your database installation.

```
service postgresql initdb
chkconfig postgresql on
```

On Fedora 24 and other later derived distributions:

```
postgresql-setup initdb
systemctl enable postgresql.service systemctl start
postgresql.service
```

Installers for Windows and Mac

The easiest way to install is through installers. One-click installers provide a graphical wizard for installation. These installers have options for choosing your installation and data directory locations, as well as ports, user, passwords, etc.

Download the installers from here (according to your operating system): https://www.openscg.com/bigsql/postgresql/installers/

Double-click on the installer and follow the GUI wizard.

Setting Environment Variables

It is very important to set up these environment variables for trouble-free startup/shutdown of the database server.

- PATH: Should point to the correct bin directory

- PGDATA: Should point to the correct data cluster directory

- PGPORT: Should point to the correct port on which the database cluster is running. You will get the port number of the instance from the port parameter in the postgresql.conf file.

- PGUSER: specifies the default database user name.

Edit the .profile or .bash_profile file to set these variables. In Windows, set these variables using the My Computer Properties page. More environment variables are found here: https://www.postgresql. org/docs/current/static/libpq-envars.html.

Getting Started with PostgreSQL

This section talks about some basic commands that are very helpful on a day-to-day basis. The following examples involving service startup are on Linux. However, these commands work across all platforms.

The pg_ctl command can be used to control the PostgreSQL database. To check the status of the PostgreSQL instance:

```
$ su - root
# service postgresql-9.6 status
```

Or:

```
#su - postgres
$ /install/location/bin/pg_ctl D /location/to/data status
```

To start the PostgreSQL service:

```
 $ su - root
# service postgresql9.2 start
```

To start the Postgresql service as a Postgres user (an operating system user), use this command:

```
$ /install/location/bin/pg_ctl D /location/to/data start.
```

To stop the PostgreSQL service, use this command:

```
$ su - root
# service postgresql-9.6 stop
(OR)
#su - postgres
$ /install/location/bin/pg_ctl D /location/to/data stop mf
```

Reload PostgreSQL means to force the PostgreSQL service to allow the modifications in postgresql.conf/pg_hba.conf. To reload the PostgreSQL service:

```
$ su - root
# service postgresql-9.6 reload
```

Or:

```
$/install/location/bin/pg_ctl D /location/to/data reload
```

Use the psql utility to connect to the database. It needs a port, username, hostname, and database name to be passed. An example:

```
$/install/location/bin/psql -p port -h hostname -U username -d dbname
$/install/location/bin/psql -p 5432 -h localhost -U postgres -d postgres
```

To get the object details, PostgreSQL has meta-commands that help you get the list of objects. Connect to the psql prompt and execute these commands.

```
postgres=# \dt
          List of relations
 Schema |  Name   | Type  |  Owner
--------+---------+-------+----------
 test   | test_1  | table | postgres
 test   | test_2  | table | postgres
 test   | test_3  | table | postgres
 test   | test_5  | table | postgres
 test   | test_6  | table | postgres
(5 rows)

postgres=#
```

- \dv: Meta command to get the list of views

- \di: List of indexes

- \d: Table description

You can find all these meta-commands by executing \? in the psql terminal. These commands are not supported in any other applications.

To monitor the database connections, such as which application user executes which query from which IP, you can use the following query to list all the connection details of a cluster.

```
postgres=# select * from pg_stat_activity;
```

To list all the active connections (the connections that are doing some actions on the database), use this command:

```
postgres=# select * from pg_stat_activity where waiting is
false; --(for <= PostgreSQL 9.5)
```

To list all the connections that are waiting, use this command.

```
postgres=# select * from pg_stat_activity where waiting is
true; --(for <= PostgreSQL 9.5)
```

To get the current locks in database, use this command.

```
postgres=# select * from pg_locks;
```

Configuration Parameters

postgresql.conf is the configuration file in PostgreSQL. You can find it under the DATA directory. It's used to set configuration parameters. There are many configuration parameters that affect the behavior of the database system. All the parameter names are case-insensitive. Every parameter takes a value of one of four types: boolean, integer, floating point, or string.

- postgresql.conf holds parameters used by clusters. Parameters are case-insensitive.

- postgresql.conf is normally stored in data directory.

- Initdb installs a default copy of the config file.

- Some parameters take effect only on server restart (pg_ctl), while others go into effect by signaling the postmaster.

- # is used for comments.

- One parameter allowed per line.

- They can also be specified as command-line option.

Some parameters can be changed per session using the SET command and some parameters can be changed at the user level using ALTER USER. Some parameters can be changed at the database level using ALTER DATABASE. The SHOW command can be used to see settings. The pg_settings catalog table lists the settings information.

Connection Settings

- `listen_addresses` (default `localhost`): Specifies the addresses on which the server is to listen for connections or from which hosts you can connect to instance. Provide user-comma separated host IPs or use * for all hosts.

- `port` (default 5432): The port the server listens on. The default is 5432; however, you can use any port number that is free on the server.

- `max_connections` (default 100): The maximum number of concurrent connections the server can support. If you want to increase this parameter, remember that you can see an increase in memory in case of all concurrent sessions.

- `superuser_reserved_connections` (default 3): Number of connection slots reserved for superusers. If max_connections are 100, the normal user connections would be 100 – `superuser_reserved_connections`. These are reserved for the worst case when an instance is running out of connections for normal users.

- `unix_socket_directory` (default `/tmp`): Directory to be used for UNIX socket connections to the server.

Security and Authentication Settings

- `authentication_timeout` (default 1 minute): Maximum time to complete client authentication, in seconds. Default is one minute and it will error out after one minute.

- `ssl` (default `off`): Enables SSL connections for more security.

- `ssl_ciphers`: List of SSL ciphers that may be used for secure connections.

Memory Settings

- `shared_buffers` (default really small): Size of PostgreSQL shared buffer pool in shared memory. Rule of thumb is 25% of system memory to a maximum of 8GB on Linux; or 512MB on Windows.

- `temp_buffers` (default 8MB): Amount of memory used by each backend for caching temporary table data. It is used only when temporary tables are created.

- `work_mem` (default 1MB): Amount of memory used for each sort or hash operation before switching to temporary disk files. Default is conservative, but don't overdo it. If you increase, it may cause the system to go out of memory. Rule of thumb is 25% of RAM/`max_connections`.

- `maintenance_work_mem` (default 16MB): Amount of memory used for each index build or `VACUUM`. It is useful to increase it at the session level when you are running `VACUUM` or `CREATE INDEX`, but not at the instance level.

Query Planner Settings

- `random_page_cost` (default 4.0): Estimated cost of a random page fetch, in abstract cost units. May need to be reduced to account for caching effects. It is used during index scans.

- `seq_page_cost` (default 1.0): Estimated cost of a sequential page fetch, in abstract cost units. May need to be reduced to account for caching effects. Must always set `random_page_cost >= seq_page_cost` to get better performance. However, the planner decides which scan is to be performed based on the stats. You can force `seq scan` or `index scan` by altering these parameters, when necessary.

- `effective_cache_size` (default 128MB): Used to estimate the cost of an index scan. Rule of thumb is 75% of system memory.

Write Ahead Log Settings

- `wal_level` (default `minimal`): Determines how much information is written to the WAL. Other values are `archive` and `hot_standby`. Set to `archive` if you want to enable only archiving for point in time recovery and set to `hot_standby` if you want to set up a replication.

- `fsync` (default on): Turn this off to make your database much faster and silently cause arbitrary corruption in case of a system crash. It is not recommended to turn it off.

- `wal_buffers` (default 64KB): The amount of memory used in shared memory for WAL data. May need to be raised to 1-16 MB on busy systems.

- `checkpoint_timeout` (default 5 minutes): Maximum time between checkpoints. After this much time, the checkpoint will be performed automatically.

- `max_wal_size` (integer): Maximum size to let the WAL grow to between automatic WAL checkpoints. This is a soft limit; WAL size can exceed `max_wal_size` under special circumstances, like under heavy load, a failing archive command, or a high `wal_keep_segments` setting. The default is 1GB. Increasing this parameter can increase the amount of time needed for crash recovery. This parameter can only be set in the `postgresql.conf` file or from the server command line.

- `min_wal_size` (integer): As long as WAL disk usage stays below this setting, old WAL files are always recycled for future use at a checkpoint, rather than removed. This can be used to ensure that enough WAL space is reserved to handle spikes in WAL usage. For example, when running large batch jobs. The default is 80MB. This parameter can only be set in the `postgresql.conf` file or from the server command line.

Where to Log

- `log_destination`: Destination to log written types. Valid values are combinations of `stderr`, `csvlog`, `syslog`, and `eventlog`, depending on the platform.

- `logging_collector`: Enables advanced logging features. `csvlog` requires `logging_collector`. Enabling it creates a utility process called "logger process," which takes care of writing into log files.

- `log_directory`: Directory where log files are written. Requires logging collector to be turn on.

- `log_filename`: Format of log file name (e.g., `postgresql-%Y-%M- %d.log`). Allows regular log rotation. Requires logging collector.

- `log_rotation_age`: Automatically rotates logs after this much time. Requires `logging_collector` to be turn on.

- `log_rotation_size`: Automatically rotates logs when they get this big. Requires `logging_collector` to be turn on.

When to Log

- `client_min_messages` (default `NOTICE`): Messages of this severity level or above are sent to the client. Other severity levels are `LOG`, `WARNING`, `ERROR`, `FATAL`, and `PANIC`.

- `log_min_messages` (default `WARNING`): Messages of this severity level or above are sent to the database log files.

- `log_min_error_statement` (default `ERROR`): When a message of this severity or higher is written to the server log, the statement that caused it is logged along with it.

- `log_min_duration_statement` (default `-1`, disabled): When a statement runs for at least this long (specified in milliseconds), it is written to the server log, with its duration.

What to Log

- `log_connections` (default `off`): Log successful connections to the server log. Useful when generating reports on the number of connections based on log files.

- `log_disconnections` (default `off`): Log some information each time a session disconnects, including the duration of the session. Useful when generating reports on number of connections based on log files.

- `log_error_verbosity` (default "`default`"): Can also select "`terse`" or "`verbose`".

- `log_duration` (default `off`): Log duration of each statement. Useful when you want to see the duration of each statement that is logged.

- `log_line_prefix`: Additional details to log with each line. You can log details of each statement such as hostname, pid, database/username, duration, etc.

- `log_statement` (default `none`): Legal values are `none`, `ddl`, `mod` (DDL and all other data-modifying statements), or `all`. Though `all` is specified, it will not log error statements, as this is applicable to the statements that pass parsing.

- `log_temp_files` (default `-1`): Log temporary files of this size or larger in kilobytes. These files are created when `work_mem` is not sufficient during the sorting of the queries.

Background Writer Settings

- `bgwriter_delay` (default 200 ms): Specifies time between activity rounds for the background writer. Resting time of background writer after it writes and before it starts writing again.

- `bgwriter_lru_maxpages` (default 100): Maximum number of pages that the background writer may clean per activity round. Increasing it makes the background writer write more buffers and may cause some I/O on the server.

- `bgwriter_lru_multiplier` (default 2.0): Multiplier on buffers scanned per round. By default, if the system thinks 10 pages will be needed, it cleans 10 * `bgwriter_lru_multiplier` of 2.0 = 20.

Vacuum Cost Settings

- `vacuum_cost_delay` (default 0 ms): The length of time, in milliseconds, that the process will wait when the cost limit is exceeded. By default, it does not wait.

- `vacuum_cost_page_hit` (default 1): The estimated cost of vacuuming a buffer found in the PostgreSQL buffer pool.

- `vacuum_cost_page_miss` (default 10): The estimated cost of vacuuming a buffer that must be read into the buffer pool.

- `vacuum_cost_page_dirty` (default 20): The estimated cost charged when vacuum modifies a buffer that was previously clean.

- `vacuum_cost_limit` (default 200): The accumulated cost that will cause the vacuuming process to sleep.

Autovacuum Settings

- `autovacuum` (default on): Controls whether the autovacuum launcher runs and starts worker processes to vacuum and analyze tables. It may create some load on heavily active tables (update/deletes); however, it increases the performance of the table. It is not recommended to turn this off.

- `log_autovacuum_min_duration` (default -1): Autovacuum tasks running longer than this duration (in milliseconds) are logged.

- `autovacuum_max_workers` (default 3): Maximum number of autovacuum worker processes that may be running in parallel at one time.

We covered a few of the most important parameters. However, there are a lot of parameters not covered here. For more information, visit `https://www.postgresql.org/docs/9.5/static/runtime-config.html`.

Summary

This chapter covered the detailed architecture of PostgreSQL and its design and data limits. We went through the installation procedures and showed you how to get started with PostgreSQL. We also looked at the directory structure and some basic parameters. The next chapter covers one of the main PostgreSQL service cloud vendors, Amazon Cloud. We talk about the types of instances, including how to choose one, and the limitations and advantages of EC2 and RDS instances.

CHAPTER 3

Amazon Cloud

This chapter covers Amazon Web Services (AWS) and how to get started with it. We talk about availability zones and getting started with AWS and answer queries that most of the people raise before they choose AWS. We cover only a few services related to PostgreSQL, like ec2 machines and RDS instances. We describe the step-by-step process of creating each service, which will give you a better idea about which option you should choose for your environment.

Amazon Cloud or Amazon Web Services

As discussed in Chapter 1, AWS is widespread across 16 geographic regions with 43 availability zones. It is about to launch four more regions with 11 availability zones. AWS also has over 66 edge locations or CDN endpoints for CloudFront.

AWS Regions and Availability Zones

An AWS region is a geographical or physical location that hosts multiple availability zones. Figure 3-1 shows 16 geographic regions across various locations in the world.

© Baji Shaik, Avinash Vallarapu 2018
B. Shaik and A. Vallarapu, *Beginning PostgreSQL on the Cloud*,
https://doi.org/10.1007/978-1-4842-3447-1_3

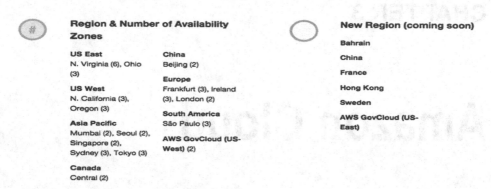

Figure 3-1. *The 16 geographic regions across various locations in the world*

As seen in Figure 3-1, each region or location has at least two availability zones (AZ) to enable high availability and disaster recovery features for production environments. An *availability zone* is a data center in simple terms. To enable high availability, all the availability zones in a region are connected through a fast and private fiber optic network with redundant power and security. Choosing multiple availability zones for your infrastructure helps you build redundant applications that manage failover automatically. You can build replication between multiple regions or within the same region using availability zones.

Getting Started with AWS

Before starting your deployment of PostgreSQL on AWS, you may have a few questions. This chapter addresses the following questions:

- How do you create an AWS account?

- What is the difference between an RDS and EC2 instance?

- When do you choose between an RDS and an EC2 for PostgreSQL?

- How do you create a PostgreSQL RDS instance or an EC2 instance on AWS?

- How do you choose a region? When should you choose a multi-availability zone and how?

- How should you determine the correct specifications or instance type?

- What are all services you need to know to implement PostgreSQL on AWS?

- How can you monitor PostgreSQL on AWS?

- Is PostgreSQL on AWS secured?

- How do you choose a VPC?

- How do you encrypt data in motion and data at rest?

- How do you take backups of PostgreSQL on AWS?

- How is user management and privileged access control achieved on AWS?

- What is Aurora PostgreSQL and how is it different from Community PostgreSQL?

All these questions are answered in the next pages.

Creating an AWS Account

Creating an AWS account is very easy and user friendly. Using the following link, you can directly land on the page that requires you to enter your AWS account name, email address, and password. See `https://portal.aws.amazon.com/billing/signup`.

On the next page, you see an option asking you to select whether it is a company or personal account (see Figure 3-2). In fact, it does not matter. If you are creating the account for your organization, feel free to select the company account and complete the rest of the fields.

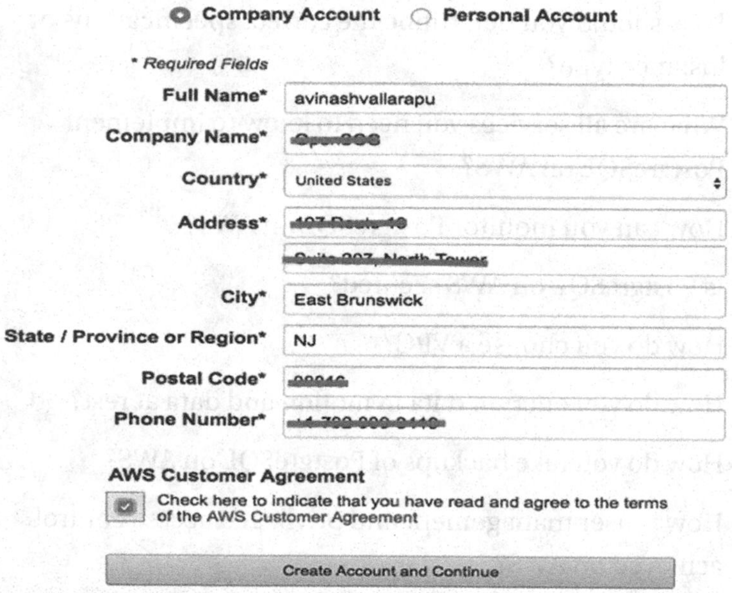

Figure 3-2. *Creating the account*

Once you click on Create Account and Continue, you are asked to enter your credit card number and choose the billing address for the card. You are then asked to provide a telephone number for a confirmation call. The verification stage is then complete. See Figure 3-3.

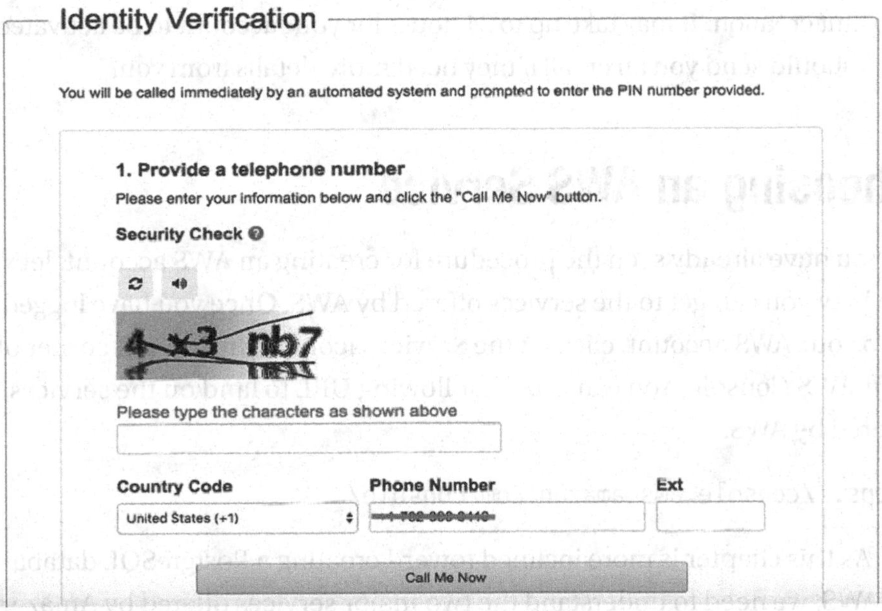

Identity Verification

You will be called immediately by an automated system and prompted to enter the PIN number provided.

1. Provide a telephone number

Please enter your information below and click the "Call Me Now" button.

Security Check ❷

4×3 nb7

Please type the characters as shown above

Country Code

United States (+1)

Phone Number

Ext

Call Me Now

Figure 3-3. *Provide a phone number for verification*

The final step is to choose a support plan. Here are the four support plans available for users on AWS:

- Basic support plan

- Developer support plan

- Business support plan

- Enterprise support plan

If you are planning to try AWS for the first time, feel free to choose the Basic support plan, which is available at no extra cost. To see more details on the support plans offered by AWS, visit https://aws.amazon.com/premiumsupport/compare-plans/.

Once you have selected your support plan, you are done with AWS account creation. It may take up to 24 hours for your account to be activated. AWS should send you an email if they need more details from you.

Choosing an AWS Service

As you have already seen the procedure for creating an AWS account, let's see how you can get to the services offered by AWS. Once you have logged in to your AWS account, click on the Services icon on the top-left corner of your AWS Console. You can use the following URL to land on the services offered by AWS.

https://console.aws.amazon.com/console/

As this chapter is more inclined toward creating a PostgreSQL database on AWS, we need to understand the two major services offered by Amazon for this purpose.

- Relational Database Service (RDS)
- Elastic Compute Cloud (EC2)

RDS

As discussed in the Chapter 1, Amazon RDS is a managed relational database service or a DBaaS (Database as a Service) offered by AWS.

Amazon RDS offers a customizable database service that allows scaling of components like CPU, memory, storage, and IOPS independently. RDS enables developers to focus on building their applications, as many of the time-consuming tasks such as database provisioning, administration, backups, database software installation, database setup, upgrades, patching, and monitoring can be automated and left to AWS. Amazon provides this service for a variety of database software products such as PostgreSQL and MySQL.

Choosing an RDS Instance

Amazon allows you to choose an instance type of your choice from a list of several instance types. Every instance type varies in terms of the CPUs, memory, IOPS, and network capacity. You can choose an instance type that is optimal for your requirements. This list may vary but should give you an understanding that you have a list of instances from which you can select your RDS instance. See Figure 3-4.

Instance Type	vCPU	Memory (GiB)	PIOPS-Optimized	Network Performance
Standard - Latest Generation				
db.m4.large	2	8	Yes	Moderate
db.m4.xlarge	4	16	Yes	High
db.m4.2xlarge	8	32	Yes	High
db.m4.4xlarge	16	64	Yes	High
db.m4.10xlarge	40	160	Yes	10 Gigabit
Standard - Previous Generation				
db.m3.medium	1	3.75	-	Moderate
db.m3.large	2	7.5	-	Moderate
db.m3.xlarge	4	15	Yes	High
db.m3.2xlarge	8	30	Yes	High
Memory Optimized - Current Generation				
db.r3.large	2	15	-	Moderate
db.r3.xlarge	4	30.5	Yes	Moderate
db.r3.2xlarge	8	61	Yes	High
db.r3.4xlarge	16	122	Yes	High
db.r3.8xlarge	32	244	-	10 Gigabit
Burstable Performance - Current Generation				
db.t2.micro	1	1	-	Low
db.t2.small	1	2	-	Low
db.t2.medium	2	4	-	Moderate
db.t2.large	2	8	-	Moderate

Figure 3-4. *List of instance types*

Amazon offers two types of storage for RDS instances.

- General Purpose (SSD) Storage
- Provisioned IOPS (SSD) Storage

General Purpose (SSD), or gp2, is suitable for applications that don't require guaranteed and consistent IOPs and are not concerned about huge IO intensive transactions. IOPS is the number of input/output operations second. This storage type scales at a rate of three IOPS per gigabyte of storage. For example, 33.33GB of storage gets you 100 IOPS. There is also a hard limit of 10,000 IOPS being the maximum for gp2 storage when you choose a storage of size 3,334GB and above. To get more IOPS, you need to choose more storage. Choosing 100GB General Purpose (SSD) storage gets you 300 IOPS. Choosing gp2 type of storage gets you an initial credit balance of IOPS (5.4 million IOPS), which can be used automatically by the instance to sustain a burst performance when large amounts of IO are happening. These credits can sustain 3000 IOPS for 30 minutes. Hence, if you are building an OLTP environment that gets a huge number of transactions for longer durations, needing more IOPS, you may not choose this storage type.

Provisioned IOPS (SSD) Storage is a storage type that lets you provision your instance IOPS between 3 to 10 times of your storage, unlike General Purpose Storage. That means that choosing a storage of size 1,000GB lets you choose an IOPS between 3,000 to 10,000, incremented by 1000. 300GB of storage would let you choose an IOPS between 1000 to 3000, which are always rounded off to multiples of 1000. This is why the minimum storage you can choose while choosing the Provisioned IOPS Storage type is 100GB and it's scalable up to 6144GB.

You can choose up to 30,000 IOPS per database instance irrespective of the instance type you choose. Hence, your instance is now capable of processing a bigger number of I/O requests concurrently if you have chosen this storage type. Provisioned IOPS storage is highly suitable for

OLTP workloads. Increased IOPS refers to decreased IO latency in a system with huge transactions, which makes your transactions complete more quickly. If you want to modify your storage type from gp2 to Provisioned IOPS, doing so requires downtime. Storage, once allocated, can be upgraded without downtime, but it is not possible to downgrade your storage size.

Creating PostgreSQL on an RDS

Follow these steps to create a PostgreSQL RDS instance:

1. As you saw earlier, you need to search for the RDS service in the AWS Console. Once you click on RDS, you should land on an RDS Dashboard. Click on Instances and you should see an option to launch a DB instance. Figure 3-5 shows the options highlighted for your understanding.

Figure 3-5. *Launching the DB instance*

2. Once you click on Launch DB Instance, you should select your engine. Since we are talking about PostgreSQL, lets select PostgreSQL, as highlighted in Figure 3-6. Click Next to continue.

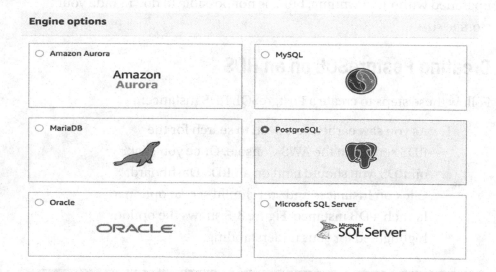

Figure 3-6. *Select PostgreSQL as the engine*

3. Now you need to select your use case from the two options—production and development (see Figure 3-7). If you are building this service for production, select production. However, there is no difference between production and development except for the Multi-AZ and Provisioned IOPS selected by default. You can choose the same options if you select development as your use case. Click Next to proceed.

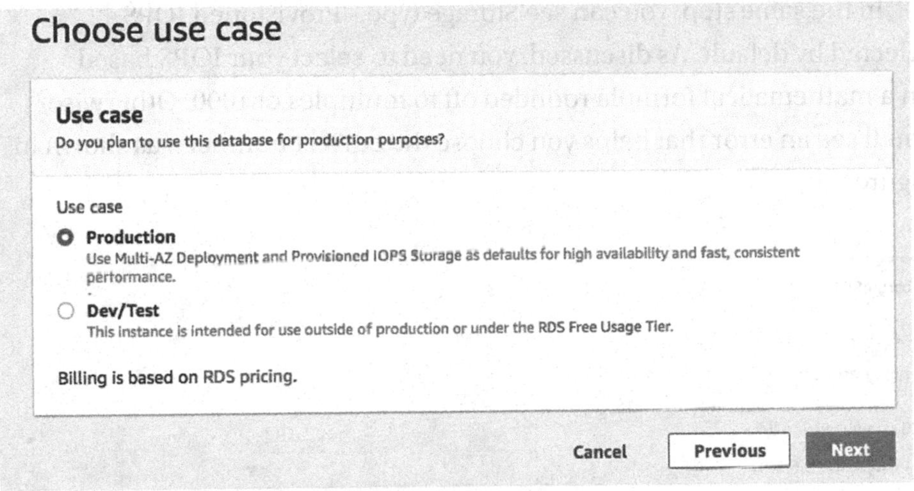

Choose use case

Use case

Do you plan to use this database for production purposes?

Use case

○ **Production**
Use Multi-AZ Deployment and Provisioned IOPS Storage as defaults for high availability and fast, consistent performance.

○ **Dev/Test**
This instance is intended for use outside of production or under the RDS Free Usage Tier.

Billing is based on RDS pricing.

Cancel   Previous   Next

Figure 3-7. *Select the use case*

4. This step is crucial. You need to select the PostgreSQL version you want to install on your RDS instance. AWS takes care of the installation automatically. You see an option to choose your instance class or instance type. Among the list of instances available, you need to select the type that suits your environment in terms of CPU and memory. As seen in Figure 3-8, Create Replica In Different Zone is automatically highlighted for you. As discussed at the beginning of this chapter, there are at least two availability zones in every region. Amazon creates a replica that can be used for reads and high availability when you select this option. Choosing a use case as production will select this option automatically for you.

In the same step, you can see Storage type - Provisioned IOPS selected by default. As discussed, you need to select your IOPS based on a mathematical formula rounded off to multiples of 1000. Otherwise, you'll see an error that helps you choose the correct numbers, as shown in Figure 3-8.

DB engine
PostgreSQL

License model info

| postgresql-license | ▼ |

DB engine version info

| PostgreSQL 9.6.2-R1 | ▼ |

DB instance class info

| db.m3.xlarge — 4 vCPU, 15 GiB RAM | ▼ |

Multi-AZ deployment info

○ **Create replica in different zone**
  Creates a replica in a different Availability Zone (AZ) to provide data redundancy, eliminate I/O freezes, and minimize latency spikes during system backups.

○ No

Storage type info

| Provisioned IOPS (SSD) | ▼ |

Allocated storage

| 1000 | ⊝ | **GB** |

(Minimum: 100 GB, Maximum: 6144 GB)

Provisioned IOPS info

| 1000 | ⊝ |

⚠ postgres requires 3000–10000 IOPS for 1000 GB storage

Figure 3-8. *The error tells you the correct range for the entry*

On the same page, once you scroll down to the end, you should see Settings (see Figure 3-9). Choose a name that will help you identify this instance. Look at the standard naming conventions at your organizational level. You can choose your own username and passport that helps you get superuser access to this instance. Click Next to proceed.

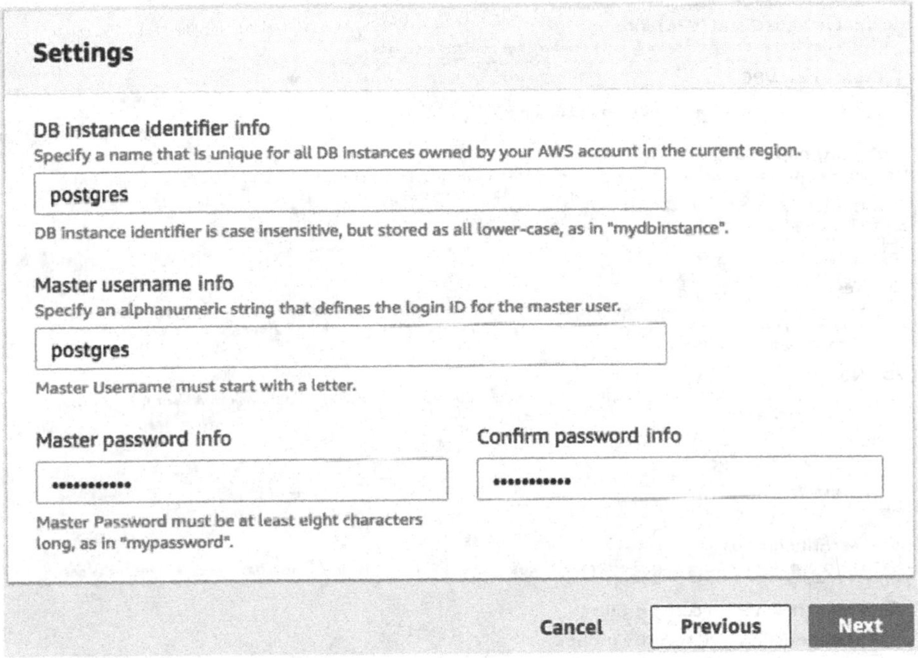

Settings

DB instance identifier info
Specify a name that is unique for all DB instances owned by your AWS account in the current region.

postgres

DB instance identifier is case insensitive, but stored as all lower-case, as in "mydbinstance".

Master username info
Specify an alphanumeric string that defines the login ID for the master user.

postgres

Master Username must start with a letter.

Master password info

••••••••••••

Master Password must be at least eight characters long, as in "mypassword".

Confirm password info

••••••••••••

Cancel   Previous   **Next**

Figure 3-9.   Fill in the settings here

5.   Now you'll land on the Advanced Settings page (see Figure 3-10). You can create your own VPC or choose an existing VPC. One of the important decision is whether to let your instance be publicly accessible. If you need to let other EC2 instances or devices outside the VPC of your instance connect to your instance, you need to choose Yes. However, you need to specifically choose the VPC so devices can connect to your instance explicitly.

There are multiple availability zones in every region, and you can choose one AZ from your region in which to create this instance using the dropdown under Availability Zone.

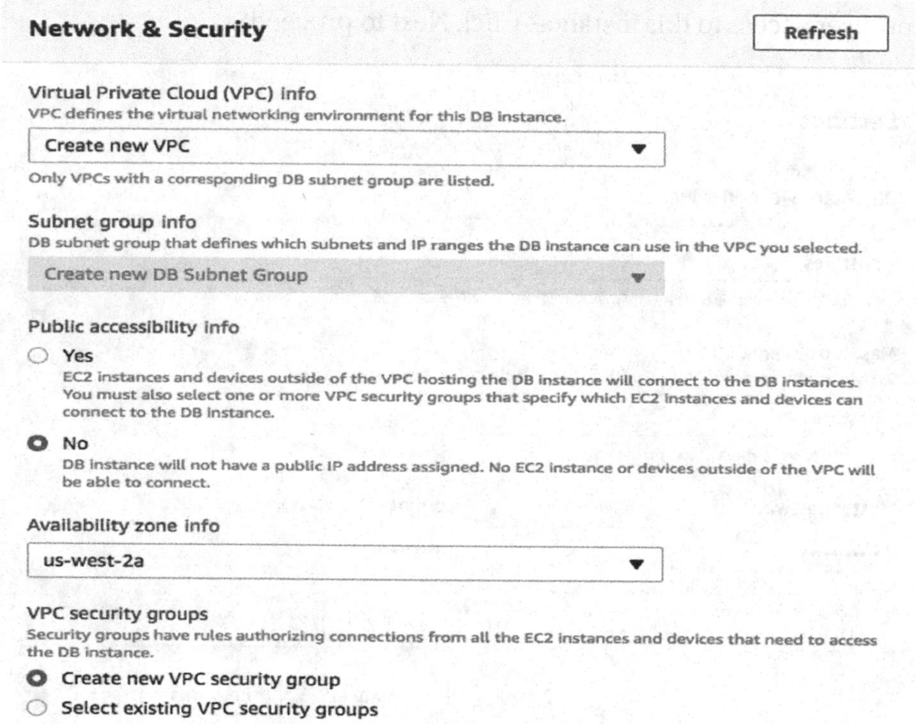

Network & Security   Refresh

Virtual Private Cloud (VPC) info
VPC defines the virtual networking environment for this DB instance.

Create new VPC   ▼

Only VPCs with a corresponding DB subnet group are listed.

Subnet group info
DB subnet group that defines which subnets and IP ranges the DB instance can use in the VPC you selected.

Create new DB Subnet Group   ▼

Public accessibility info

○ Yes
   EC2 instances and devices outside of the VPC hosting the DB instance will connect to the DB instances.
   You must also select one or more VPC security groups that specify which EC2 instances and devices can
   connect to the DB instance.

● No
   DB instance will not have a public IP address assigned. No EC2 instance or devices outside of the VPC will
   be able to connect.

Availability zone info

us-west-2a   ▼

VPC security groups
Security groups have rules authorizing connections from all the EC2 instances and devices that need to access
the DB instance.

● Create new VPC security group
○ Select existing VPC security groups

Figure 3-10. *The advanced settings page*

6. On the same page, choose your default database name and the port on which this instance should run. You can select Yes for encryption if you would like to encrypt your data at rest, such as database storage, snapshots, backups, etc. See Figure 3-11.

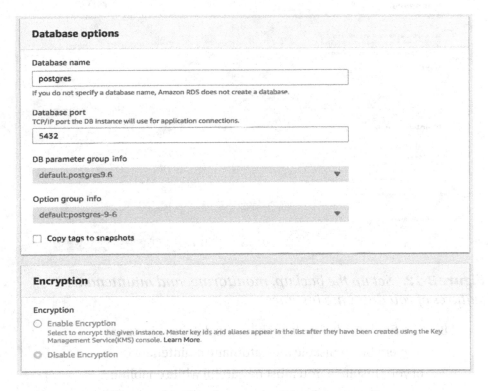

Figure 3-11. *Choose the database name and port*

7. Once you scroll down, you can choose your backup retention period, which is modifiable at later stages. AWS automatically takes care of your backups. You can enable more detailed monitoring by selecting Enable Enhanced Monitoring under Monitoring. See Figure 3-12.

Figure 3-12. *Set up the backup, monitoring, and maintenance features of you database instance*

8. The final step before launching the database instance is to enable or disable the automatic maintenance of your instance. You must be careful while enabling automatic maintenance, as it can perform minor version upgrades of your PostgreSQL instance automatically during a scheduled maintenance window. You can choose your maintenance window or let AWS proceed with the maintenance window, which would be announced in their community forums. I prefer to choose No to take care of such maintenance in my production environments through a planned downtime.

Now, click on Launch DB Instance to finish creating your RDS instance.

EC2

EC2 stands for Elastic Compute Cloud. Unlike an RDS instance, this web service allows users to configure a compute capacity in the cloud with complete control over it. EC2 instances can be provisioned in no time, irrespective of the number of instances you create simultaneously. It is much easier to scale capacity on demand. EC2 instances get root access to users and allow them to install any external applications and software on the server without hassle. Amazon EC2 also commits to a Service Level Agreement of 99.95%.

There are currently five types of instances that you need to understand before creating an EC2 instance the first time.

- Spot instances

- Reserved instances

- Dedicated hosts

- Dedicated instances

- Elastic GPUs

EC2 Spot Instances

Spot instances help users save more money for a workload that is tolerant for interruption. Users can create a spot instance for non-mission critical requirements such as analytics and testing. Using spot instances, you can choose a price you want to pay for an instance you choose, per hour, through a bid. You can view the current spot price and choose a price higher than that through a bid. This way, you can provision your spot instances at the same time. The history of spot pricing is available on the

Amazon website and it will help you understand the spot price in the last 90 days. Using this history, you can choose a price that can sustain for a longer period. When the bid reaches or exceeds the spot price chosen by the user, the service is interrupted. The reason that many users choose a spot instance is because it is very cheap when compared to a EC2 reserved instance but has the same performance.

Reserved Instances

There are several attributes that help you choose a reserved instance and avail a better discounted price. These attributes include instance type, region, and commitment (1 or 3 years). If you choose to delete your instance and not worry about your contract, you can sell it in the Amazon Marketplace. It does not make any difference if you choose a Reserved Instance that is sold in the Marketplace or directly on the AWS Dashboard, because it is the same hardware that is being managed by Amazon. Within Reserved Instances (RIs), you have three categories.

- **Standard RIs:** Help you choose an instance with a great discount without the feature of changing the instance family and other attributes.

- **Convertible RIs:** Gets you a good discount (could be less than standard RIs) but allows you to change the attributes of the RI at the same or higher value.

- **Scheduled RIs:** These instances best suit a predictable workload. For example, I perform a month-end report on the last day of the month or a weekly report every Sunday. You can select a Scheduled RI that would be available for launch for a specified time through a one-year term.

Dedicated Hosts

EC2 dedicated hosts help you create your own physical server. This makes it easier to launch your instances on your own dedicated host, which helps you meet your organizational compliance requirements. Dedicated hosts also allow you to use your existing software licenses, which are calculated on per socket, per core (or VM core) basis, subject to the terms and conditions of the software. You can let Amazon create your instance on your dedicated host explicitly.

Dedicated Instances

Dedicated instances run on hardware that is dedicated to a single customer. You may choose to launch an instance on your dedicated host. However, by choosing a dedicated instance, you would only pay per hour billing for the dedicated instance.

Elastic GPUs

AWS allows you to add virtual graphics, which is as easy as adding an EBS volume to an EC2 instance. Users do not have to choose a physical GPU that is very costly and choose a fraction of resources using elastic GPUs. Elastic GPU instances save users who are involved in 3D gaming and designing a lot of money.

Let's now see how AWS categorizes their instances into five groups/types of instances:

- General purpose
- Compute optimized
- Memory optimized
- Accelerated computing
- Storage optimized

General Purpose

General purpose instances include the T2, M4, and M3 family of instances.

- **T2 instances:** These instances are also referred to as *burstable performance instances*. These instances allow users to get more CPU performance than the baseline through CPU credits. CPU credits are accumulated depending on the idle time of an instance. More CPU credits can be accumulated by a bigger instance type. Environments or applications that are idle most of the time but require a burst performance while running a certain activity or analysis find this instance type better. Currently, you can choose up to 8 vCPUs and 32GB of RAM with EBS-Only. See Figure 3-13.

Model	vCPU	CPU Credits / hour	Mem (GiB)	Storage
t2.nano	1	3	0.5	EBS-Only
t2.micro	1	6	1	EBS-Only
t2.small	1	12	2	EBS-Only
t2.medium	2	24	4	EBS-Only
t2.large	2	36	8	EBS-Only
t2.xlarge	4	54	16	EBS-Only
t2.2xlarge	8	81	32	EBS-Only

Figure 3-13. *The T2 instances*

- **M3 instances:** These instances are SSD-based storage Instances for fast I/O performance. You can choose up to eight vCPUs and 30GB RAM and 2 x 80GB of SSD storage. See Figure 3-14.

Model	vCPU	Mem (GIB)	SSD Storage (GB)
m3.medium	1	3.75	1 x 4
m3.large	2	7.5	1 x 32
m3.xlarge	4	15	2 x 40
m3.2xlarge	8	30	2 x 80

Figure 3-14. *M3 instances*

- **M4 instances:** These instances provide a great balance of CPU, memory, and network resources. Thus, it can be one of the instance types chosen by many applications. These instances are EBS optimized by default. They use 2.3GHz and 2.4GHz of Intel Xeon processors. See Figure 3-15.

Model	vCPU	Mem (GiB)	SSD Storage (GB)	Dedicated EBS Bandwidth (Mbps)
m4.large	2	8	EBS-only	450
m4.xlarge	4	16	EBS-only	750
m4.2xlarge	8	32	EBS-only	1,000
m4.4xlarge	16	64	EBS-only	2,000
m4.10xlarge	40	160	EBS-only	4,000
m4.16xlarge	64	256	EBS-only	10,000

Figure 3-15. *M4 instances*

Compute Optimized

Compute Optimized instances consist of the C5, C4, and C3 family of instances. Let's learn more about these family of instances.

- **C5 instances:** These instances are chosen by users who deal with time-series data collection and machine learning, and gaming and video encoding, or by users who have a demand for high-performance web servers. This instance features a 3.0 GHz Intel Xeon processor, which can go up to 3.5 GHz using Intel Turbo Boost. The highest instance in this family consists of 72 vCPUs and 144GB of RAM with a dedicated network bandwidth. Figure 3-16 shows the type of instances available in this family of instances.

Model	vCPU	Mem (GiB)	Storage	Dedicated EBS Bandwidth (Mbps)
c5.large	2	4	EBS-Only	Up to 2,250
c5.xlarge	4	8	EBS-Only	Up to 2,250
c5.2xlarge	8	16	EBS-Only	Up to 2,250
c5.4xlarge	16	32	EBS-Only	2,250
c5.9xlarge	36	72	EBS-Only	4,500
c5.18xlarge	72	144	EBS-Only	9,000

Figure 3-16. *C5 instances*

- **C4 instances:** These instances are built with Intel Xeon E5-2666 processors and are EBS-optimized. Applications needing high performance and users with gaming needs should choose an instance from this instance class. See Figure 3-17.

Model	vCPU	Mem (GiB)	Storage	Dedicated EBS Bandwidth (Mbps)
c4.large	2	3.75	EBS-Only	500
c4.xlarge	4	7.5	EBS-Only	750
c4.2xlarge	8	15	EBS-Only	1,000
c4.4xlarge	16	30	EBS-Only	2,000
c4.8xlarge	36	60	EBS-Only	4,000

Figure 3-17. *C4 instances*

- **C3 instances:** These Instances are good for high performance with local SSD-based storage. They include Intel Xeon E5 processors with EBS-optimization available at an extra cost. See Figure 3-18.

Model	vCPU	Mem (GiB)	SSD Storage (GB)
c3.large	2	3.75	2 x 16
c3.xlarge	4	7.5	2 x 40
c3.2xlarge	8	15	2 x 80
c3.4xlarge	16	30	2 x 160
c3.8xlarge	32	60	2 x 320

Figure 3-18. *C3 instances*

Memory Optimized Instances

Memory Optimized Instances include X1e, X1, R4, and R3 instances. Let's learn what these four instances include.

- **X1e instances:** X1e instances are designed for high performance in-memory databases and memory intensive applications. These instances include a high frequency Intel Xeon E7 processor and the highest instance of this class can be configured with up to 3,904GB of RAM. These instances include SSD and are EBS-optimized by default. See Figure 3-19.

Model	vCPU	Mem (GiB)	SSD Storage (GB)	Dedicated EBS Bandwidth (Mbps)
x1e.32xlarge	128	3,904	2 x 1,920	14,000
x1e.16xlarge	64	1,952	1 x 1,920	7,000
x1e.8xlarge	32	976	1 x 960	3,500
x1e.4xlarge	16	488	1 x 480	1,750
x1e.2xlarge	8	244	1 x 240	1,000
x1e.xlarge	4	122	1 x 120	500

Figure 3-19. X1e instances

- **X1 instances:** Designed for memory intensive applications and databases that are designed for in-memory. These instances can scale up to 128 vCPUs and 1,952GB of RAM. These instances include SSD and are EBS-optimized by default. See Figure 3-20.

Model	vCPU	Mem (GiB)	SSD Storage (GB)	Dedicated EBS Bandwidth (Mbps)
x1.32xlarge	128	1,952	2 x 1,920	14,000
x1.16xlarge	64	976	1 x 1,920	7,000

Figure 3-20. X1 instances

- **R4 instances:** R4 instances are considered for memory intensive applications with less memory and vCPUs requirements when compared to the X1e and X1 instances. These instances include SSD by default and reach up to 25GB of network performance. See Figure 3-21.

Model	vCPU	Mem (GiB)	Networking Perf.	SSD Storage (GB)
r4.large	2	15.25	Up to 10 Gigabit	EBS-Only
r4.xlarge	4	30.5	Up to 10 Gigabit	EBS-Only
r4.2xlarge	8	61	Up to 10 Gigabit	EBS-Only
r4.4xlarge	16	122	Up to 10 Gigabit	EBS-Only
r4.8xlarge	32	244	10 Gigabit	EBS-Only
r4.16xlarge	64	488	25 Gigabit	EBS-Only

Figure 3-21. *R4 instances*

- **R3 instances:** RS instances are chosen for memory
  intensive applications but with less memory and vCPUs
  requirements than R4 instances. These instances
  include SSD storage by default. See Figure 3-22.

Model	vCPU	Mem (GiB)	SSD Storage (GB)
r3.large	2	15.25	1 x 32
r3.xlarge	4	30.5	1 x 80
r3.2xlarge	8	61	1 x 160
r3.4xlarge	16	122	1 x 320
r3.8xlarge	32	244	2 x 320

Figure 3-22. *R3 instances*

Accelerated Computing

These instances are an example of Elastic GPU instances. P3, P2, G3, and
F1 instances are considered Accelerated Computing instances. Let's learn
more about what these instances offer.

- **P3 instances:** These instances better suit applications
  that deal with high-performance computing, speech
  recognition, high-end gaming, and 3D graphics. These
  instances offer up to 128GB of graphics memory and
  488GB of RAM. These instances include eight NVIDIA
  Tesla V100 GPUs and a high frequency Intel Xeon E5
  processor. Figure 3-23 shows the list of P3 instances
  currently available.

Model	GPUs	vCPU	Mem (GiB)	GPU Mem (GiB)	GPU P2P
p3.2xlarge	1	8	61	16	-
p3.8xlarge	4	32	244	64	NVLink
p3.16xlarge	8	64	488	128	NVLink

Figure 3-23. *P3 instances*

- **P2 instances:** P2 instances suit environments with massive parallel graphics processing and high performance computing dealing with 3D graphics rendering, etc. These instances have higher configurations available than P3 instances. You can choose up to 16 GPUs with 64 vCPUs and 732GB of RAM and 192GB of GPU memory. Figure 3-24 shows the list of instances available in P2.

Model	GPUs	vCPU	Mem (GiB)	GPU Memory (GiB)
p2.xlarge	1	4	61	12
p2.8xlarge	8	32	488	96
p2.16xlarge	16	64	732	192

Figure 3-24. *P2 instances*

- **G3 instances:** These instances suit graphics intensive applications better. G3 instances feature an Intel Xeon E5 series processor with NVIDIA Tesla M60 GPUs, each with 2048 parallel processing cores and 8GB of memory. These instances are good for users looking for 3D visualizations, 3D rendering, and video encoding. These instances consist of an elastic network adapter with 25GBs of network bandwidth. Figure 3-25 shows the list of instances within the G3 instances family.

Model	GPUs	vCPU	Mem (GiB)	GPU Memory (GiB)
g3.4xlarge	1	16	122	8
g3.8xlarge	2	32	244	16
g3.16xlarge	4	64	488	32

Figure 3-25. *G3 instances*

- **F1 instances:** These instances offer high frequency Intel Xeon E5 series processors and SSD storage with an enhanced networking support. These instances especially offer customizable hardware with FPGAs (field programmable gate arrays). Users looking for Big Data analytics and genomics searches may choose this as their preferred instance type.

Figure 3-26 shows a list of instances available within this family.

Model	FPGAs	vCPU	Mem (GiB)	SSD Storage (GB)	Networking Performance
f1.2xlarge	1	8	122	470	Up to 10 Gigabit
f1.16xlarge	8	64	976	4 x 940	25 Gigabit

Figure 3-26. *F1 instances*

Storage Optimized Instances

These instances consists of I3: High I/O instances and D2: Dense-storage instances. Let's learn more about these instances:

- **I3 - high I/O instances:** These instances use NVMe SSD Storage up to 8 x 1.9 TB, which is good for a very high random I/O performance and a much higher sequential read throughout. These instances are preferred for data warehouse and NoSQL databases such as Cassandra, MongoDB, and Redis. Figure 3-27 shows a list of instances available in this instance class.

Model	vCPU	Mem (GiB)	Networking Performance	Storage (TB)
i3.large	2	15.25	Up to 10 Gigabit	1 x 0.475 NVMe SSD
i3.xlarge	4	30.5	Up to 10 Gigabit	1 x 0.95 NVMe SSD
i3.2xlarge	8	61	Up to 10 Gigabit	1 x 1.9 NVMe SSD
i3.4xlarge	16	122	Up to 10 Gigabit	2 x 1.9 NVMe SSD
i3.8xlarge	32	244	10 Gigabit	4 x 1.9 NVMe SSD
i3.16xlarge	64	488	25 Gigabit	8 x 1.9 NVMe SSD

Figure 3-27. *I3 instances*

- **D2 - Dense-storage instances:** These instances offer up to 48TB of local HDD-based storage with a high disk throughout and enhanced networking support. These instances are better for MPP data warehousing environments, such as MapReduce and Hadoop. Figure 3-28 shows the list of instances available in this family.

Model	vCPU	Mem (GiB)	Storage (GB)
d2.xlarge	4	30.5	3 x 2000 HDD
d2.2xlarge	8	61	6 x 2000 HDD
d2.4xlarge	16	122	12 x 2000 HDD
d2.8xlarge	36	244	24 x 2000 HDD

Figure 3-28. D2 instances

Creating an EC2 Instance

You have seen the type of instances available with EC2, so now you can create your first EC2 instance. AWS gives you the option to configure a free-tier instance that is free for an year with certain terms and conditions.

1. In the AWS Services Dashboard, search for EC2. Once you see EC2 listed as one of your services, click on it.

2. You should see the screen similar to Figure 3-29. What you see here is an EC2 Dashboard that helps you launch an EC2 instance for the first time and manage your EC2 instances that are already created.

You could see options to request spot instances, reserved instances, and dedicated hosts in the same EC2 dashboard.

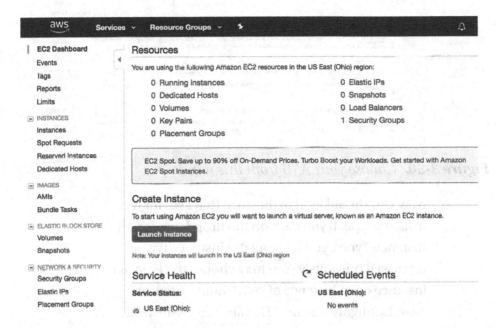

Figure 3-29. *The EC2 Dashboard*

3. Click on Launch Instance to launch your first EC2 instance. Once you click on Launch Instance, you should see an option to choose your AMI (see Figure 3-30). You can proceed to choose the Amazon Linux AMI or any option of your choice.

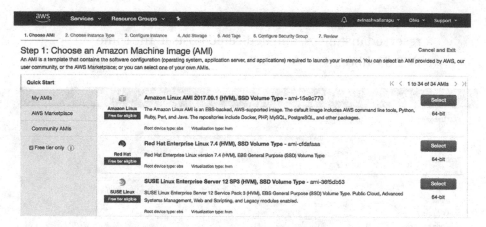

Figure 3-30. *Choose your AMI from this window*

4. Now you should land to the page that asks for the
    instance type. If you click on the dropdown for All
    Instance Types, you'll see all the instance types
    discussed previously. You may choose the Free tier
    instance or an instance of your choice. Click on
    New: Configure Instance Details. See Figure 3-31.

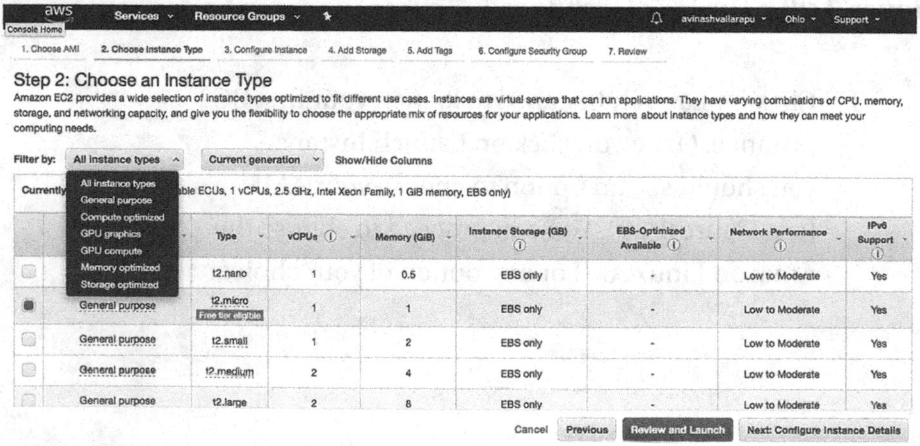

Figure 3-31. *Choose an instance type*

5. You get an option to configure your instance details, as shown in Figure 3-32. Leave the defaults if you are trying this for the first time. We discuss VPC and subnet more in the next chapters. If you click on Request Spot Instance, you can see if Spot Instances are currently available for the instance type you choose.

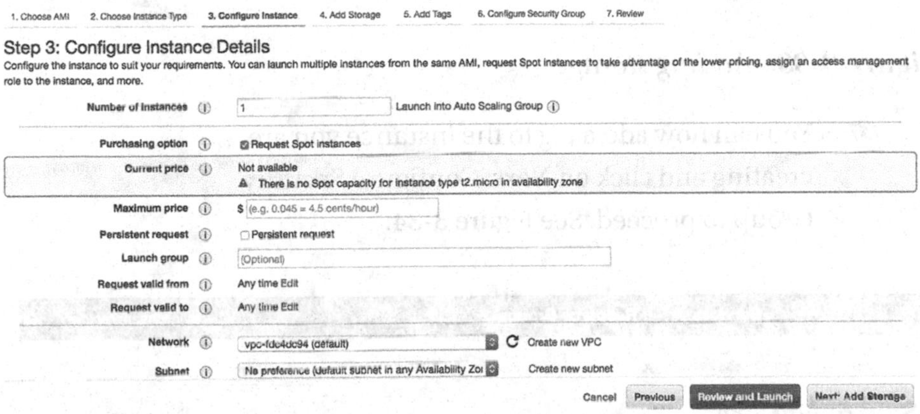

Figure 3-32. Configure your instance details here

6. Click on Next: Add Storage to add more storage. Once you click on Add Storage, you can see that the default root partition is already available (see Figure 3-33). You can click on Add New Volume and add more storage and choose the volume type that suits your needs. Free tier customers are eligible for up to 30GB of EBS General Purpose Storage for free. You can choose your preference and click Next: Add Tags.

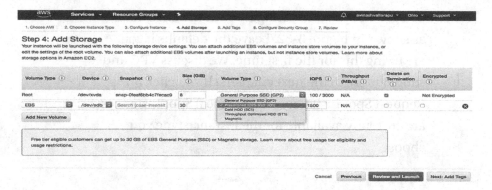

Figure 3-33. *Adding storage*

7. You can now add a tag to the instance you are
    creating and click on Next: Configure Security
    Group to proceed. See Figure 3-34.

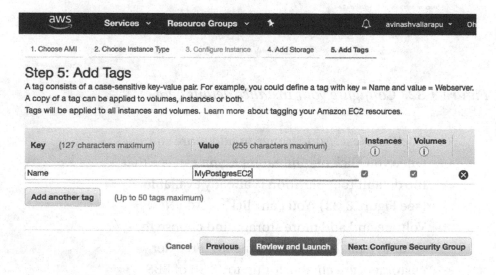

Figure 3-34. *Add a tag to your instance*

8. Configuring security groups is important. You see a default SSH rule for port 22 already added as an option. You can edit it or add more rules for TCP or HTTP.

   In Figure 3-35, a new rule is added which is the custom TCP for port 5432 from 10.0.0.0/32 series of IPs.

   You should also see a warning that 0.0.0.0/0 is accessible by all IPs. You may modify it per your requirements. Once you have selected your rules, click on Review and Launch.

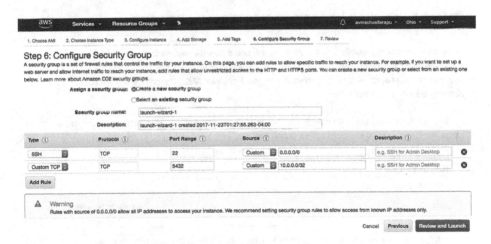

Figure 3-35. *Configuring security groups*

9. Now you get a box that asks you to select an existing key pair or create a new one. If it is the first time you are creating an EC2 instance, you can select Create a New Key Pair and type a key pair. Once you type a name, click on Download Key Pair. The downloaded key pair should be kept safe to ensure that you can connect to your EC2 instance once it has been created. It should take some time to launch your first EC2 instance. The status can be seen on the EC2 Dashboard.

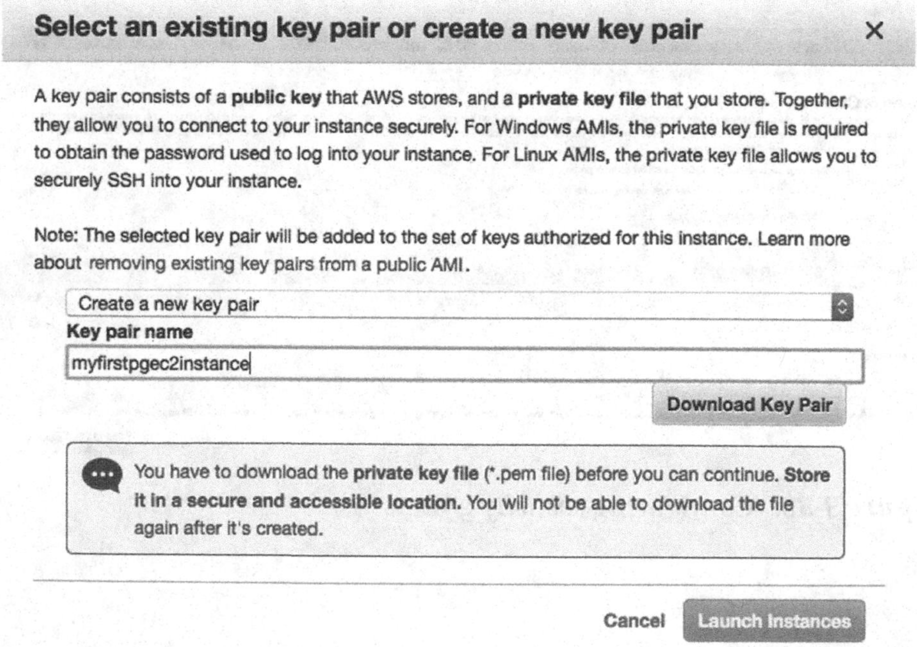

Select an existing key pair or create a new key pair   ✕

A key pair consists of a **public key** that AWS stores, and a **private key file** that you store. Together, they allow you to connect to your instance securely. For Windows AMIs, the private key file is required to obtain the password used to log into your instance. For Linux AMIs, the private key file allows you to securely SSH into your instance.

Note: The selected key pair will be added to the set of keys authorized for this instance. Learn more about removing existing key pairs from a public AMI.

Create a new key pair   ⌄

Key pair name

myfirstpgec2instance

Download Key Pair

⋯   You have to download the **private key file** (*.pem file) before you can continue. **Store it in a secure and accessible location.** You will not be able to download the file again after it's created.

Cancel   Launch Instances

Figure 3-36. *Creating a key pair*

Connecting to Your First EC2 Instance

Once your EC2 instance has been successfully launched, you need to connect to it for the first time using the .pem file you downloaded in the last step before launching. Follow these steps:

1. You can see the public IP or the public DNS that you can use to connect to your EC2 instance under Description, as seen in Figure 3-37.

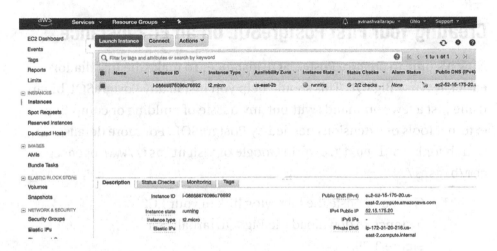

Figure 3-37. *Look for the public IP or public DNS*

2. Let's say you are using Linux or a Mac. You can safely copy the .pem file to a location and modify its permissions so that only the owner has read and write access. Once that's done, SSH to the EC2 instance using the default user ec2-user. See Figure 3-38.

101

```
Avinash-OpenSCG:~ avinash$ chmod 700 myfirstpgec2instance1.pem
Avinash-OpenSCG:~ avinash$ ssh -i myfirstpgec2instance1.pem ec2-user@52.15.175.20
Last login: Thu Nov 23 05:59:26 2017 from 24.222.43.68

     __|  __|_  )
     _|  (     /   Amazon Linux AMI
    ___|\___|___|

https://aws.amazon.com/amazon-linux-ami/2017.09-release-notes/
[ec2-user@ip-172-31-20-216 ~]$
```

Figure 3-38. *Copy the .pem file*

This way, you can connect to your EC2 instance.

Creating Your First PostgreSQL on an EC2 Instance

Now it's time to create a PostgreSQL instance. To make the Installation easier, lets use BigSQL. This should help you install any PostgreSQL binary using just a few commands without any hassle of building or compiling external tools or extensions needed by PostgreSQL. For more details, search for `bigsql postgresql` in Google or visit `https://www.openscg.com/bigsql/`.

1. Copy and paste the following link in your EC2 instance to download the BigSQL tarball. See Figure 3-39.

    ```
    python -c "$(curl -fsSL https://s3.amazonaws.com/pgcentral/install.py)"
    ```

```
[ec2-user@ip-172-31-20-216 ~]$ python -c "$(curl -fsSL https://s3.amazonaws.com/pgcentral/install.py)"
Downloading BigSQL PGC 3.3.4 ...

Unpacking ...

Cleaning up

Setting REPO to https://s3.amazonaws.com/pgcentral

Updating Metadata

BigSQL PGC installed.  Try 'bigsql/pgc help' to get started.
[ec2-user@ip-172-31-20-216 ~]$
```

Figure 3-39. *Downloading BigSQL*

2. Now install PostgreSQL 9.6 or PostgreSQL 10. See
   Figure 3-40.

```
[ec2-user@ip-172-31-20-216 ~]$ bigsql/pgc list
Category      | Component   | Version   | ReleaseDt  | Status | Updates
PostgreSQL      pg10          10.1-1      2017-11-09
PostgreSQL      pg93          9.3.20-1    2017-11-09
PostgreSQL      pg94          9.4.15-1    2017-11-09
PostgreSQL      pg95          9.5.10-1    2017-11-09
PostgreSQL      pg96          9.6.6-1     2017-11-09
Servers         gpdb5         5.2.0-1     2017-11-17
Servers         pgbouncer17   1.7.2-1b    2017-02-09
Servers         pgdevops      2.0-2       2017-11-09
Applications    backrest      1.25        2017-11-04
Applications    ora2pg        18.2        2017-09-18
Applications    pgbadger      9.2         2017-07-31
Frameworks      java8         8u151       2017-11-04

[ec2-user@ip-172-31-20-216 ~]$ bigsql/pgc install pg96
  ['pg96']
Get:1 https://s3.amazonaws.com/pgcentral pg96-9.6.6-1-linux64
  Unpacking pg96-9.6.6-1-linux64.tar.bz2
```

Figure 3-40. *Downloading the tarball*

3. Now start the installed PostgreSQL software. When
   you start it the first time, you will be asked to select
   your superuser password and re-enter it. This will be
   your Postgres superuser password. See Figure 3-41.

```
[ec2-user@ip-172-31-20-216 ~]$ bigsql/pgc start pg96

## Initializing pg96 ######################

Superuser Password [password]:
Confirm Password:
Setting directory and file permissions.

Initializing Postgres DB with:
   /home/ec2-user/bigsql/pg96/bin/initdb -U postgres -A md5 -E UTF8 --no-locale
bigsql/pg96/.pgpass" > "/home/ec2-user/bigsql/data/logs/pg96/install.log" 2>&1

Using PostgreSQL Port 5432

Password securely remembered in the file: /home/ec2-user/.pgpass

to load this postgres into your environment, source the env file:
   /home/ec2-user/bigsql/pg96/pg96.env

pg96 starting on port 5432
[ec2-user@ip-172-31-20-216 ~]$ ▌
```

Figure 3-41. *Enter the superuser password*

Now you can connect to your first PostgreSQL instance to your first
EC2 instance. See Figure 3-42.

```
[ec2-user@ip-172-31-20-216 ~]$ /home/ec2-user/bigsql/pg96/bin/psql -U postgres -p 5432
psql (9.6.6)
Type "help" for help.

postgres=# \l
                               List of databases
   Name    |  Owner   | Encoding | Collate | Ctype |   Access privileges
-----------+----------+----------+---------+-------+------------------------
 postgres  | postgres | UTF8     | C       | C     |
 template0 | postgres | UTF8     | C       | C     | =c/postgres          +
           |          |          |         |       | postgres=CTc/postgres
 template1 | postgres | UTF8     | C       | C     | =c/postgres          +
           |          |          |         |       | postgres=CTc/postgres
(3 rows)

postgres=# select version();
                                         version
-------------------------------------------------------------------------------------------
 PostgreSQL 9.6.6 on x86_64-pc-linux-gnu, compiled by gcc (GCC) 4.4.7 20120313 (Red Hat 4.4.7-17), 64-bit
(1 row)

postgres=# ▌
```

Figure 3-42. *Your first PostgreSQL instance*

Summary

This chapter introduced AWS and its available zones. As only a few services are related to PostgreSQL, we covered only those. You learned about EC2 and RDS instances and how to create these services with the step-by-step process using snapshots for each step. We hope this chapter helps you get started with AWS services for PostgreSQL. In the next chapter, we cover Rackspace cloud and its services. We talk about the services that it provides for PostgreSQL and its backups.

CHAPTER 4

Rackspace Cloud

This chapter covers Rackspace solutions like Managed Hosting and Managed Cloud. Under Managed Hosting, we cover creation and configuration of dedicated or bare metal server and virtual servers. Under Managed Cloud, we cover the support that Rackspace provides for customers who are using other cloud venders like Amazon, Google Cloud, and Microsoft Azure. We also cover managed data storage of Rackspace.

Rackspace is a managed cloud computing company that provides cloud services/solutions that are based on other venders as well as its own. This book is specific to PostgreSQL database on the cloud, so we cover the solutions that relate to a database.

- Managed Hosting
- Managed Cloud

Managed Hosting

Rackspace's Managed Hosting service provides dedicated as well as VMware servers, which means you can create on-metal (on-premises) servers or a virtual machine.

To start, you have to sign up at `https://cart.rackspace.com/cloud`.

Once you are done with the signup, it will take some time (around 24 hours) for Rackspace to review and activate the account. You can access the products only after they are activated. You will get an email to register

© Baji Shaik, Avinash Vallarapu 2018
B. Shaik and A. Vallarapu, *Beginning PostgreSQL on the Cloud*,
https://doi.org/10.1007/978-1-4842-3447-1_4

an email ID once the account is approved. After your account is approved, you have to log in at `https://login.rackspace.com`.

Your Rackspace portal dashboard looks like Figure 4-1 after you log in.

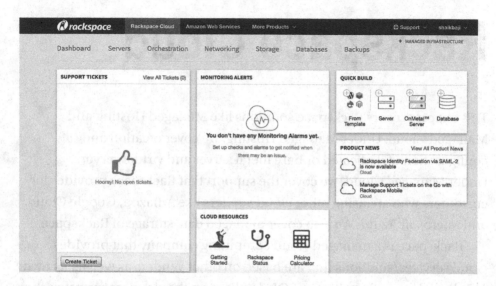

Figure 4-1. *The Rackspace portal dashboard*

You can see your profile settings in the right-top corner, as shown in Figure 4-2. These settings include user management, changing the password, enabling/disabling multi-factor authentication, etc.

Figure 4-2. *The profile settings*

We'll start by creating a dedicated server. Rackspace will help you design a server that's the right fit for your workload. These dedicated servers are on-metal servers, which means the virtual machine is installed directly on the hardware rather than within the host operating system. To solve existing permanent problems (in terms of compromised speed/ performance due to the hypervisor and other virtualization overhead

109

and complexity) with shared virtual machines, use on-metal servers. Rackspace on-metal cloud servers are high-performance, reliable servers designed to help you grow and scale your business quickly and easily.

Features of dedicated or virtual servers that Rackspace provides include:

- High performance

- Options are available for optimized workloads

- Hybrid flexibility with dedicated or private cloud environments

- Provision on-metal bare metal cloud servers for large, demanding workloads

- Highly reliable, with fully redundant networking and power

Rackspace also provides virtual servers so you do not need to walk away from VMware to get the benefits of the cloud. It gives you customized dedicated hardware and your choice of management and control levels. Rackspace provides VMWare Certified Professional to manage your virtual machines, so whichever solution you choose, you will reap the benefits.

Here are some features of the virtual server that Rackspace provides:

- As Rackspace has VMWare Certified Professionals, it builds and manages the world's largest VMware vSphere footprints. It will help you to architect, deploy, and troubleshoot your environments irrespective of how complex they are.

- 100% network uptime and hardware uptime guarantees with consistent, reliable performance.

- Provide full level of control and flexibility.

- Get the enhanced security of a customized single-tenant environment with fully-dedicated network, compute, and storage hardware.

Creating a Dedicated Server

Here are the steps to create a dedicated server:

1. On the dashboard (after you log in), you can click on
    the Servers tab and select Cloud Servers, as shown
    in Figure 4-3.

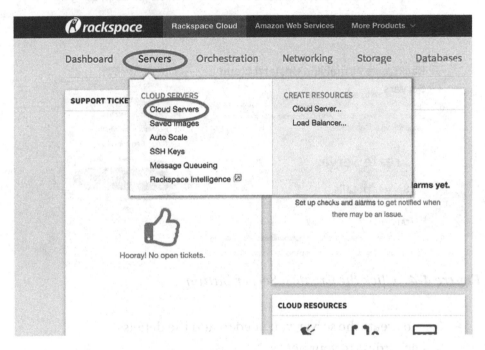

Figure 4-3.   *Choose a cloud server*

2.   Click on Create a Server, as shown in Figure 4-4.

Figure 4-4.   *Click the Create a Server button*

3.   To create the server, you need to add the details
according to your needs.

Server name: Name of the server, just like a tag
name, to differentiate your servers.

Region: Multiple data centers are available. Choose
a data center near your application and users to
introduce geographic redundancy. You will get the
list of available data centers from the dropdown, as
shown in Figure 4-5.

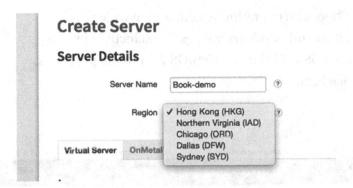

Figure 4-5. *List of available data centers*

4. Select the OnMetal Server, as shown in Figure 4-6.

Figure 4-6. *Choose the OnMetal Server option*

Note that OnMetal Servers are available only for the
Northern Virginia (IAD) and Dallas (DFW) regions.

5. Choose an operating system from a wide range of
    Linux and Windows images. We selected Linux ➤
    CentOS ➤ OnMetal - CentOS 7 for demo purposes.
    See Figure 4-7.

Image

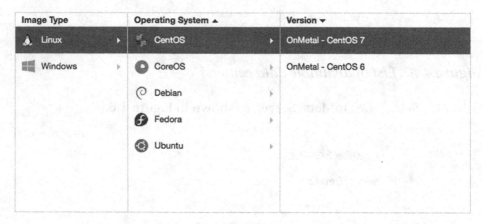

Figure 4-7. *Choose an operating system*

6. Select an OS flavor. There are some predefined
    configurations from Rackspace. With dozens of
    hardware options optimized for popular workloads,
    you will find the right match for your needs.
    Currently, there are five workloads, as shown in
    Figure 4-8. The purpose and hardware configuration
    of each flavor, including pricing, is clearly
    mentioned.

Flavor

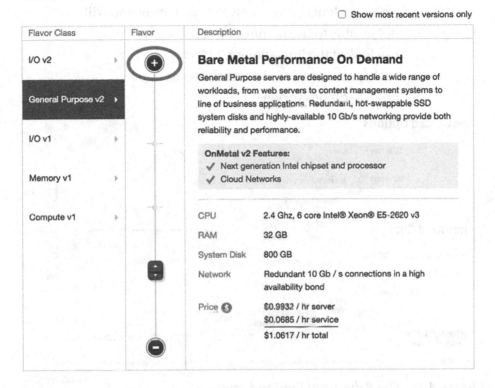

Figure 4-8. *Choose among the five workload flavors*

We selected General Purpose v2 for demo purposes. You can click on the + sign to increase the hardware in terms of RAM/CPU/storage.

7. In the Advanced Options area (see Figure 4-9), notice the SSH Key and Networks options.

- *SSH Key*: Add a public key that you want for the server.

- *Networks*: You can add networks (IP ranges) from where you want to connect. You can see a couple of networks already added that are used for certain Rackspace products, including monitoring and

115

backups. If you deselect any of the networks, the
server no longer has access to the Internet and will
not be able to use monitoring and backups. You
can look at the limitations at `https://support.`
`rackspace.com/how-to/removing-networks-`
`from-a-cloud-server`.

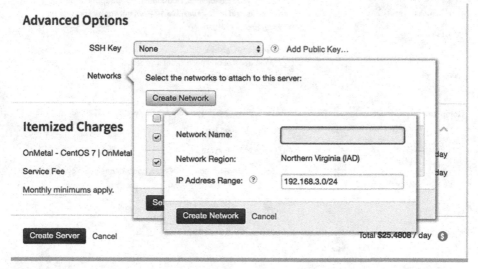

Figure 4-9. The Advanced Options area

8. You can see your charges per day for the selected
    type of server before you create it. This pricing is the
    raw infrastructure plus the managed infrastructure
    rate, with a minimum service charge of $50/month
    after the first 30 days across all cloud servers (virtual
    and bare metal).

9. Click on Create Server once you done with all
    options to create the final product, as shown in
    Figure 4-10.

Itemized Charges   ∧

OnMetal - CentOS 7 | OnMetal General Purpose v2 Small $23.8368 / day

Service Fee $1.644 / day

Monthly minimums apply.

Create Server   Cancel   Total $25.4808 / day

Figure 4-10. *Create the server when you're ready*

Creating a Virtual Server

Creating a virtual server is basically the same as creating a dedicated
server. Steps 1-3 are essentially the same as when you're creating a
dedicated server, except for a few minor changes. Follow Steps 1-3 from
the previous section and then use these steps to create a virtual server:

1. Create Virtual Server instead of OnMetal Server.

2. Choose an operating system as before.

3. Virtual servers have different flavors than OnMetal
    Servers. The purposes and hardware configurations
    are mentioned in the Description field shown in
    Figure 4-11.

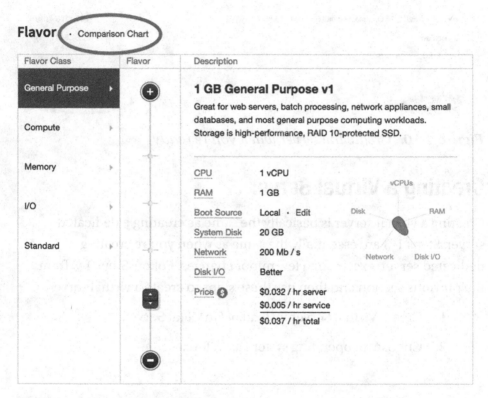

Figure 4-11. *Virtual server flavors*

We selected the General Purpose flavor for demo
purposes. You can use the Comparison Chart option
shown in Figure 4-11. If you click on that option, you
can see a clear comparison of all available flavors, as
shown in Figure 4-12.

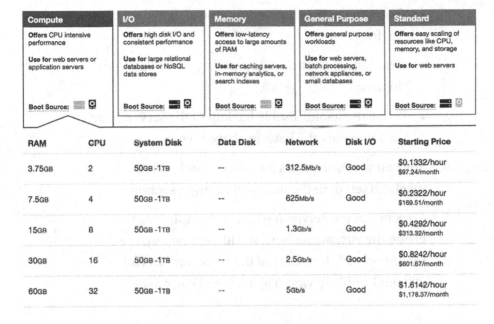

Compute	I/O	Memory	General Purpose	Standard
Offers CPU intensive performance	Offers high disk I/O and consistent performance	Offers low-latency access to large amounts of RAM	Offers general purpose workloads	Offers easy scaling of resources like CPU, memory, and storage
Use for web servers or application servers	Use for large relational databases or NoSQL data stores	Use for caching servers, in-memory analytics, or search indexes	Use for web servers, batch processing, network appliances, or small databases	Use for web servers
Boot Source:	Boot Source:	Boot Source:	Boot Source:	Boot Source:

RAM	CPU	System Disk	Data Disk	Network	Disk I/O	Starting Price
3.75GB	2	50GB-1TB	--	312.5Mb/s	Good	$0.1332/hour $97.24/month
7.5GB	4	50GB-1TB	--	625Mb/s	Good	$0.2322/hour $169.51/month
15GB	8	50GB-1TB	--	1.3Gb/s	Good	$0.4292/hour $313.32/month
30GB	16	50GB-1TB	--	2.5Gb/s	Good	$0.8242/hour $601.67/month
60GB	32	50GB-1TB	--	5Gb/s	Good	$1.6142/hour $1,178.37/month

Figure 4-12. *Comparison of all available flavors*

4. Fill in the Advanced Options area the same as the previous section for the dedicated server.

5. You will be prompted with some recommendations for your server, as shown in Figure 4-13, before you create it.

Recommended Installs

The following options are recommended by Rackspace Fanatical Support Specialists. All checked options will be automatically installed and configured.

☑ Monitor recommended server metrics   Free

☑ Operating system security patches applied on selected images   Free

☐ Protect your data with weekly Cloud Backups   Starts at $0.329 / day $

🚹 Without Cloud Backup your data will not be backed up to help prevent data and configuration loss.

Figure 4-13. *Server setup recommendations*

- You can enable/disable monitoring for your server for free.

- You can select to apply operating system patches for free.

- You can enable/disable backup of the server. Note that enabling the backup charges you.

6. You can see the charges for the selected virtual machine server in the Itemized Charges section.

7. Click on Create Server. It will take few minutes to create the virtual machine. It will then pop up the root password. Take note of the password, as you will not be able to view it again (see Figure 4-14).

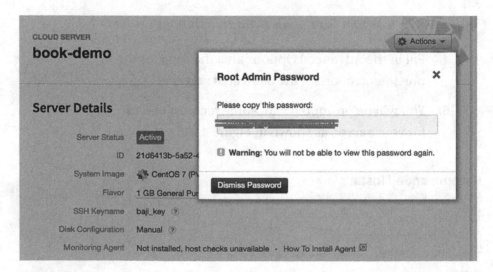

Figure 4-14. *Be sure to make note of the password before exiting*

Connecting to the Virtual Machine and Installing PostgreSQL

The following steps explain how to connect to the virtual server you created and install PostgreSQL on it:

1.   Once you have created your virtual machine choose
     Servers ➤ Cloud Servers from the dashboard. You
     can then see the virtual server you created, as shown
     in Figure 4-15.

Figure 4-15.   *The virtual server you created*

2.   If you click on the virtual server, you can see the
     details of your server and commands (as highlighted
     in Figure 4-16) to connect to the virtual server. If you
     want to reboot/resize or delete the server, go to the
     Actions tab, as highlighted in Figure 4-16.

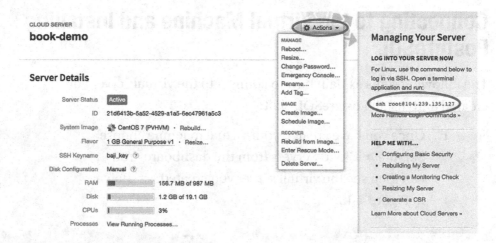

Figure 4-16. *The details of the virtual server*

3. Once you have the public IP of the virtual server, you
can connect the server, as shown in Figure 4-17.

```
C1MQV0FZDTY3:bin bajishaik$ ssh root@23.253.109.31
The authenticity of host '23.253.109.31 (23.253.109.31)' can't be established.
RSA key fingerprint is d2:42:cf:64:0d:3e:4a:31:61:7a:11:b2:90:8d:20:cc.
Are you sure you want to continue connecting (yes/no)? yes
Warning: Permanently added '23.253.109.31' (RSA) to the list of known hosts.
Last login: Wed Nov  1 21:24:25 2017 from 10.191.200.5
[root@book-demo ~]#
[root@book-demo ~]# hostname
book-demo
[root@book-demo ~]# hostname -I
23.253.109.31 10.209.129.107 2001:4800:7819:104:be76:4eff:fe04:5a40
[root@book-demo ~]#
[root@book-demo ~]# df -h
Filesystem      Size  Used Avail Use% Mounted on
/dev/xvda1       20G  1.3G   18G   7% /
devtmpfs        484M     0  484M   0% /dev
tmpfs           494M     0  494M   0% /dev/shm
tmpfs           494M   13M  481M   3% /run
tmpfs           494M     0  494M   0% /sys/fs/cgroup
tmpfs            99M     0   99M   0% /run/user/0
[root@book-demo ~]#
[root@book-demo ~]#
```

Figure 4-17. *Connecting the new server*

As we already added the public key when we created
the virtual server, it does not need a password to
connect.

4. Go to `https://www.openscg.com/bigsql/`.

5. Click on the Downloads section.

6. Click on the Usage Instructions link, as shown in
    Figure 4-18.

Figure 4-18. *Click on usage instructions*

7. As per the usage instructions, for Linux machines,
    you can execute this command to install BigSQL
    package.

```
python -c "$(curl -fsSL
https://s3.amazonaws.com/pgcentral/install.py)"
```

BigSQL uses a command-line utility called pgc (pretty good command-line). For example, to list the available PostgreSQL binaries, extensions, and tools for PostgreSQL, users can run the following command.

```
pgc list
```

To install PostgreSQL 9.6, just fire the following command.

```
pgc install pg96
```

To install an extension called `pg_repack`, use the following command.

```
pgc install pg_repack
```

Users don't have to worry about several dependencies such as a gcc compiler or any other packages that need to be installed while installing Postgres or its extensions. BigSQL takes care of all the dependencies and makes it very easy for users to deal with PostgreSQL.

One of the most advanced features of BigSQL is its pgDevOps. pgDevOps is a UI that allows users to install and manage PostgreSQL instances in a few clicks. Users can upgrade PostgreSQL minor version or install or update an extension in a few clicks. PgDevOps also helps users analyze queries and database metrics like connections, checkpointing, temp file generation, etc., through pgBadger reports on its UI, as requested.

Users can also tune their complex procedural language using an excellent tool embedded in its UI, called plProfiler console. Using plProfiler console, users can look at the complete call stack of a complex PostgreSQL function and concentrate on the code that consumed more time of execution in its entire call stack.

Thus, BigSQL helps users install and manage PostgreSQL and its extensions in a few clicks. BigSQL, combined with any cloud service, can easily build a very economic PostgreSQL database on the cloud.

Cloud Block Storage

Cloud block storage allows us to create persistent block-level storage volumes that can be used with Rackspace cloud servers. So it allows us to scale storage independently of whatever servers are already created.

More information on this storage is available at `https://developer.`
`rackspace.com/docs/user-guides/infrastructure/cloud-config/`
`storage/cloud-block-storage-product-concepts/#cloud-block-`
`storage-product-concepts`.

Let's look at creating a block storage volume and attaching it to the
server that we already created.

1. From the dashboard, choose Storage ➤ Block
    Storage Volumes.

2. You will see a list of created volumes if there are any;
    otherwise, you can create a volume by clicking on
    the Create Volume button, as shown in Figure 4-19.

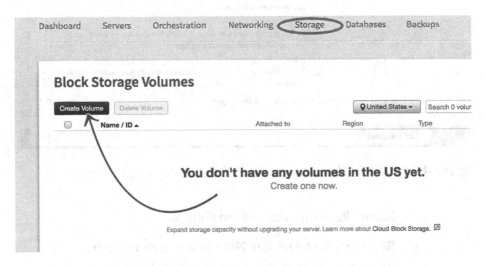

Figure 4-19. *Creating a block storage volume*

3. You will need to fill in the details to create the volume, as shown in Figure 4-20.

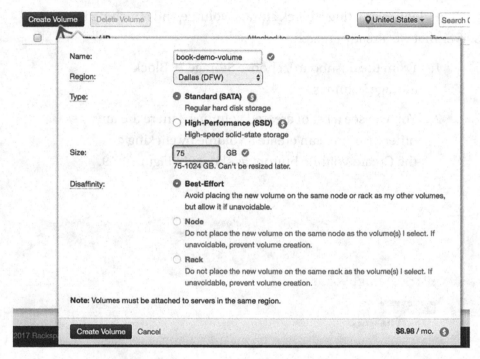

Figure 4-20. *Fill in the details about the block storage volume*

- **Name:** Refers to name of the volume.

- **Region:** Select a region. Note that you can attach volumes to servers that are in same region. So select the region that your servers are in.

- **Type:** Type of volume. It can be a regular hard disk storage (SATA) or high speed solid state drives (SSD).

- **Size:** The size of the volume. Minimum 75GB to maximum 1TB.

- **Disaffinity:** This can be

  - Best-Effort

    Avoid placing the new volume on the same node or rack as my other volumes, but allow it if unavoidable.

  - Node

    Do not place the new volume on the same node as the volume(s) I select. If unavoidable, prevent volume creation.

  - Rack

    Do not place the new volume on the same rack as the volume(s) I select. If unavoidable, prevent volume creation.

4. Click on Create Volume.

5. Once the volume is created, you can see the details
    of volume, as shown in Figure 4-21, with actions like
    Rename/Attach/Create/Clone/Delete Volume.

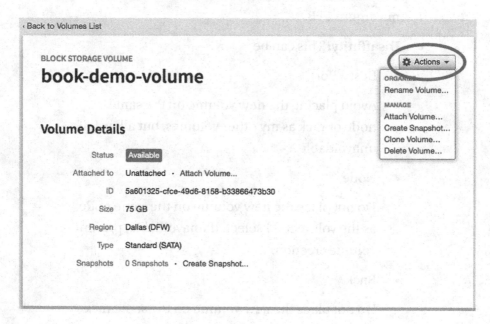

Figure 4-21. Volume details and actions

6. Click on the Attach Volume option from the Actions
    dropdown and attach the volume to one of the
    servers (see Figure 4-22). It will take few minutes to
    attach the volume.

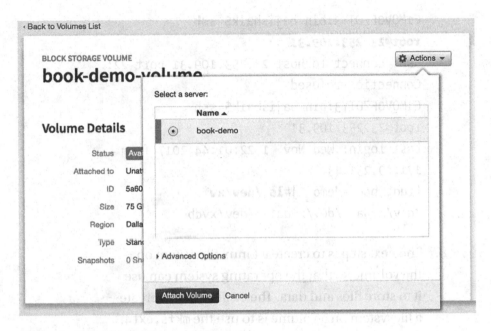

Figure 4-22. *Attaching a volume*

Note that book-demo is the virtual server that was
created for demo purposes here.

7. Once you have attached the new volume, it is visible to your virtual server. You can check using the following command after connecting to your virtual server:

```
C1MQVOFZDTY3:bin bajishaik$ ssh
root@23.253.109.31
ssh: connect to host 23.253.109.31 port 22:
Connection refused
C1MQVOFZDTY3:bin bajishaik$ ssh
root@23.253.109.31
Last login: Wed Nov  1 22:01:44 2017 from
171.49.231.43
[root@book-demo ~]#ls /dev/xv*
/dev/xvda   /dev/xvda1   /dev/xvdb
```

8. The next step is to create a Linux filesystem on the volume so that the operating system can use it to store files and data. The easiest way to create a filesystem on a volume is to use the mkfs.ext4 utility, which takes as arguments the label and the volume device:

```
[root@book-demo ~]# /sbin/mkfs.ext4 -L /
new_volume /dev/xvdb
mke2fs 1.42.9 (28-Dec-2013)
Filesystem label=/new_volume
OS type: Linux
Block size=4096 (log=2)
Fragment size=4096 (log=2)
Stride=0 blocks, Stripe width=0 blocks
4915200 inodes, 19660800 blocks
```

983040 blocks (5.00%) reserved for the super
user
First data block=0
Maximum filesystem blocks=2168455168
600 block groups
32768 blocks per group, 32768 fragments per
group
8192 inodes per group
Superblock backups stored on blocks:
        32768, 98304, 163840, 229376,
        294912, 819200, 884736, 1605632,
        2654208,
        4096000, 7962624, 11239424

Allocating group tables: done
Writing inode tables: done
Creating journal (32768 blocks): done
Writing superblocks and filesystem
accounting information: done

9. Now mount the filesystem so that you can see and
    use the volume in the virtual server.
    ```
    [root@book-demo ~]# mkdir /new_volume
    [root@book-demo ~]# mount /dev/xvdb /new_
    volume/
    [root@book-demo ~]# mount | grep new_volume
    /dev/xvdb on /new_volume type ext4 (rw,relat
    ime,seclabel,data=ordered)
    [root@book-demo ~]#
    [root@book-demo ~]# df -h
    ```

```
Filesystem          Size  Used  Avail  Use%  Mounted on
/dev/xvda1          20G   1.3G  18G    7%    /
devtmpfs            484M  0     484M   0%    /dev
tmpfs               494M  0     494M   0%    /dev/shm
tmpfs               494M  13M   481M   3%    /run
tmpfs               494M  0     494M   0%    /sys/fs/cgroup
tmpfs               99M   0     99M    0%    /run/user/0
/dev/xvdb           74G   53M   70G    1%    /new_volume
[root@book-demo ~]#
[root@book-demo ~]# cd /new_volume/
[root@book-demo new_volume]# ls -ltrh
total 16K
drwx------. 2 root root 16K Nov  1 22:10
lost+found
[root@book-demo new_volume]# touch test
[root@book-demo new_volume]# ls -ltrh
total 16K
drwx------. 2 root root 16K Nov  1 22:10
lost+found
-rw-r--r--. 1 root root   0 Nov  1 22:15
test
[root@book-demo new_volume]#
```

Summary

This chapter talked about Rackspace solutions like Managed Hosts and Managed Cloud. We covered creating/configuring bare metal and virtual servers, which are part of the Managed Host solution, and installation of PostgreSQL on top of the servers. We also talked about the storage volumes that Rackspace provides. In the next chapter, we talk about Google cloud in terms of what services it provides and how to create/configure those services.

CHAPTER 5

Google Cloud

This chapter talks about using the Google Cloud Console to create projects and instances in order to build/install PostgreSQL and your applications. The chapter also covers some of the Google Could Platforms (GCP), like Compute Engine, Could Storage, and Cloud SQL, in detail. You'll learn how to install PostgreSQL on machines created using Compute Engine and on the PostgreSQL service, which is part of Cloud SQL.

Getting Started with GCP

As with the other cloud vendors, Google Cloud has a console through which you can see all the available services and create/modify/delete services that you need.

The first step to creating an instance or a service using GCP is to sign in to its console from https://console.cloud.google.com/. This console requires you to sign in using an existing email account with no hassles. It took me 10 seconds to access the Google Cloud Console.

Before going further with GCP, we cover why you'll need a project in GCP.

What Is a GCP Project?

This is something interesting, as it is not something you see with most of the cloud vendors. Consider an organization that has 10 applications. It uses 300 servers for application servers/web servers and another 10 servers for databases. It may look confusing to view the console with such a huge list of servers. If you cannot segregate the servers by application on the console, managing these accounts could be difficult.

I still remember working with a console that had several hundred servers. I started to search the entire list to understand the database servers of an application that was getting retired. Decommissioning those database servers took a few days, as I had to confirm several times before deleting those instances.

GCP forces you to create a project before creating an instance. A simple solution to the previous problem is to create one project for every application and create your instances within those projects. This makes life simple. GCP allows you to create multiple projects using a single account.

Considering the example without such segregation on the console, if I have 10 applications running in my organization, I create 10 projects and create all the 300 application servers and 10 database servers within their respective projects. In this case, I don't have to scan through the entire list of instances if I have to retire an application. I can just delete the instances in that project.

Project Quota

Have you ever thought about the project quota, which is the number of projects that are allowed to be created using a single account? Yes, there is a limit and it's 12 projects. However, Google allows you to request more projects considering a variety of factors, including resources that most legitimate customers use, the customer's previous usage and history with Google Cloud, and previous abuse penalties. When you try to create your 13th project, you are automatically prompted to fill out a form.

You need to pay to increase your quota, but it is then available as a credit in a later billing cycle.

Creating a Project Using the Console

Once you log in to your Google Cloud Console, you have two options to create your first project. As shown in Figure 5-1, you can click on Select a Project from the top-left corner or click on Create an Empty Project from the bottom-left corner of your console.

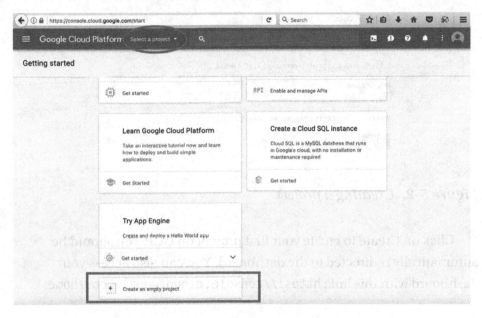

Figure 5-1. *Getting started window*

Once you click on Create an Empty Project, you see a rectangular box that allows you to choose a project name. Your project name can only include letters, numbers, quotes, hyphens, spaces, and exclamation points. As shown in Figure 5-2, you could see a message that says that you have 11 projects remaining in your quota. Every time you create a project, you'll see the number of projects you have left.

One interesting observation is the Project ID. We will discuss its
significance later in the chapter. You may want to edit the Project ID and
choose your own for your project. Otherwise, GCP automatically chooses a
Project ID for you.

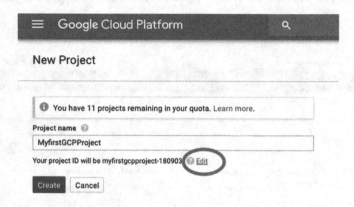

Figure 5-2. *Creating a project*

Click on Create to create your first project on GCP. You should be
automatically redirected to the dashboard. You can also access your
dashboard with this link: `https://console.cloud.google.com/home`.

Deleting a Project

It is easy to delete an entire project that consists of several instances.
However, the registered user will be notified. A project delete is a
scheduled event. It will not take place immediately. The registered user
can click the link sent to his email within a month to retrieve his project.
The deletion email is shown in Figure 5-3.

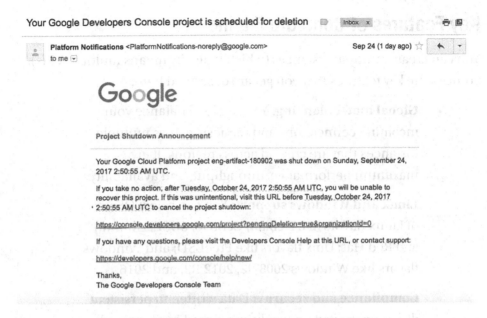

Figure 5-3. *Email stating the project is being deleted*

Types of Google Cloud Platforms

There are several categories in GCP that you might be interested in. However, as per the subject of this book, we are going to cover only these platforms:

- Compute Engine
- Cloud Storage
- Cloud SQL

Compute Engine

Compute Engine provides virtual machines running on Google data centers. As with the other cloud venders, it provides a powerful network that makes you connect your machines without any interruptions and comes with a persistence disk that persists during the crashes and delivers a consistent performance.

Key Features of Compute Engine

You can create multiple instances (which typically means multiple VMs). Some of the key features that you get are described here:

- **Global load balancing:** You can load balance your incoming connections and requests across multiple instances that are created across regions. It gives maximum performance, throughput, and availability.

- **Linux and Windows support:** You can select OSes of Linux flavors like Debian, CentOS, SUSE, Ubuntu, and Red Hat; Unix flavors like FreeBSD; and Windows flavors like Windows 2008 R2, 2012 R2, and 2016.

- **Compliance and security:** Data written to persistent disk is encrypted on the fly and stored in encrypted form. Google Compute Engine has completed ISO 27001, SSAE-16, SOC 1, SOC 2, and SOC 3 certifications, demonstrating their commitment to information security.

- **Transparent maintenance:** You do not need to worry about maintenance of your infrastructure selected with Compute Engine. It provides innovative data centers that are secure, migrate data without downtime, and enable proactive infrastructure maintenance such as patching OS. This transparent maintenance improves reliability and security.

- **Automatic discounts:** If you have long-running workloads, Google automatically gives you discounted prices with no sign-up fees or up-front commitment.

- **Customer machine types:** You can select your VMs and shape them based on how many vCPUs and GB of RAM you actually need, with increments of two vCPUs and 0.25GB at a time. By customizing your machines, you can save money and pay only for what you use.

- **Per-minute billing:** This is an excellent feature that GCP has. Google bills in minute-level increments. After a 10-minute minimum charge, you pay only for the actual compute time that you use.

More information about Google Compute Engine is available at
`https://cloud.google.com/compute/docs/`.

Create an Instance

When you log in to the Google Cloud Console, it typically looks Figure 5-4. Note the Cloud Launcher, which typically contains all the solutions available in Google Cloud.

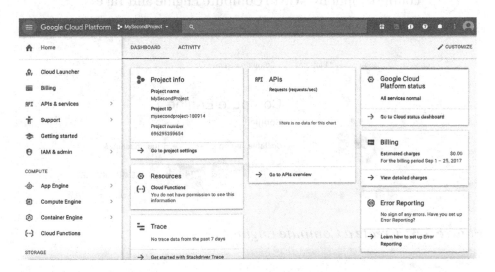

Figure 5-4. *Dashboard*

Once you click on Cloud Launcher, it will direct you to a window where you can see the GCP (Google Cloud Platform) on the left side. Just clicking on that shows all available solutions for GCP. The typical steps to create a VM are as follows:

1. Log in to the Google Cloud Console using your Gmail account.

2. Create a project in which you want to initialize your services. Read the "How to Create a Project Using the Console" section in this chapter to create a project.

3. Click on Cloud Launcher on the left side panel.

4. Click on Google Cloud Platform on the left side panel.

5. Click on Compute Engine in the Compute section.

6. You will be directed to a page where you see a couple of options—Go to Compute Engine and Take Quickstart (see Figure 5-5).

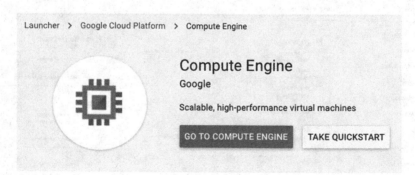

Figure 5-5. *Create a Compute Engine*

7. You can click on Take Quickstart to get quick
    10-minute video on this process.

8. Once you're done with the quickstart, come back
    and select the Go To Compute Engine option. You
    can instead directly open the `https://console.`
    `cloud.google.com/compute/instances` link, which
    takes you to the Create Instance page, as shown in
    Figure 5-6.

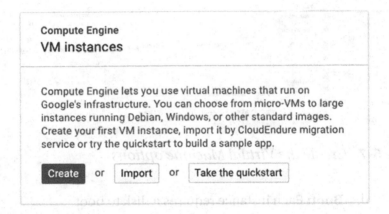

Compute Engine
VM instances

Compute Engine lets you use virtual machines that run on
Google's infrastructure. You can choose from micro-VMs to large
instances running Debian, Windows, or other standard images.
Create your first VM instance, import it by CloudEndure migration
service or try the quickstart to build a sample app.

Create   or   Import   or   Take the quickstart

Figure 5-6. *Create Virtual Machine*

9. You need to fill in the details of the instance before
    you create it (see Figure 5-7).

    a. **Name:** Must start with a lowercase letter
        followed by up to 63 lowercase letters, numbers,
        or hyphens, and cannot end with a hyphen.

    b. **Zone:** Determines what computing resources
        are available and where your data is stored and
        used.

    c.   **Machine Type:** The type of machine that you want to create. You can choose CPU Cores and Memory for your instance. It can be upgraded later if you choose a machine with low configuration.

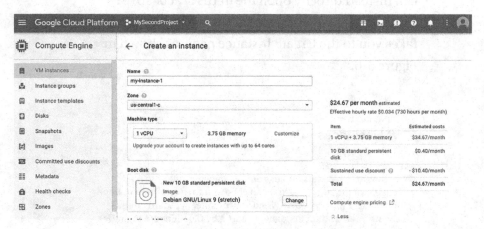

Figure 5-7. *Create the Virtual Machine options*

    d.   **Boot:** Each instance requires a disk to boot from. Select an image or snapshot to create a new boot disk or attach an existing disk to the instance. Be sure to choose the operating system that you want, as shown in Figure 5-8.

Boot disk

Select an image or snapshot to create a boot disk; or attach an existing disk

OS images   Application images   Custom images   Snapshots   Existing disks

---

○ **Ubuntu 16.04 LTS**
   amd64 xenial image built on 2017-09-19
○ **Ubuntu 17.04**
   amd64 zesty image built on 2017-09-22
○ **Container-Optimized OS 62-9901.21.0 beta**
   Kernel: ChromiumOS-4.4.79 Kubernetes: 1.7.6 Docker: 17.03.2
○ **Container-Optimized OS 63-9956.0.0 dev**
   Kernel: ChromiumOS-4.4.86 Kubernetes: 1.7.6 Docker: 17.03.2
○ **Container-Optimized OS 61-9765.66.0 stable**
   Kernel: ChromiumOS-4.4.70 Kubernetes: 1.6.10 Docker: 17.03.2
○ **Red Hat Enterprise Linux 6**
   x86_64 built on 2017-09-18
○ **Red Hat Enterprise Linux 7**
   x86_64 built on 2017-09-18
○ SUSE Linux Enterprise Server 11 SP4
   x86_64 built on 2017-06-21
○ SUSE Linux Enterprise Server 12 SP2

Boot disk type ❓   **Size (GB)** ❓

| Standard persistent disk   ▼ | 10 |

Figure 5-8. *Selecting the OS*

    e.   **Identity and API access:** Applications running on the VM use the service account to call Google Cloud APIs. Select the service account you want to use and the level of API access you want to allow. Access Scopes is selecting the type and level of API access to grant the VM. The defaults are read-only access to storage and service management, write access to stackdriver logging and monitoring, and read/write access to service control.

f.   You can see more options on managing disks, networking, and SSH keys by clicking on the Management, Disks, Networking, SSH Keys option, as shown in Figure 5-9.

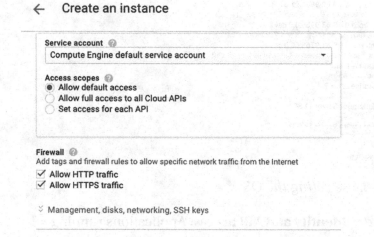

Figure 5-9.   Creating the VM security options

10.   Click on Create to create the instance.

11.   Once the instance is created, the page looks like Figure 5-10. Clicking on the new instance (as highlighted) gives you the details about your instance, as shown in Figure 5-11.

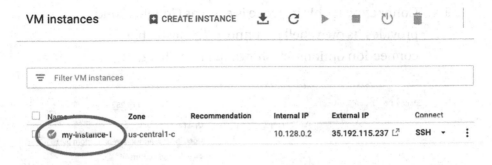

Figure 5-10. *Virtual machine*

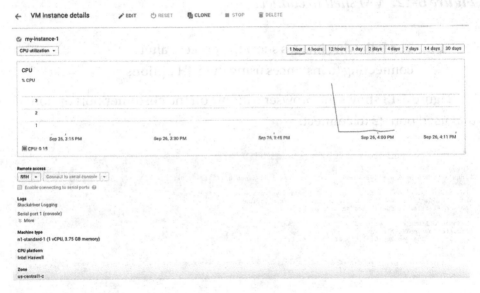

Figure 5-11. *VM details*

12.   Connecting to this instance is easy, as Google Cloud
provides its own shell to connect. The available
connection options are shown in Figure 5-12.

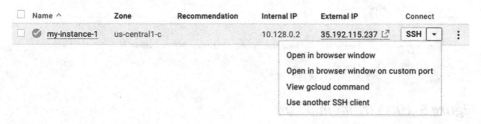

Figure 5-12. *VM shell to connect*

13.   The following images show the process after
connecting to instances using the SSH options.

Figure 5-13 shows the browser window on the customer port option
that used port 22 to connect.

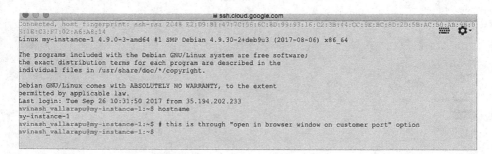

Figure 5-13. *VM open in browser*

Figure 5-14 shows the result of the `view gcloud` command option. You should click on Run In Cloud Shell.

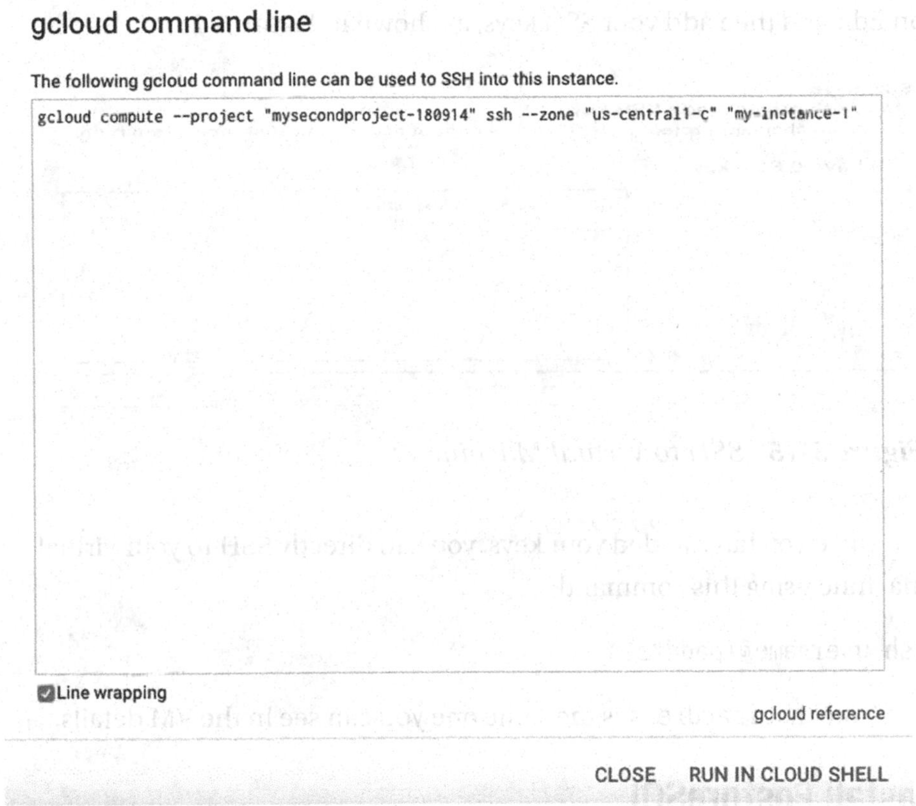

gcloud command line

The following gcloud command line can be used to SSH into this instance.

```
gcloud compute --project "mysecondproject-180914" ssh --zone "us-central1-c" "my-instance-1"
```

☑ Line wrapping

gcloud reference

CLOSE   RUN IN CLOUD SHELL

Figure 5-14. *VM gcloud result*

147

How to Connect from Your Machine

If you want to connect through your machine, edit the instance by clicking on Edit and then add your SSH keys, as shown in Figure 5-15.

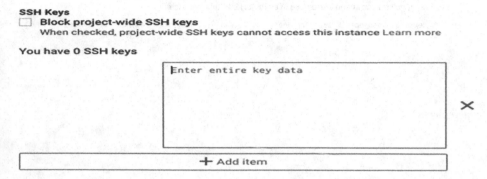

SSH Keys
☐ **Block project-wide SSH keys**
When checked, project-wide SSH keys cannot access this instance Learn more

You have 0 SSH keys

Enter entire key data

✕

＋ Add item

Figure 5-15. *SSH to Virtual Machine*

Once you have added your keys, you can directly SSH to your virtual machine using this command:

`ssh username@ipaddress`

Note that `ipaddress` is the same one you can see in the VM details.

Install PostgreSQL

Once you have created your instance, you will have a VM/machine ready for PostgreSQL installation. There are several ways to choose your PostgreSQL installation. You can use RPMs or use source installation.

One of the most easiest and most reliable ways to perform a PostgreSQL installation is through BigSQL, which is an Open Source DevOps platform designed for PostgreSQL. BigSQL binaries are portable across any Linux and Windows operating system. A user may want to install additional extensions and tools to build a complete PostgreSQL server for production. BigSQL combines a carefully selected list of extensions deployed in several PostgreSQL production environments after rigorous testing. This makes it easy for users to choose the extension they want to install using BigSQL. Then they can use very easy command-line features to install BigSQL.

To install PostgreSQL using BigSQL, follow these steps:

1. Go to `https://www.openscg.com/bigsql/`.

2. Click on the Downloads section.

3. Click on Usage Instructions, as shown in Figure 5-16.

Figure 5-16. *BigSQL usage instructions*

4. As per the usage instructions, for Linux machines, you can execute the following command to install the BigSQL package.

```
python -c "$(curl -fsSL
https://s3.amazonaws.com/pgcentral/install.py)"
```

BigSQL uses a command-line utility called pgc (pretty good command-line).

149

Here are some example commands.

To list the available PostgreSQL binaries and extensions for PostgreSQL, run the following command.

```
pgc list
```

To install PostgreSQL 9.6, run the following command.

```
pgc install pg96
```

To install an extension called pg_repack, run this command.

```
pgc install pg_repack
```

You need not worry about dependencies, such as gcc compiler or any other packages that need to be installed while installing postgres or its extensions. BigSQL takes care of all the dependencies and makes it very easy for you to deal with PostgreSQL.

One of the most advanced features of BigSQL is pgDevOps. pgDevOps is a UI that allows users to install and manage PostgreSQL instances in a few clicks. Users can upgrade PostgreSQL minor version or install and update an extension in a few clicks. BigSQL also helps users generate the queries/connections metrics through PgBadger reports on its UI, as requested. Users can also tune their complex procedural language using an excellent tool embedded in its UI, called plProfiler Console. Using plProfiler Console, users can look at the complete call stack of a complex PostgreSQL function and concentrate on the code that consumed more time of the execution in its entire call stack.

Thus, BigSQL helps users install and manage PostgreSQL and its extensions in a few clicks. BigSQL, combined with a cloud service, can easily build a very economic PostgreSQL database on the cloud.

Google Cloud Storage

Google Cloud Storage (GCS) offers object storage that's simple, secure, durable, and highly available. It can be used by developers and IT organizations. GCS's simple capacity pricing is highly effective across all storage classes with no minimum fee. It's a pay for what you use model.

Storage Classes

GCS has four storage classes:

- Multi-regional storage

- Regional storage

- Nearline storage

- Coldline storage

Multi-regional storage is a redundant storage model across geographical locations and it has the highest level of availability and performance. It is ideal for low-latency, high QPS content serving to users distributed across geographic regions.

Regional storage is only for a single region and provides the same level of availability and performance as multi-regional. It is ideal for compute, analytics, and Machine Learning (ML) workloads in a particular region.

The other two—the Nearline and Coldline storage classes—are fast and low-cost. Both have highly durable storage with consistent APIs. Use cases for these two storage options are:

- Nearline is designed for data that you do not want to access frequently. So, it is useful infrequently accessed data.

- Coldline is designed for cold data, such as archive and disaster recovery.

In addition, with lifecycle management, Google Cloud storage allows you to reduce your costs even further by moving your objects to Nearline and Coldline, and through scheduled deletions. Google Cloud Storage stores and replicates your data, thereby allowing a high level of persistence, and all the data is encrypted both in-flight and at rest.

Key Features of GCS

Google Cloud Storage is almost infinitely scalable. It can support applications irrespective of whether they are small or large or in a multi-exabyte system.

All four storage classes that we talked about offer very high availability. Multi-regional storage offers 99.95% monthly availability in its Service Level Agreement. Regional storage offers 99.9% availability, and the Nearline and Coldline storage classes offer 99%.

Like very few venders, Google Cloud Storage is designed for 99.999999999% durability. This is because it stores multiple copies redundantly across multiple disks, racks, power and network failure domains, with automatic checksums to ensure data integrity. As we already discussed, with the Multi-Regional storage class, data is also geo-redundant across multiple regions and locations

GCS has very consistent data and guarantees that when a write succeeds, the latest copy of the object will be returned to any GET, globally (applies to PUTs, new or overwritten objects, and DELETEs).

More information about Google Cloud Storage is available at https://cloud.google.com/storage/docs/.

We cover this storage option more in Chapter 8, "Backups on the Cloud."

Cloud SQL

Google Cloud SQL is a fully managed database service from GCP. Like other cloud vendors for RDBMS, Google Cloud SQL makes it easy to set up, manage, and maintain relation databases. It makes the administrator's job easy.

There are two relational databases available with Cloud SQL.

- Cloud for MySQL

- Cloud for PostgreSQL (beta)

Let's talk about the PostgreSQL service.

Cloud for PostgreSQL

This service was introduced recently and is still in its beta version. However, still you can choose this for your POCs and test your applications. As this is still in beta, some important features when compared to other cloud vendors for PostgreSQL are not available. They will likely be introduced in later releases. Due to storage security and durability, you can still consider your applications deployed on Cloud SQL. This product might change in backward-incompatible ways and is not subject to any SLA or deprecation policy. Let's look at key features of this service.

Advantages:

- The latest version of PostgreSQL 9.6 is available in the cloud, which is fully managed.

- You can choose machine types according to your application demand. Custom machine types with up to 208GB of RAM and 32 CPUs are available.

- You can create and manage instances in the Google Cloud Platform Console just like with other cloud vendors.

- Instances are available in US, EU, and Asia.

- You do not need worry about storage in the case of large applications. Up to 10TB of storage is available, with the ability to automatically increase storage as needed.

- There is more security for your data as customer data is encrypted on Google's internal networks and in database tables, temporary files, and backups.

- Has support for secure external connections using Cloud SQL Proxy or SSL protocol.

- Support for PostgreSQL client-server protocol and standard PostgreSQL connectors.

- You can import and export databases using SQL dump files.

- Backup are automated and you can have on-demand backups too.

- Monitoring and logging are available.

Because Cloud SQL for PostgreSQL is in beta, some PostgreSQL features are not yet available:

- Replication

- High-availability configuration

- Point-in-time recovery (PITR)

- Import/export in CSV format

Cloud SQL for PostgreSQL supports many types of PostgreSQL extensions. A few of them are:

- PostGIS

- Data type extensions like `btree_gin`, `btree_gist`, `cube`, `hstore`, etc.

- Language extensions like `plpgsql`

- Miscellaneous extensions like `pg_buffercache`, `pgcrypto`, `tablefunc`, etc.

For a complete list, visit this link: `https://cloud.google.com/sql/docs/postgres/extensions`.

Cloud SQL for PostgreSQL supports the PL/pgSQL SQL procedural language.

Support for languages, in terms of front-end or application languages for an application that is going to connect PostgreSQL, is robust. Without a cloud (or a on-premises database), you can use applications written in several languages. Just like on-premise, Cloud SQL provides a flexible environment for applications that are written in Java, Python, PHP, Node.js, Go, and Ruby. You can also use Cloud SQL for PostgreSQL with external applications using the standard PostgreSQL client-server protocol.

You can connect to a Google Cloud SQL instance for PostgreSQL from the following:

- A psql client: `https://cloud.google.com/sql/docs/postgres/connect-admin-ip`

- Third-party tools that use the standard PostgreSQL client-server protocol

- External applications: `https://cloud.google.com/sql/docs/postgres/connect-external-app`

- Google App Engine applications: `https://cloud.google.com/sql/docs/postgres/connect-app-engine`

- Applications running on Google Compute Engine: `https://cloud.google.com/sql/docs/postgres/connect-compute-engine`

- Applications running on Google Container Engine: `https://cloud.google.com/sql/docs/postgres/connect-container-engine`

Connecting from Google Cloud functions or by using Private Google access is not supported.

So, what are the differences between Cloud SQL and the standard PostgreSQL functionality? The PostgreSQL functionality provided by a Cloud SQL instance is generally the same as that provided by a local PostgreSQL instance. However, there are a few differences between a standard PostgreSQL instance and a Cloud SQL for PostgreSQL instance.

- You cannot have SUPERUSER privileges for your users. However, an exception to this rule is made for the `CREATE EXTENSION` statement, but only for supported extensions.

- It has custom background workers.

- The psql client in the Cloud Shell does not support operations that require a reconnection, such as connecting to a different database using the `\c` command.

- Some PostgreSQL options and parameters are not enabled for editing as Cloud SQL flags. Google advises: "If you need to update a flag that is not enabled for editing, start a thread on the Cloud SQL Discussion group."

Create a PostgreSQL Instance Using Cloud SQL

When you log in to the Google Cloud Console, it typically looks like
Figure 5-17. You can see Cloud Launcher, which typically contains all the
solutions available in Google Cloud.

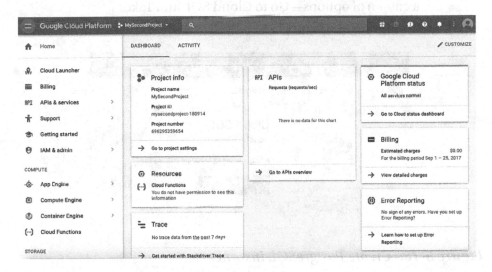

Figure 5-17. *The Google Cloud Dashboard*

Once you click on Cloud Launcher, it will direct you to a window where
you can see the GCP (Google Cloud Platform) on the left side. Clicking
on that shows all available solutions for GCP. The typical steps to create a
PostgreSQL service instance are as follows:

1. Log in to the Google Cloud Console using your
    Gmail account.

2. Create a project in which you want to initialize your
    services. Look at the "How to Create a Project Using
    the Console" section earlier in this chapter to create
    a project.

3. Click on Cloud Launcher on the left side panel.

157

4. Click on Google Cloud Platform on the left side panel.

5. Click on Cloud SQL in the Storage section.

6. You will be directed to a page where you will see a couple of options—Go to Cloud SQL and Take Quickstart. See Figure 5-18.

Figure 5-18. *Create PostgreSQL instance*

7. If you want to look at the documentations/pricing/ APIs related information, click on Take Quickstart. Click on PostgreSQL, as highlighted in Figure 5-19.

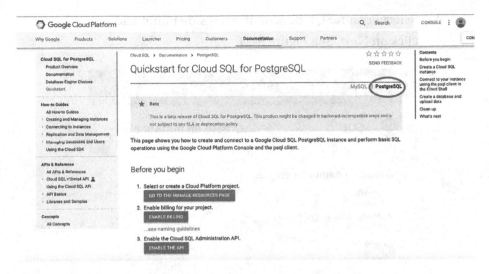

Figure 5-19. *Quickstart for Cloud SQL for PostgreSQL*

8. Once you're done with the quickstart, you select the Go to Cloud SQL option. You can also directly open the `https://console.cloud.google.com/sql/instances` link, which takes you to the create instance page shown in Figure 5-20.

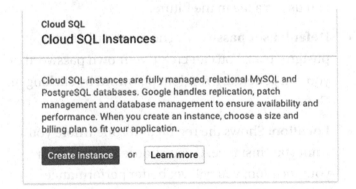

Figure 5-20. *Create PostgreSQL instance*

9. Select PostgreSQL Beta on the left side panel and click on Next. See Figure 5-21.

Figure 5-21. *Choose PostgreSQL instance*

10. The creation instance window in shown in Figure 5-22. Set the following options:

- **Instance ID:** The name of your instance, which you can use as a tag in the future.

- **Default user password:** The password of your postgres user. You can create your own password or you can generate a random password by clicking on Generate.

- **Location:** Shows the region and zone where you want your instance. If you choose a region near your location, you will get better performance.

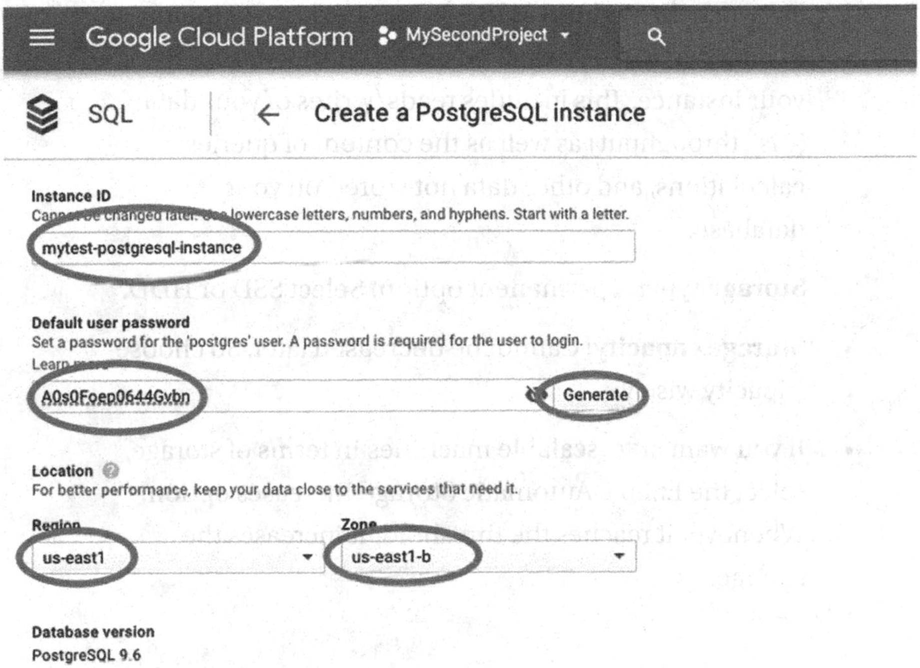

Figure 5-22. *Create PostgreSQL instance options*

You can click on Show Configuration Options to expand it and choose the options (see Figure 5-23):

- **Machine type:** Determines the virtualized hardware resources available to your instance, such as memory, virtual cores, and persistent disk limits. This choice affects billing. Constraints on dedicated core machine types are that memory must be at least 3.75GB, memory must be a multiple of 0.25GB, vCPU count must be one or even, and memory per vCPU must be between 0.9GB and 6.5GB per vCPU, inclusive. Some zones do not support machine types with 32 vCPUs.

- **Network throughput (MB/s):** The maximum amount of data that can be delivered over a connection to your instance. This includes reads/writes of your data (disk throughput) as well as the content of queries, calculations, and other data not stored on your database.

- **Storage type:** A permanent option. Select SSD or HDD.

- **Storage capacity:** Cannot be decreased later. So choose capacity wisely.

- If you want auto-scalable machines in terms of storage, select the Enable Automatic Storage Increases option. Whenever it reaches the threshold, it increases the storage.

≡   Google Cloud Platform   **⁖•** MySecondProject ▾

⊜   SQL | ←   **Create a PostgreSQL instance**

1   **Configure machine type and storage**   ∧

Machine type ⊘

• • •

Network throughput (MB/s) ⊘   250 of 2,000

▬▬▬▬▬▬▬▬▬▬▬▬▬▬▬▬▬▬▬▬▬▬▬▬▬

Storage type ⊘
Choice is permanent.
◉ **SSD (Recommended)**
  Most popular choice. Lower latency. Higher QPS and data throughput.
◯ **HDD**
  Lower performance than SSD. Much cheaper per GB stored. May be
  preferable for infrequently read data and long-term storage.

Storage capacity ⊘
10 – 10230 GB. Higher capacity improves performance, up to the limits set by
the machine type. Capacity cannot be decreased later.

| 10| GB |

☑ **Enable automatic storage increases**
  Whenever you're near capacity, space will be incrementally increased. All
  increases are permanent. Learn more

Disk throughput (MB/s) ⊘		**IOPS** ⊘	
Read: 4.8	Max: 250.0	Read: 300	Max: 15,000
Write: 4.8	Max: 75.8	Write: 300	Max: 15,000

| Close |

Figure 5-23. *Configure the machine type and storage*

- **Enable auto backups:** Enables auto backups of your databases. You can schedule a time for your backups. As they affect performance, it is recommended to schedule backups during your off-peak hours. See Figure 5-24.

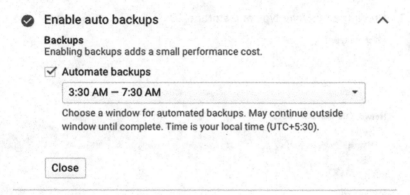

Figure 5-24. *Enabling auto backups*

- **Authorize Networks:** Add IP4 addresses that you want
  to allow to connect to the database. You can provide a
  particular IP or a range of IPs. See Figure 5-25.

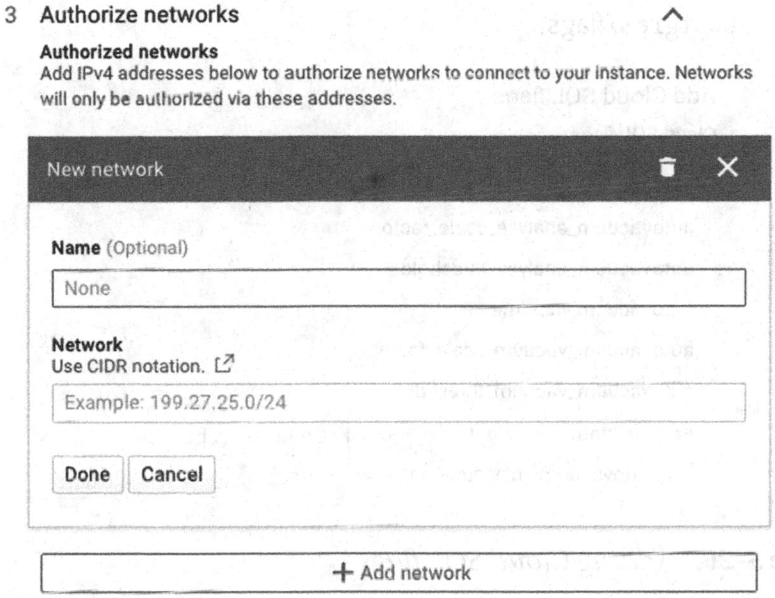

3   Authorize networks   ∧

Authorized networks
Add IPv4 addresses below to authorize networks to connect to your instance. Networks
will only be authorized via these addresses.

New network   🗑   ✕

Name (Optional)

None

Network
Use CIDR notation. ↗

Example: 199.27.25.0/24

Done   Cancel

➕ Add network

Figure 5-25. *Authorizing networks*

165

- **Add Cloud SQL flags:** You can add parameters that
  you want to change. Currently it allows only a few
  parameters to change (see Figure 5-26). The full list is
  available at `https://cloud.google.com/sql/docs/`
  `postgres/flags`.

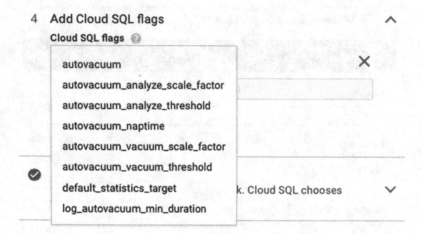

Figure 5-26. Adding Cloud SQL flags

- **Set maintenance schedule:** Allows you to set a time
  for the database maintenance activities. The instance
  will automatically restart to apply updates during a
  one-hour maintenance window. Updates happen once
  every few months. Choose a window, or leave it as Any
  window and Cloud SQL will pick a day and hour. See
  Figure 5-27.

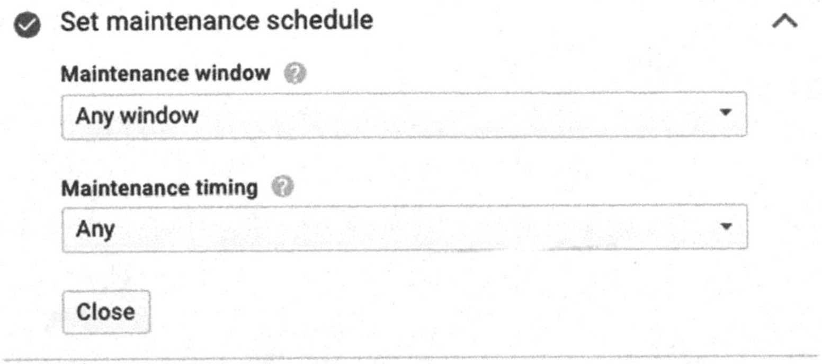

✓ Set maintenance schedule   ⌃

Maintenance window ?

Any window   ▾

Maintenance timing ?

Any   ▾

Close

Figure 5-27. *Set the maintenance mode*

Once you have set all the PostgreSQL instance options the way you want them, click on Create to create the instance.

Summary

This chapter explained the Google Cloud Console (GCC) and how to start using it. You learned how to create projects in GCC and how to create instances using GCC under Google Cloud Platforms like Compute Engine. We also covered PostgreSQL installation on instances. This chapter covered cloud storage, Cloud SQL, and the PostgreSQL service under Cloud SQL. We hope that it helps you start your applications on Google Cloud. The next chapter covers Microsoft Azure, including how to start it and the services available. It also covers how to create virtual machines and focuses on the PostgreSQL service that was introduced recently.

CHAPTER 6

Azure Cloud

This chapter covers products that Microsoft provides and how you can
use them with PostgreSQL. We cover how to initialize VMs and install/
configure PostgreSQL on them. This chapter provides basic information
on the storage that Azure provides, which we cover in further chapters in
detail. There is also an overview, initialization, and API discussion for the
PostgreSQL service recently introduced by Microsoft Azure.

Although Microsoft Azure provides a lot of services, we are going to
cover only a few services that are specific to PostgreSQL. See this link for a
list of services that it provides: `https://docs.microsoft.com/en-us/azure/`
`#pivot=products&panel=all`.

The following services are covered in this chapter:

- Virtual machines

- Storage

- Azure database for PostgreSQL

We discuss each service in detail.

Virtual Machines

Azure provides a way to create Windows or Linux virtual machines in a few
seconds. It is all about the choice of your operating system. You can choose
to be on-premises, in the cloud, or both. Choose your own operating

© Baji Shaik, Avinash Vallarapu 2018
B. Shaik and A. Vallarapu, *Beginning PostgreSQL on the Cloud*,
https://doi.org/10.1007/978-1-4842-3447-1_6

system virtual machine image or download a certified preconfigured image from the Azure marketplace.

You can scale your machine depending on needs. You can create a large cluster with cloud scalability. You can scale globally with a growing number of regional Azure data centers, which makes you closer to your customers.

You can encrypt your data to protect it from viruses using encrypting options available. Using the security options, you can easily meet your compliance requirements. More details on security are here: `https://azure.microsoft.com/en-us/services/security-center/`.

You can control your budget by paying for what you use. You can go for per-minute billing as well, which gives you better budget allocation for resources. Pricing details are based on need. Details are here: `https://azure.microsoft.com/en-us/pricing/details/virtual-machines/linux/`.

You can start using Azure with a free account. Go to `https://azure.microsoft.com/en-us/free/` and click on Start Free, as shown in Figure 6-1.

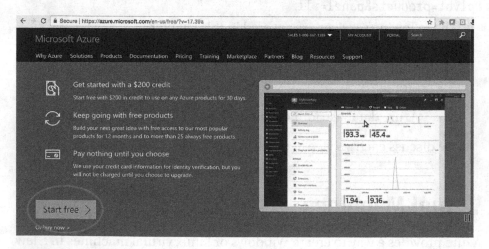

Figure 6-1. *Click Start Free to begin using Azure*

Once you click on Start Free, it will take you to a window where you can sign up for a free account by filling in the details, as shown in Figure 6-2.

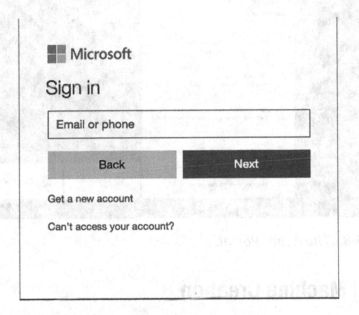

Figure 6-2. *Fill in the details of your free account*

Once you sign up, you can log in in to the Azure Portal to use the services provided by Azure. Here is the Portal login link: `https://portal.azure.com/`.

The Azure Portal is shown in Figure 6-3.

Figure 6-3. *The Azure Portal*

Virtual Machine Creation

This section explains how to create a virtual machine. Here are the high-level steps to doing so:

1. After logging in to the Azure Portal, click on Virtual Machines on left side and then choose Create Virtual Machines on right side, as highlighted in Figure 6-4.

172

Figure 6-4. *Create a virtual machine*

2. The available operating systems are listed in
    Figure 6-5.

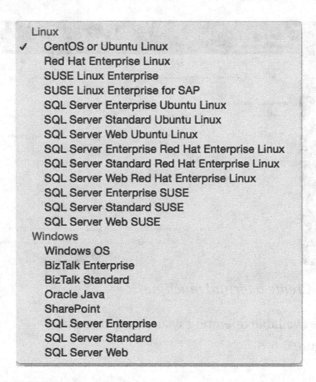

Figure 6-5. *The list of available operating systems is long*

3. By default, the section goes to Red Hat Enterprise
    Linux 7.4, but you can select whichever OS you
    want from the Recommended section. Look at the
    legal terms once you click Create. As RHEL OS is
    not covered under free trail, we selected Ubuntu for
    demo purposes.

4. The basic configuration settings are shown in
    Figure 6-6 and described in the following list.

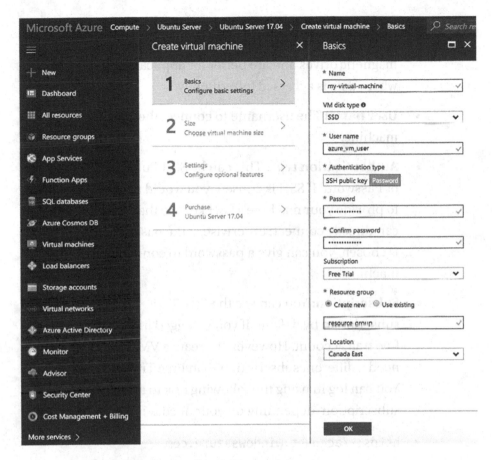

Figure 6-6. *The basic configuration settings*

- **Name:** The name of the virtual machine to differentiate.

- **VM disk type:** The type of disk. You can choose SSD or HDD. Premium (SSD) disks are backed by solid state drives and offer consistent, low-latency performance. They provide the best balance between price and performance and are ideal for I/O-intensive applications and production workloads. Standard (HDD) disks are backed by magnetic drives and are better for applications where data is accessed infrequently.

- **User name:** The username to connect the virtual machine.

- **Authentication type:** This can be SSH Public Key or Password. If SSH is chosen, you would need to provide your machine's SSH keys so that you can directly connect; otherwise, if the password is chosen, you can give a password to connect to machine.

- **Subscription:** You can see the Free Trail subscription by default, if you're logged in with a free trail account. However, to create a VM, you need a different subscription than Free Trail. You can log in using the following link to add a subscription, depending on your needs.

  https://account.windowsazure.com

- **Resource group:** You can create a new one or use an existing resource group if you have created one already. You can create a resource by clicking on Resource Group on left side panel.

- **Location:** The region in which you want your virtual machine. Available locations are shown in Figure 6-7.

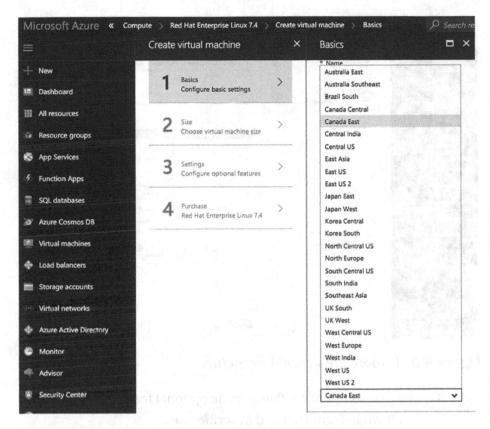

Figure 6-7. *Locations available for the virtual machine*

5. The next step is to choose the size of the machine that you want. Figure 6-8 shows the available sizes. You can also click on View All, as highlighted in Figure 6-8, to see all available sizes.

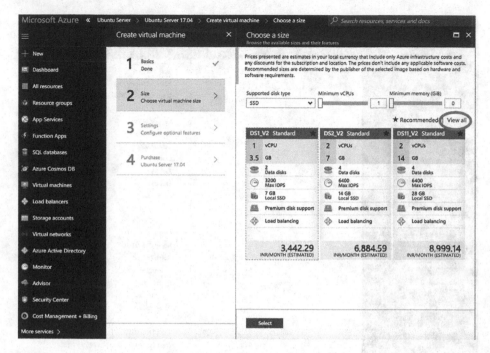

Figure 6-8. *Choose the size of the machine*

6. The next step is to configure some optional features, as shown in Figure 6-9 and described next.

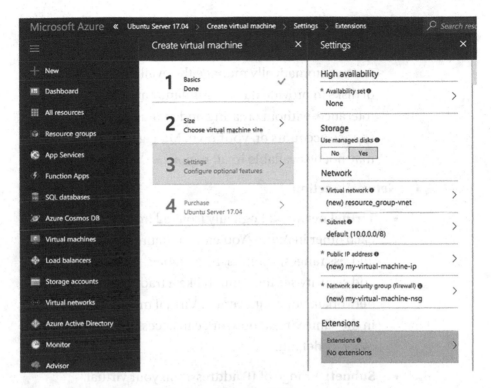

Figure 6-9. *Optional features for the VM*

- **High Availability Section**
  - **Availability set:** Provides redundancy to your application; we recommend that you group two or more virtual machines in an availability set. This configuration ensures that during a planned or unplanned maintenance event, at least one virtual machine will be available and meet the 99.95% Azure SLA. The availability set of a virtual machine can't be changed after it is created.

179

- **Storage Section**

  - **Use managed disks:** Enable this feature to have
    Azure automatically manage the availability
    of disks to provide data redundancy and fault
    tolerance, without creating and managing
    storage accounts on your own. Managed disks
    may not be available in all regions.

- **Network Section**

  - **Virtual network:** Logically isolated from
    each other in Azure. You can configure the IP
    address ranges, subnets, route tables, gateways,
    and security settings, much like a traditional
    network in your data center. Virtual machines
    in the same virtual network can access each
    other by default.

  - **Subnet:** A range of IP addresses in your virtual
    network, which can be used to isolate virtual
    machines from each other or from the Internet.

  - **Public IP address:** Use this if you want to
    communicate with the virtual machine from
    outside the virtual network.

  - **Network security group(firewall):** A set of
    firewall rules that control traffic to and from the
    virtual machine.

- **Extensions Section**

  - **Extensions:** These add new features, like
    configuration management or antivirus
    protection, to your virtual machine. See
    Figure 6-10.

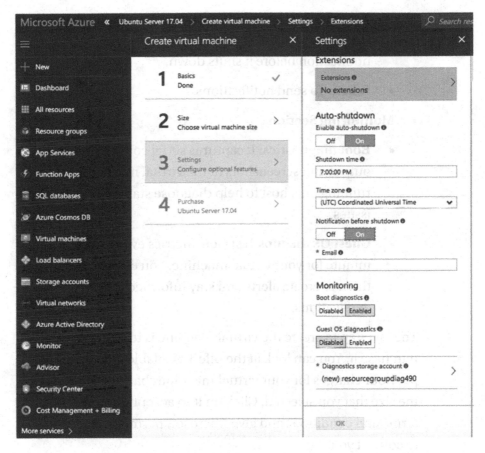

Figure 6-10. *The Extensions section*

- **Auto-Shutdown Section**

    - **Enable auto-shutdown:** Configures your virtual machines to shut down daily.

    - **Shutdown time:** The time when virtual machines shut down daily.

    - **Timezone:** Refers to the timezone for the time you selected.

181

- **Notifications before shutdown:** If you subscribe using your email ID, it sends notification before it shuts down.

- **Email:** To send notifications.

- **Monitoring Section**

  - **Boot diagnostics:** It captures serial console output and screenshots of the virtual machine running on a host to help diagnose startup issues.

  - **Guest OS diagnostics:** Gets metrics every minute for your virtual machine. You can use them to create alerts and stay informed of your applications.

7. The last step to create the virtual machine is to purchase it. You can look at the offers available and per hour charges for your virtual machines based on the size that you selected. Click on it to accept the terms and conditions and give Microsoft permission to contact you.

Once you click on Purchase, it will start initializing/deployment of the virtual machine. It may take a few seconds.

You can click on Notifications to see the process of deployment of your virtual machine, as highlighted in Figure 6-11.

Figure 6-11. *The deployment process*

Once the virtual machine is created, you can see the details by clicking on Virtual Machines on left panel and then on the virtual machine name on the right panel. You'll see all the details that you have chosen while creating the virtual machine. It shows monitoring metrics as well. Figure 6-12 is an example.

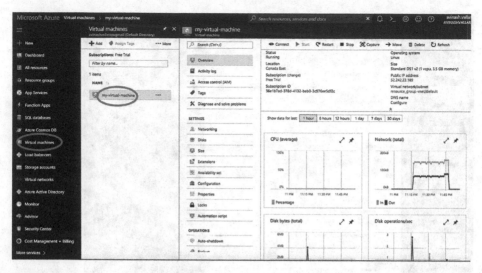

Figure 6-12. *The virtual machine's data and metrics*

Connecting to Virtual Machines

The virtual machine is created using a password, so you can directly use `ssh` to log in to Linux virtual machine using the public IP. You can get the public IP from the overview of the virtual machine, as shown in Figure 6-13.

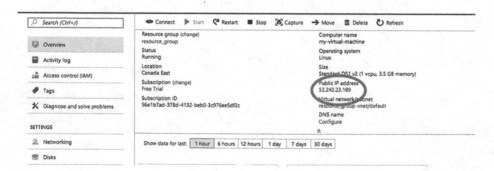

Figure 6-13. *The public IP of the Linux virtual machine*

You can `ssh` from your local machine, as shown in Figure 6-14. However, make sure that your IP is open. Take a look at Network Section in Step 6 to open IPS to connect.

```
C1MQV0FZDTY3:Documents bajishaik$ ssh azure_vm_user@52.242.23.189
azure_vm_user@52.242.23.189's password:
Welcome to Ubuntu 17.04 (GNU/Linux 4.10.0-35-generic x86_64)

 * Documentation:  https://help.ubuntu.com
 * Management:     https://landscape.canonical.com
 * Support:        https://ubuntu.com/advantage

 * What are your preferred Linux desktop apps?  Help us set the default
   desktop apps in Ubuntu 18.04 LTS:
   - https://ubu.one/apps1804

  Get cloud support with Ubuntu Advantage Cloud Guest:
    http://www.ubuntu.com/business/services/cloud

0 packages can be updated.
0 updates are security updates.


The programs included with the Ubuntu system are free software;
the exact distribution terms for each program are described in the
individual files in /usr/share/doc/*/copyright.

Ubuntu comes with ABSOLUTELY NO WARRANTY, to the extent permitted by
applicable law.

To run a command as administrator (user "root"), use "sudo <command>".
See "man sudo_root" for details.

azure_vm_user@my-virtual-machine:~$ █
```

Figure 6-14. Use ssh from your local machine

Installing PostgreSQL on a Virtual Machine

One of the easiest and most reliable ways to perform a PostgreSQL installation is through BigSQL, which is an Open Source DevOps platform designed for PostgreSQL. BigSQL binaries are portable across any Linux and Windows operating system. A user might want to install additional extensions and tools to build a complete PostgreSQL server for production. BigSQL combines a carefully selected list of extensions deployed in several

PostgreSQL production environments after rigorous testing. It makes it easy for users to choose the extension they want to install and then they can use the easy command-line features to install BigSQL.

To install PostgreSQL using BigSQL, follow these steps:

1. Go to `https://www.openscg.com/bigsql/`.

2. Click on the Downloads section.

3. Click on Usage Instructions, as shown in Figure 6-15.

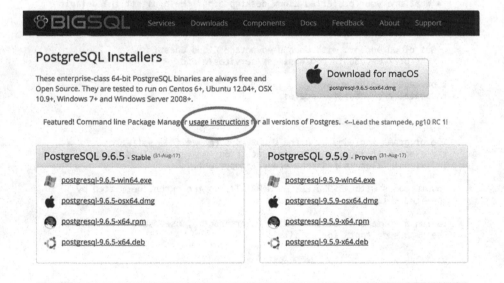

Figure 6-15. *Click on usage instructions*

4. As per the usage instructions, for Linux machines, you can simply execute the following command to install the BigSQL package.

```
python -c "$(curl -fsSL https://s3.amazonaws.com/
pgcentral/install.py)"
```

BigSQL uses a command-line utility called pgc (pretty good command-line).

- To list the available PostgreSQL binaries and extensions available for PostgreSQL, users can run the following command.

```
pgc list
```

- To install PostgreSQL 9.6, users can simply fire the following command.

```
pgc install pg96
```

- To install an extension called pg_repack, users can run the following command.

```
pgc install pg_repack
```

Users need not worry about several dependencies—such as gcc compiler or any other packages that need to be installed—while installing postgres or its extensions. BigSQL takes care of all the dependencies and makes it very easy to deal with PostgreSQL.

One of the most advanced features of BigSQL is its pgDevOps. pgDevOps is a UI that allows users to install and manage PostgreSQL instances in a few clicks. Users can upgrade the PostgreSQL minor version or install or update an extension in a few clicks. PgDevOps also helps users analyze queries and other database metrics like Connections, checkpointing, temp file generation, etc., through pgBadger reports on its UI, as requested. Users can also tune their complex procedural language using an excellent tool embedded in the UI, called plProfiler console. Using plProfiler console, users can look at the complete call stack of a complex PostgreSQL function and concentrate on the code that consumed more time of execution in its entire call stack.

Thus, BigSQL helps users install and manage PostgreSQL and its extensions in a few clicks. BigSQL, combined with any cloud service, can easily build a very economic PostgreSQL database on the cloud.

Dealing with Storage

Microsoft Azure provides scalable, durable cloud storage. It can be used for backup and recovery solutions for any volume of data, whether it is big or small. You can plan your database backups to upload to the cloud storage. If you have virtual machines created already, you can add more storage required by your application cost-effectively, whereas additional storage could be unstructured text or binary data such as video, audio, and images.

There are several storage types available, such as:

- Blob storage

- File storage

- Disk storage

- Table storage

- Queue storage

However, we cover only blob storage, as it is used for streaming and storing documents, videos, pictures, backups, and other unstructured text or binary data.

For blob store accounts, you can the Access Tier attribute, which you can see during account creation. Based on the access pattern, there are two types of access tiers:

- A hot access tier for the objects that you access frequently

- A cool access tier for the objects that you do not access frequently

The pricing details for dedicated Blob storage accounts with hot, cool, and archive (where available) access tiers are here: https://azure. microsoft.com/en-us/pricing/details/storage/blobs/.

We cover more about this storage in Chapter 8, "Backups on the Cloud."

Azure Database for PostgreSQL

After looking at the popularity of PostgreSQL in the Open Source world and listening to what customers wanted, Microsoft Azure announced Azure Database for PostgreSQL in May of 2017. It was the most frequently asked for service from its customers.

Advantages of Azure Database

This section looks at the advantages/benefits of this service. Azure Database for PostgreSQL provides a managed database service that can be set up in minutes and used for app development and deployments. You can scale on the fly.

With its low price (there are different pricing models), you will get much needed features like high-availability, security, and recovery—all built in. No need to pay extra for these features.

There is also no need to worry about database administration, as Azure Database for PostgreSQL provides managed database service, which means it provides automatic database patching, built-in monitoring, automatic backups, security, high-availability, and more. You don't need to worry about database administration. You can only focus on your applications, however, not on the infrastructure.

Scale without downtime. You can provision this service in minutes. And you can scale it on the fly to improve the performance without any downtime.

Built-in high availability. Azure Database for PostgreSQL provides built-in high availability and it needs no extra manual work from the user end, such as configuration or replication. There is no additional cost.

Use your favorite languages. You don't need to change your application programming language. You can just use what you're currently using with this service. It supports all the application programming languages that a stand-alone PostgreSQL installation supports.

Pay one simple price for everything. Features like point-in-time-recovery and high availability for Azure database for PostgreSQL come at no extra cost. They are included in the basic pricing.

Rest assured knowing you are backed by Azure. Once you create Azure Database for PostgreSQL, your data will be in Microsoft's global network of data centers, which are secure and have round-the-clock monitoring.

Azure Database for PostgreSQL Service Creation

You need to sign up to create the service. As explained in the "Virtual Machines" section, you may create a free account from `https://azure.microsoft.com/en-us/free/`.

Later you can add subscriptions that you want.

Follow these high-level steps to create an Azure Database for PostgreSQL instance:

1. Once you log in to the Azure Portal, click on + on the left panel and type `Azure Database for PostgreSQL`. Click on Azure Database on PostgreSQL, which you see from search and then you can see a window, which shows a Create button, as shown in Figure 6-16.

Figure 6-16. *Create an Azure Database for PostgreSQL instance*

2. After clicking Create, you'll see the window shown in Figure 6-17, where you need to fill in the details as explained.

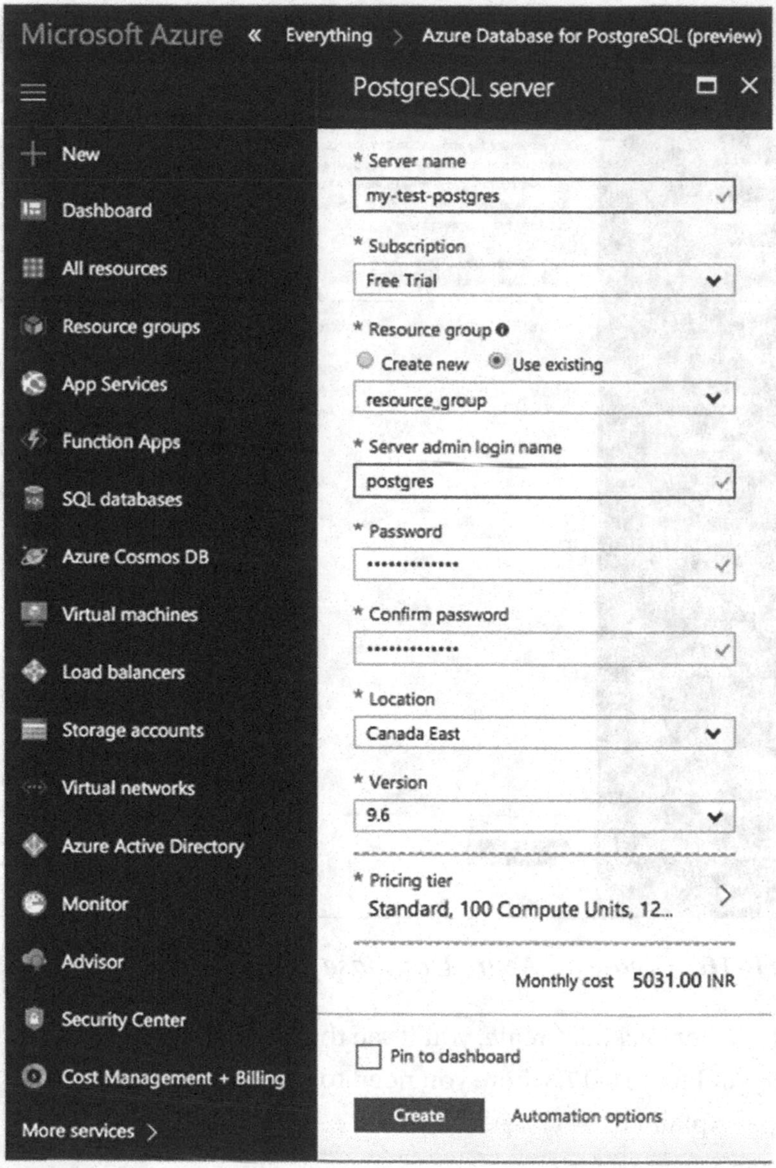

Figure 6-17. *Fill in the details for your PostgreSQL instance*

- **Server name:** The name of the instance. It's like a tag that differentiates it from other instances. You have to use the same name while staring/stopping/removing the instance.

- **Subscription:** If you added a subscription other than Free Trail, use it here.

- **Resource group:** A collection of resources that share the same lifecycle, permissions, and policies. If you have already created one, use it; otherwise, it creates one for you with the details you provide.

- **Server admin login name:** The database user that you use to connect.

- **Location:** The region in which you want your instance.

- **Version:** The PostgreSQL version. Currently, only 9.5 and 9.6 versions are available.

- **Price tier:** The type of instance that you want. Two types are currently available:

  - *Basic*: For workloads that scale with variable IOPS.

  - *Standard*: For workloads that require on-demand scaling optimized for high throughput with provisioned IOPS.

- **Compute Units:** A measure of CPU processing throughput that is guaranteed to be available to a single Azure Database for PostgreSQL server. A compute unit is a blended measure of CPU and memory resources. In general, 50 compute units equate to half a core. 100 compute units equate to one core. 2000 compute units equate to 20 cores of guaranteed processing throughput available to your server. The amount of memory per compute unit is optimized for the Basic and Standard pricing tiers. Doubling the compute units by increasing the performance level equates to doubling the set of resource available to that single Azure Database for PostgreSQL.

For example, a standard 800 compute units provides eight times more CPU throughput and memory than a standard 100 compute units configuration. However, while standard 100 compute units provide the same CPU throughput, as does basic 100 compute units, the amount of memory that is preconfigured in the Standard pricing tier is double the amount of memory configured for the Basic pricing tier. Therefore, the Standard pricing tier provides better workload performance and lower transaction latency than does the Basic pricing tier with the same compute units selected.

More details about compute units are found here: https://docs.microsoft.com/en-us/azure/ postgresql/concepts-compute-unit-and- storage.

- **Storage:** The storage required for your database.

Once you have entered the Compute Units and Storage, it will show the monthly cost for your instance, as shown in Figure 6-18.

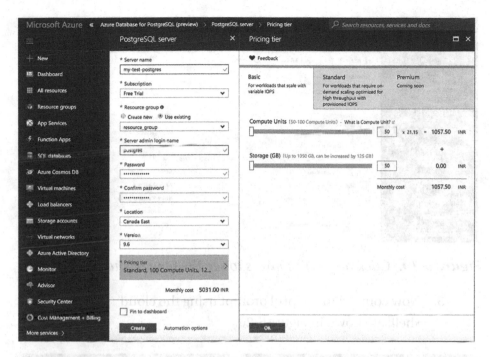

Figure 6-18. *The pricing tier*

> Click on OK and then Create so that it will start creating the instance.

3. See the Notifications tab on the right-side top to see the deployment process. The deployment takes a few minutes.

4. Once the instance is created, you can click on All Resources to see the instance, as shown in Figure 6-19.

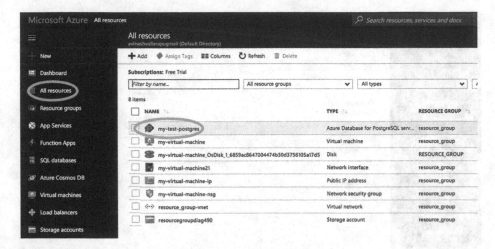

Figure 6-19. *Click on All Resources to see the new resource*

5.   Now connect to the psql prompt using the cloud
     shell, as shown in Figure 6-20.

Figure 6-20. *Connecting to the psql prompt using the cloud shell*

6.   Once you click on the cloud shell, you need to
     choose a Bash shell or a Power shell and then create
     storage to store your files. As psql is already installed
     on the cloud shell, you can do a quick psql to your
     instance, as shown in Figure 6-21. You can get the
     connection properties from your Connection Strings
     instance, as highlighted in Figure 6-21.

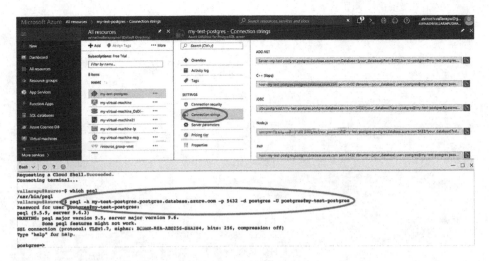

Figure 6-21. *The Connection Strings instance*

7. Migrating to your Azure instances is covered in further chapters.

Summary

This chapter covered Microsoft Azure services like virtual machines, storage, and Azure database for PostgreSQL and how can you use them with PostgreSQL. It covered the steps needed to create and configure a virtual machine and installing PostgreSQL on it. You got a little introduction to storages and learned which storage types we cover in further chapters. We also covered Azure Database for PostgreSQL service creation/connection. In the next chapter, we cover available options for securing data on each cloud. We also talk about the available tools and how to use them.

CHAPTER 7

Security on the Cloud

This chapter discusses why anyone needs security and why anyone would want to secure their data in the current world. It also covers the security options that each cloud vendor provides and how to achieve maximum security using those options. There might differences in ways of securing data for each vendor, but the ultimate goal is the same—secured data.

Security on Amazon Cloud

In previous chapters, we discussed how to create an AWS account and create our first EC2 or RDS instance. As a database administrator, my first priority is to ensure that my database is secure. In order to build such a secured environment, we need to know how we can implement proper user management and security procedures, by restricting unauthorized access and encryption of data in motion and data at rest. AWS provides a console that helps administrators achieve proper user management. This is applicable to all services created on AWS.

Identity and Access Management

Identity and Access Management (IAM) provides a mechanism that allows for user management of accounts in AWS. Users cannot use a root account to access AWS. There needs to be privileges, roles, or groups to ensure limited access to users. IAM allows us to create and manage user accounts

© Baji Shaik, Avinash Vallarapu 2018
B. Shaik and A. Vallarapu, *Beginning PostgreSQL on the Cloud*,
https://doi.org/10.1007/978-1-4842-3447-1_7

on AWS and control the access-level privileges of an AWS account. Using IAM, we can provide shared access with restricted permissions to an AWS, including temporary access to a few services. IAM allows us to use SSO (single sign-on) for an organization email account along with LinkedIn, Facebook, and Active Directory.

It is very important to secure an AWS account through several layers of security features. For example, using only password authentication is not good enough. AWS provides multi-factor authentication to secure your AWS account. You can enable password rotation policies to satisfy your organizational compliances.

Before going through the steps to use IAM to create a user, you should understand that there are two types of access that IAM provides:

- **Programmatic access:** When you select Programmatic access when creating a user, you get an access key ID and a secret access key. Programmatic access is needed for a user who uses AWS CLI and API.

- **AWS Management Console access:** Selecting this access when creating a user gives the user access to the AWS Management Console. This creates a password for every user to log in to the AWS Console.

AWS supports PCI DSS compliance. You can create a user or a *group*, which is a collection of users with one set of privileges. You can create roles and assign them to AWS resources. Policies can be created and assigned to a user, role, or a group.

A user needs to be given a certain set of privileges using policies. A *policy* is a document that defines permissions. AWS IAM enables you to create your own policies.

The policy document includes the following elements:

Effect: Whether the policy allows or denies access

Action: The list of actions that are allowed or denied by the policy

Resource: The list of resources on which the actions occur

Condition (Optional): The circumstances under which the policy grants permission

Create a User Using AWS IAM

To create a user in IAM, click on Users on the IAM Home page. You can also use the following link to do the same: https://console.aws.amazon. com/iam/home#/users. Follow these steps:

1. Click on Add User, as shown in Figure 7-1.

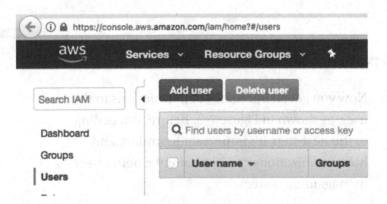

Figure 7-1. *Click on Add User*

2. Type your username and select the type of access you need. See Figure 7-2. If you want to use AWS CLI or APIs provided by AWS, you can select programmatic access. You can let AWS choose an auto-generated password that forces the user to reset it upon signing in. Click on Next to proceed to the permissions.

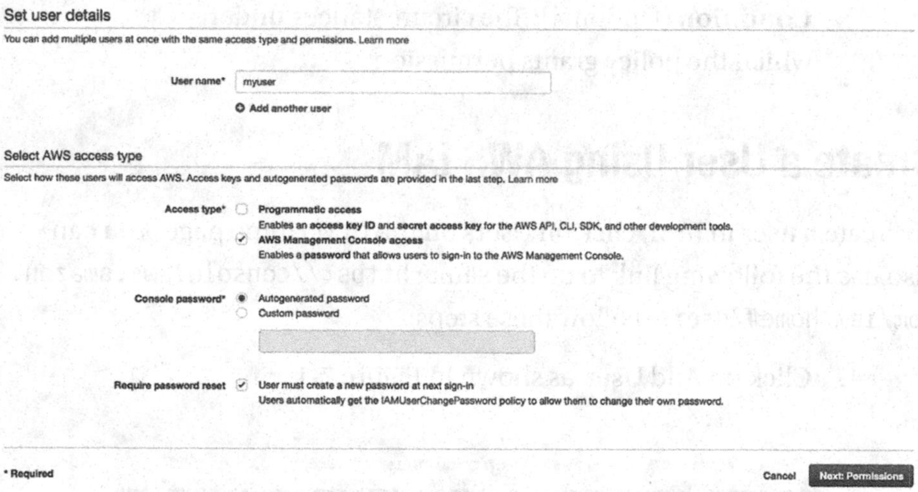

Set user details

You can add multiple users at once with the same access type and permissions. Learn more

User name* [myuser]

O Add another user

Select AWS access type

Select how these users will access AWS. Access keys and autogenerated passwords are provided in the last step. Learn more

Access type* ☐ Programmatic access
Enables an access key ID and secret access key for the AWS API, CLI, SDK, and other development tools.

☑ AWS Management Console access
Enables a password that allows users to sign-in to the AWS Management Console.

Console password* ● Autogenerated password
○ Custom password

Require password reset ☑ User must create a new password at next sign-in
Users automatically get the IAMUserChangePassword policy to allow them to change their own password.

* Required   Cancel   [Next: Permissions]

Figure 7-2. Entering the user details

3. Now you get an option to set permissions to the user, as shown in Figure 7-3. Before proceeding to the next step, it's important to understand how organizations can implement a better user management system.

    • Understand the type of users and their access requirements. For example, DBAs, developers, business analysts, infrastructure admins, etc.

- Create groups with a certain set of privileges for every type of user.

- Assign a group to a user instead of assigning individual policies every time a user is created.

  If you have not created a group yet, follow these steps to do so. As you can see in Figure 7-3, the IAM Console enables you to create a group. Click on Create Group to create a group using a set of policies.

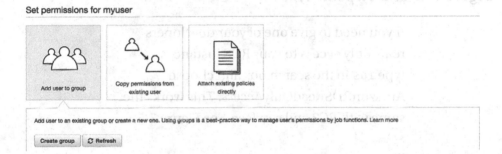

Figure 7-3. *Click on Create Group to create a group using a set of policies*

  Once you clicked on Create Group, you'll see a list of policies that clearly describes every policy, as shown in Figure 7-4. As you can see in the image, we selected AdministratorAccess, which gives the superuser full access to all the services of AWS on your AWS account.

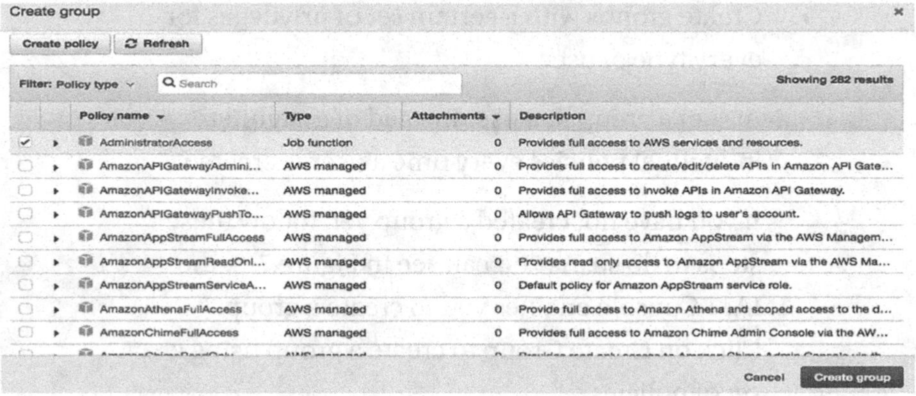

Create group   ×

| Create policy | ↻ Refresh |

Filter: Policy type ∨   🔍 Search   Showing 282 results

		Policy name ▾	Type	Attachments ▾	Description
✓	▸	AdministratorAccess	Job function	0	Provides full access to AWS services and resources.
☐	▸	AmazonAPIGatewayAdmini...	AWS managed	0	Provides full access to create/edit/delete APIs in Amazon API Gate...
☐	▸	AmazonAPIGatewayInvoke...	AWS managed	0	Provides full access to invoke APIs in Amazon API Gateway.
☐	▸	AmazonAPIGatewayPushTo...	AWS managed	0	Allows API Gateway to push logs to user's account.
☐	▸	AmazonAppStreamFullAccess	AWS managed	0	Provides full access to Amazon AppStream via the AWS Managem...
☐	▸	AmazonAppStreamReadOnl...	AWS managed	0	Provides read only access to Amazon AppStream via the AWS Ma...
☐	▸	AmazonAppStreamServiceA...	AWS managed	0	Default policy for Amazon AppStream service role.
☐	▸	AmazonAthenaFullAccess	AWS managed	0	Provide full access to Amazon Athena and scoped access to the d...
☐	▸	AmazonChimeFullAccess	AWS managed	0	Provides full access to Amazon Chime Admin Console via the AW...
☐	▸	AmazonChimeReadOnly	AWS managed	0	Provides read only access to Amazon Chime Admin Console via th...

                                                                    Cancel   **Create group**

Figure 7-4. *Select a policy type*

If you need to give one of your developers
read-only access to your RDS instances,
type rds in the search box and choose
AmazonRDSReadOnlyAccess. This works the
same with EC2 and services. See Figure 7-5.

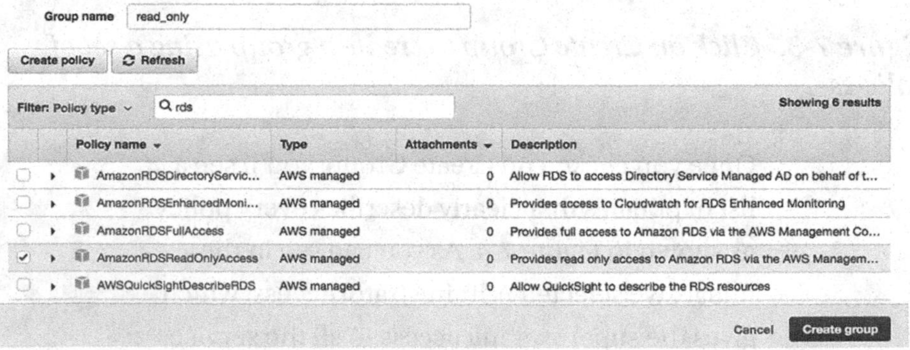

Group name   read_only

| Create policy | ↻ Refresh |

Filter: Policy type ∨   🔍 rds   Showing 6 results

		Policy name ▾	Type	Attachments ▾	Description
☐	▸	AmazonRDSDirectoryServic...	AWS managed	0	Allow RDS to access Directory Service Managed AD on behalf of t...
☐	▸	AmazonRDSEnhancedMoni...	AWS managed	0	Provides access to Cloudwatch for RDS Enhanced Monitoring
☐	▸	AmazonRDSFullAccess	AWS managed	0	Provides full access to Amazon RDS via the AWS Management Co...
✓	▸	AmazonRDSReadOnlyAccess	AWS managed	0	Provides read only access to Amazon RDS via the AWS Managem...
☐	▸	AWSQuickSightDescribeRDS	AWS managed	0	Allow QuickSight to describe the RDS resources

                                                                    Cancel   **Create group**

Figure 7-5. *Setting up read-only access*

Now, you can click on Create Group.

4.   This way, you can create multiple groups that distinguish privileges as per your organizational standard naming conventions. Now, you can select the group you want to assign to the user being created and proceed to the next step. See Figure 7-6.

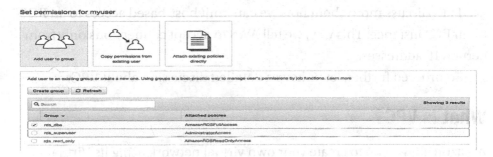

Figure 7-6. *Adding a user to a group*

5.   Once you have created the user, you'll see an URL created by AWS to let your user access the console specific to your AWS account. Using this URL, users can log in to the console and perform activities allowed by the group to which they are assigned. See Figure 7-7.

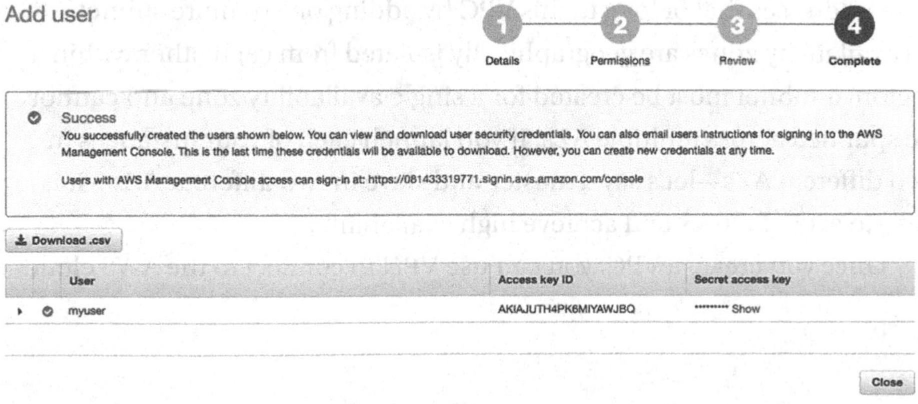

Figure 7-7. *Users log in to the console with the new URL*

Restricting Access to an RDS or an EC2 Instance

We discussed how to implement a better user management policy that helps an organization distinguish every user through the roles and activities they are intended to perform. In an organization, we need to implement multiple layers of security, which may not be achieved using a proper user management policy alone.

Let's discuss more about how we can limit host-based access to an RDS or an EC2 instance. This way, we tell AWS to accept connections only from certain IP addresses.

To proceed further, let us have a detailed discussion about VPC.

What Is VPC?

Amazon allows you to create your own virtual network using its Virtual Private Cloud (VPC) . Using AWS, you can create your own VPC that is physically within the Amazon network but logically isolated. You can define your own IP address range, subnets, security gateways, and settings while creating your VPC.

A *subnet* is a range of IP addresses within a single availability zone or region. While creating AWS instances, we can specify the subnet in which they are created. While creating a VPC, you must specify a range of IP addresses that belong to this VPC by adding one or more subnets. As availability zones are geographically isolated from each other within a region, a subnet must be created for a single availability zone and cannot be spanned across multiple AZs. If you launch each of your instances in two different AZs—let's say a master and slave in two different AZs—it is easy to avoid failures and achieve high availability.

Once you create a VPC, you can use VPN to connect to the AWS cloud.

Creating Subnet Groups

Use these steps to create subnet groups and a VPC.

1. As shown in Figure 7-8, search for VPC and
    click on it.

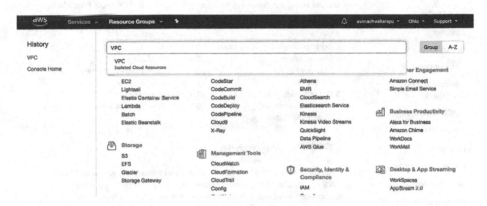

Figure 7-8. *Find VPC and click on it to begin*

2. Once you click on VPC, you should see a VPC
    dashboard, where you can get to the VPC Wizard
    and create subnets, route tables, and Internet
    gateways. See Figure 7-9.

Figure 7-9. *The VPC dashboard*

3. Click on your VPCs to create your VPC and then click on Create VPC.

Now you can choose a name tag to better identify this VPC. Select the IPv4 CIDR Block and click on Create VPC, as shown in Figure 7-10.

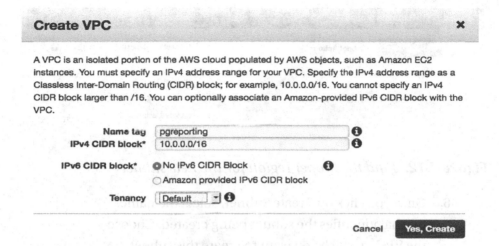

Figure 7-10. *Add a name tag to better identify the VPC*

4.   You can now click on Subnets and then choose
     Create Subnet in an availability zone.

     Click on Subnets to proceed. See Figure 7-11.

Figure 7-11. *Click on Subnets to reach this window*

5.   To create a subnet in an availability zone of a
     different region, you can change the region, as
     shown in Figure 7-12. In the top-right corner, click
     on the dropdown to modify the region in which you
     need to create your subnet.

Figure 7-12. *Find the proper region for the new subnet*

6.   Once you click on Create Subnet, select the name
tag that identifies the subnet being created. Choose
the VPC in which you want to create this subnet.
Choose the availability zone and the IPV4 CIDR
Block for this subnet as well. Once you're done, click
on Yes, Create, as shown in Figure 7-13.

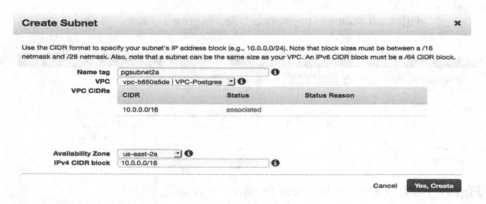

Figure 7-13. *Add the details about the subnet*

7.   Once your VPC has been created, you can now
create your EC2 instance using this VPC. This allows
you to restrict access to your EC2 instances.

While creating an RDS instance, as you learned in previous chapters, you can choose the VPC of your region. Your instance will then be created there. See Figure 7-14.

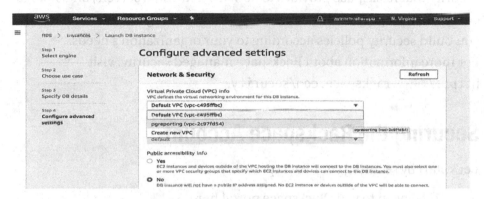

Figure 7-14. *Choose the VPC where you want to create the instance*

Likewise, you can choose a VPC while creating your EC2 instance, as shown in Figure 7-15.

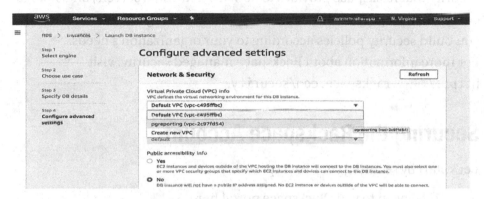

Figure 7-15. *Configuring the instance details*

Rackspace Cloud Security

In Chapter 4, we talked about how to create a Rackspace account to manage the Rackspace solutions. In this chapter, we talk about the security that Rackspace provides to its VMs, dedicated servers, and storage components. Apart from these, Rackspace has managed security that helps you build security policies according to your organization's needs. For more information about Rackspace managed security, visit https://www.rackspace.com/security.

Securing the Rackspace Account

Let's start by securing your Rackspace account.

1. Log in to your Rackspace portal here: https://login.rackspace.com.

2. Click on My profile & Settings in the top-right corner, as shown in Figure 7-16.

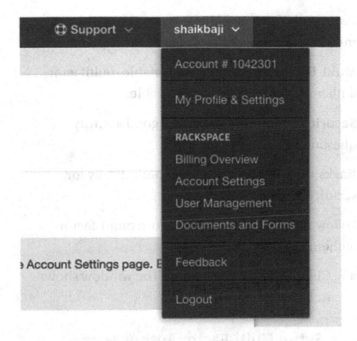

Figure 7-16. *Click on My Profile & Settings*

3. You'll then see the security settings, as shown in
    Figure 7-17.

Security Settings

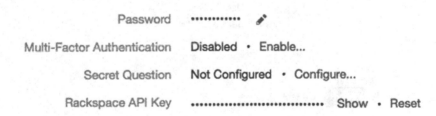

Figure 7-17. *The security settings*

213

Password: You should have strong password that meets the requirements of your security policies.

Multi-Factor Authentication: Enable multifactor authentication by clicking on Enable.

Security Question: Configure a good security question.

Rackspace API Key: Reset this periodically for security purposes.

4. Follow these sub-steps to configure multi-factor authentication.

   a. Click on the Enable option. The window shown in Figure 7-18 will pop up.

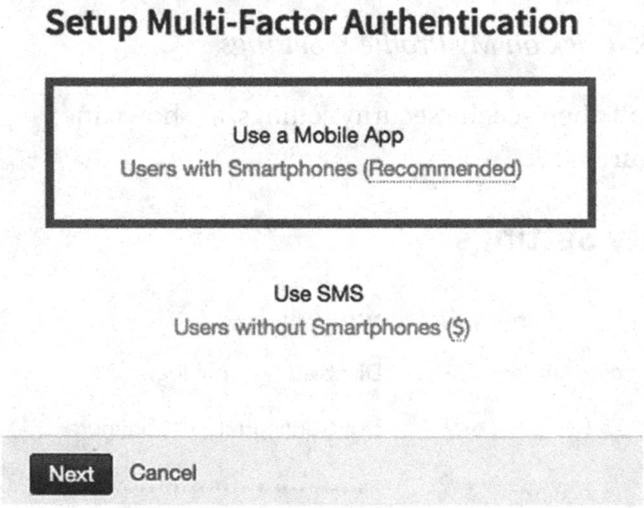

Setup Multi-Factor Authentication

Use a Mobile App
Users with Smartphones (Recommended)

Use SMS
Users without Smartphones ($)

Next   Cancel

Figure 7-18.   *Choose the recommended option of mobile app here*

b. Click on Using a Mobile App, as it is
    recommended and then Next. You will have
    to enter your device name (see Figure 7-19).
    Currently supported applications for multi-
    factor authentication are Authy, Duo, and
    Google Authenticator.

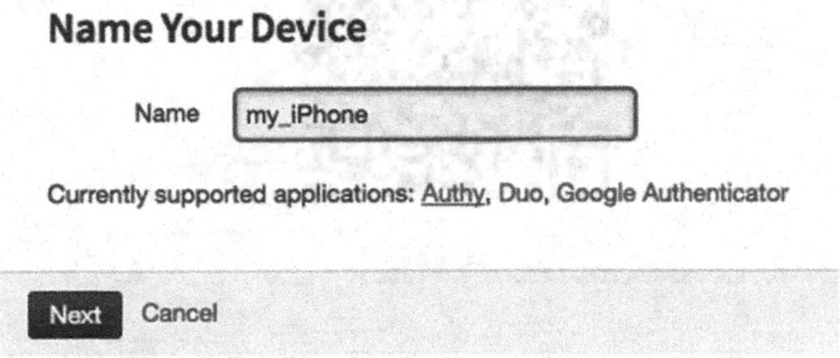

Name Your Device

Name [my_iPhone   ]

Currently supported applications: Authy, Duo, Google Authenticator

[Next] Cancel

Figure 7-19. *Name your device*

c. Install the security app on your phone
    (for example, install DUO app) and scan the
    barcode, which appears in the window in your
    phone app. See Figure 7-20.

Verify your Device

Open your mobile passcode application and scan the following barcode using your phone's camera. Below the barcode is the secret key which may also be used in your passcode application.

KU2ZUC3KFJC4TT6ALZYDOTYYJV4WECQT

Once you have scanned the barcode or copied over the secret key, enter the verification code generated by the app.

Verification Code   208583

⚠ Enabling multi-factor authentication will log you out and require you to reauthenticate using your device.

Verify   Cancel

Figure 7-20. *This barcode appears in the window in your app*

  d. Click on Verify. You will then be prompted to log in to your account again. Now, your account is configured for multi-factor authentication. Whenever you need to log in, you have to enter the code that is generated from your DUO app.

 5. If you click on User Management shown on the left corner of the same page, you can see users related to your account. See Figure 7-21.

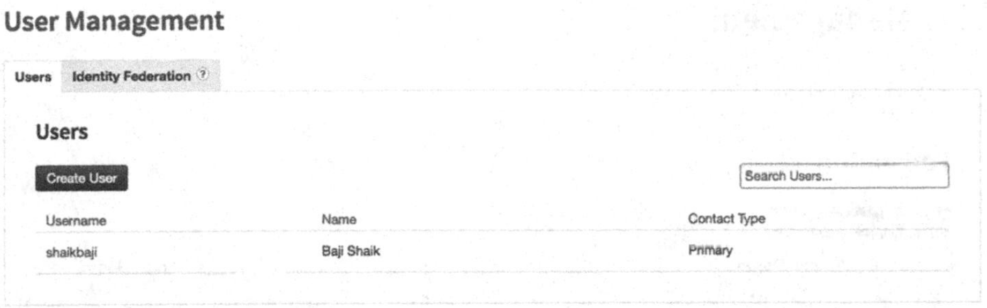

User Management

Figure 7-21. *Other users related to your account*

6. You can create users and provide only required privileges, as shown in Figure 7-22.

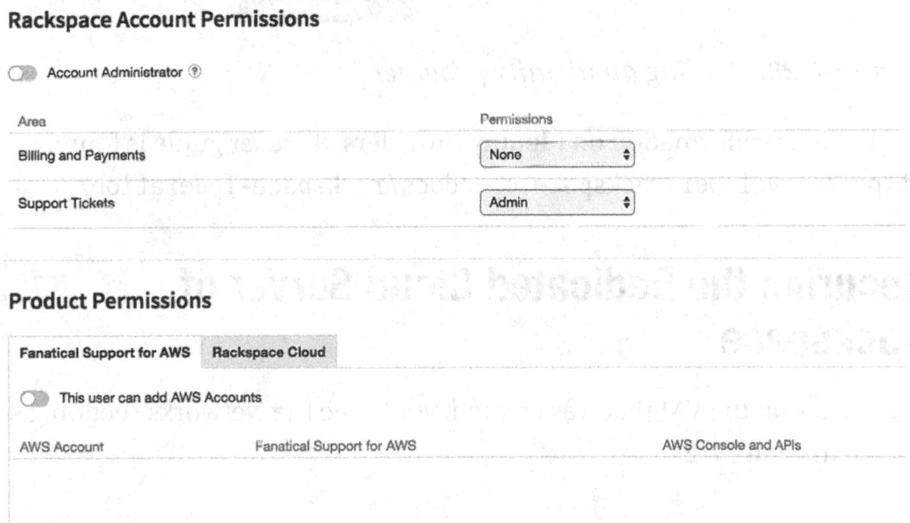

Figure 7-22. *Setting up user permissions*

7. You can also add an identity provider using the Add identity Provider button from the Identity Provider tab, as shown in Figure 7-23.

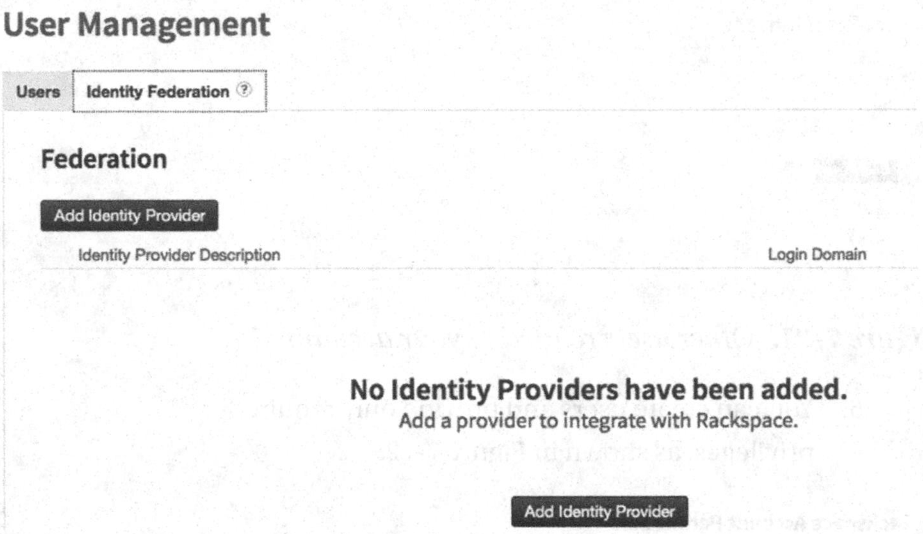

User Management

Users | **Identity Federation** ⑦

Federation

Add Identity Provider

Identity Provider Description   Login Domain

No Identity Providers have been added.
Add a provider to integrate with Rackspace.

Add Identity Provider

***Figure 7-23.** Adding an identity provider*

For more information on identity providers, the user guide is found at
`https://developer.rackspace.com/docs/rackspace-federation/`.

Securing the Dedicated Cloud Server of Rackspace

If you click on the VM that was created, you'll see the Networks section, as
shown in Figure 7-24.

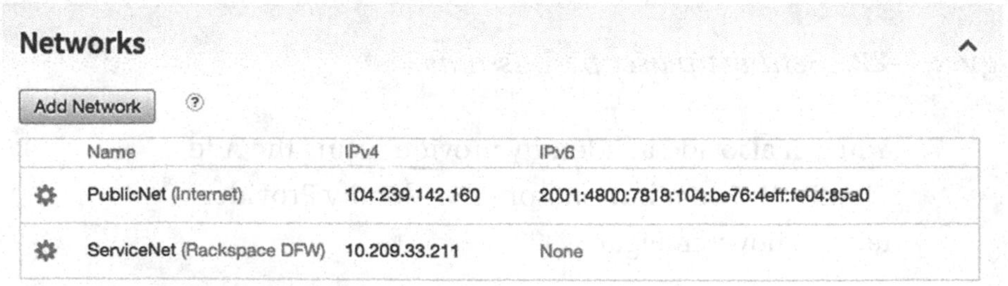

Networks   ⌃

Add Network   ⑦

	Name	IPv4	IPv6
⚙	PublicNet (Internet)	104.239.142.160	2001:4800:7818:104:be76:4eff:fe04:85a0
⚙	ServiceNet (Rackspace DFW)	10.209.33.211	None

***Figure 7-24.** Current networks on the VM*

Adding a network that allows only specific IP ranges will secure your VM because users will be prohibited from logging in from other hosts. See Figure 7-25.

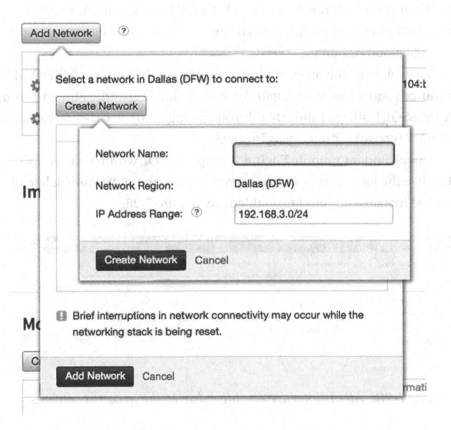

Figure 7-25. Adding a network

Security for the Google Cloud

Chapter 5 talked about creating an account to sign in to the GCP (Google Cloud Platform) console. Your user login will be the administrator of your console and can access any service. So it has no limitations.

Say there are multiple users who need read-only access to the instances of the Compute Engine or SQL databases or storage. Each user has his/her own login ID. In this case, you have to manage all the users and their respective privileges. Google Cloud has a Cloud IAM feature that enables you to control access to each user on any project in order to manage cloud resources.

To explain it with an example, say we have a GCP project with a VM instance (under Compute Engine), a storage bucket (under Storage), and a PostgreSQL instance (under SQL). You can log in to the GCP console using `https://console.cloud.google.com/`.

Check under Compute Engine, Storage, or SQL within your project. Because the login user is an admin, you can see the stop/reset/delete of the VM instance options are enabled. See Figure 7-26.

Figure 7-26. *All options are enabled due to the account settings*

Control Access to the Compute Engine

1. Log in to IAM console using the admin user and this link:

   `https://console.cloud.google.com/iam-admin/iam/project`

   You'll see the window in Figure 7-27 after you log in.

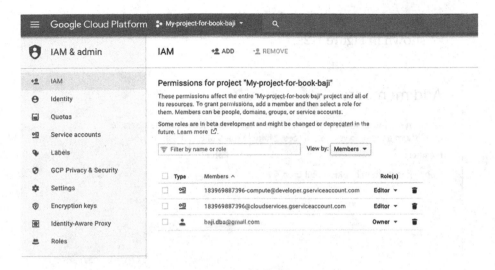

Figure 7-27. *The IAM console as viewed from the admin account*

2. You need to add a member to grant permission on
    your compute resources. Click on Add, as shown in
    Figure 7-28.

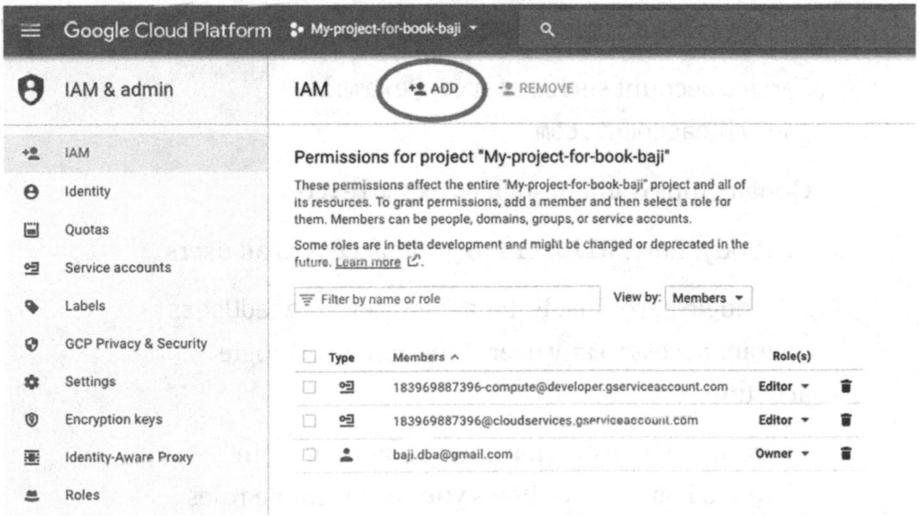

Figure 7-28. *Adding a member*

3. Once you clicked on Add, you'll can see the window shown in Figure 7-29.

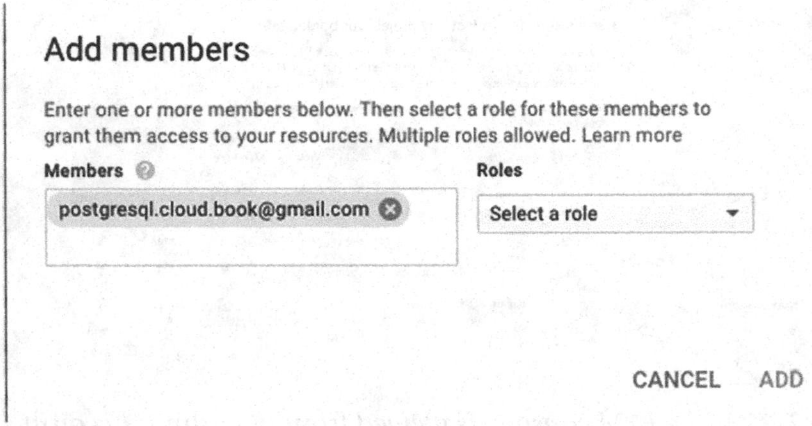

Add members

Enter one or more members below. Then select a role for these members to grant them access to your resources. Multiple roles allowed. Learn more

Members ⓘ

postgresql.cloud.book@gmail.com ⊗

Roles

Select a role ▼

CANCEL   ADD

Figure 7-29. Adding a member

To add the member, you can add any of these:

Google account email such as user@gmail.com

Google groups such as admins@googlegroups.com

Service account such as server@example. gserviceaccount.com

Google Apps domain such as example.com

Anybody: Enter allUsers to grant access to all users

All Google accounts: Enter allAuthenticatedUsers to grant access to any user signed in to a Google account

There are lot of roles that you can grant to your member. Figure 7-30 shows you the available roles for the Compute Engine service.

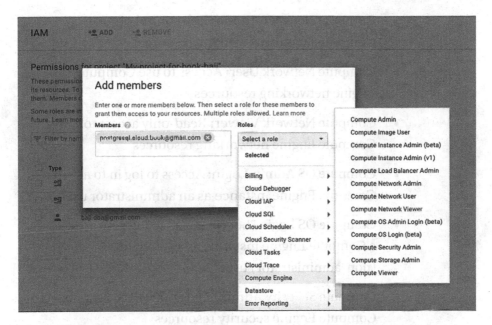

Figure 7-30. *Available roles for the Compute Engine service*

Let's look at the roles available for Compute Engine:

- Compute Admin: Full control of all Compute Engine resources

- Compute Image User: Read and use image resources

- Compute Instance Admin (beta): Full control of Compute Engine instance resources

- Compute Instance Admin (v1): Full control of Compute Engine instances, instance groups, disks, snapshots, and images. Read access to all Compute Engine networking resources

- Compute Load Balancer Admin: Full control of Compute Engine resources related to the load balancer

223

- Compute Network Admin: Full control of Compute Engine networking resources

- Compute Network User: Access to use Compute Engine networking resources

- Compute Network Viewer: Read-only access to Compute Engine networking resources

- Compute OS Admin Login: Access to log in to a Compute Engine instance as an administrator user

- Compute OS Login (beta): Access to log in to a Compute Engine instance as a standard (non-administrator) user

- Compute Security Admin: Full control of Compute Engine security resources

- Compute Storage Admin: Full control of Compute Engine storage resources

- Compute Viewer: Read-only access to get and list information about all Compute Engine resources including instances, disks, and firewalls. Allows getting and listing information about disk, images, and snapshots, but does not allow reading the data stored on them

    For this demo, we are selecting the Compute Viewer role.

    Click on Add after selecting the required role.

4. Once you have added the role, you can see the member, as shown in Figure 7-31.

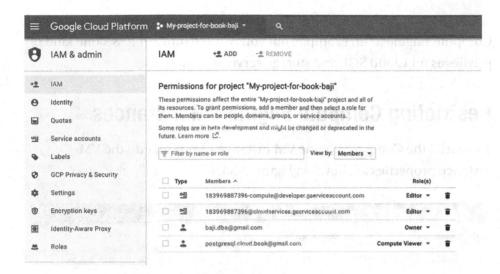

Figure 7-31. Adding the role

5. As Compute Viewer is selected, this user can only see VM instances. He can't control instances. If you click on the VM instance, all the features for Reset/Clone/Stop/Delete are disabled, as shown in Figure 7-32.

Figure 7-32. The features for Reset/Clone/Stop/Delete are disabled because of the user's permissions settings

225

In this way, you can control access to the data and services. We showed Compute Engine as an example, but you will see more or less same kind of privileges for Cloud SQL and storage services as well.

Restricting Compute Engine VM Instances

To restrict the Compute Engine VM instances, you can edit the VM instance properties as shown in Figure 7-33.

Figure 7-33. *Edit the VM properties*

Managing SSH Keys

You connect to a VM instance using an SSH key. Compute Engine manages your SSH keys for you whenever you connect to an instance from the browser or connect to an instance with the gcloud command-line tool, creating and applying public SSH keys when necessary.

However, sometimes you'll need to manage your SSH keys. Once your instance is created, you can add the SSH keys of the machines that you want to connect to the VM instance. See Figure 7-34.

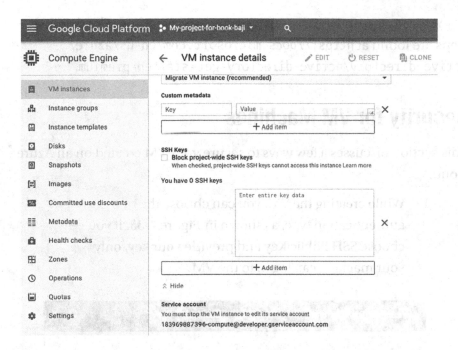

Figure 7-34. *Adding SSH keys*

Microsoft Azure Security

Chapter 6 talked about the services that Microsoft Azure provides for use with PostgreSQL. This section discusses the security that Microsoft Azure provides to their apps.

As with the other cloud venders, Microsoft Azure provides IAM with single sign-on as Microsoft Azure Active Directory Premium.

In the arms race between cyber criminals and IT security, the side with the most advanced tools wins. That means that it is not enough to rely on tools that monitor or log your systems or tools built around static policies and lists. To stay one step ahead of the other side, you need a tool that can do more.

You can sign up for Azure Active Directory Premium. The detailed steps are found at `https://docs.microsoft.com/en-us/azure/active-directory/active-directory-get-started-premium`.

Security for VM Machines

This section discusses a few ways to secure your VM created on an Azure cloud.

1. While creating the VM, you can choose the authentication type, as shown in Figure 7-35. If you choose SSH Public Key and provide your key, only your machine can log in to the VM.

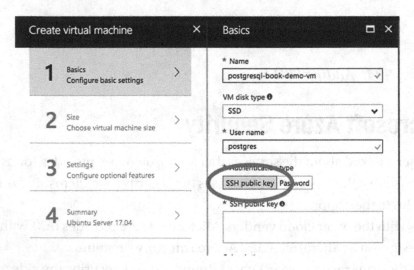

Figure 7-35. *Choose SSH Public Key to limit access*

2. While creating the VM, you can also configure IP address ranges, subnets, route tables, gateways, and security settings, much like a traditional network in your data center. See Figure 7-36.

***Figure 7-36.** Configuring security settings for the VM*

3. You can turn on Data Collection to receive security alerts and recommendations about system updates, OS vulnerabilities, and end point protection. To turn it on, choose Security Center from the left panel of the Azure Portal, and then click on Security Policy. Choose Subscription. See Figure 7-37.

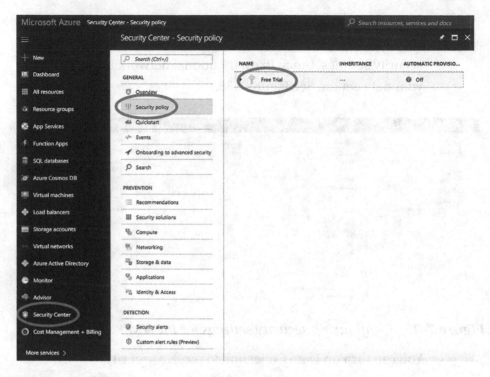

Figure 7-37. *Find your subscription settings*

Once you click on the subscription, you will see the Data Collection option on the left side panel, as shown in Figure 7-38.

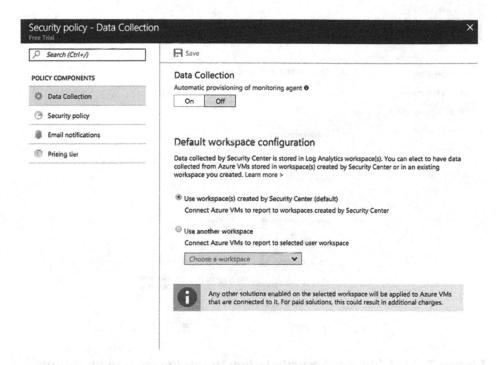

Figure 7-38. *Turn on Data Collection to receive security alerts*

If you turn it on, data collection agents will be installed on all the VMs in the subscription. If you click on Security Policy, you will see recommendations for what policies you want, as shown in Figure 7-39.

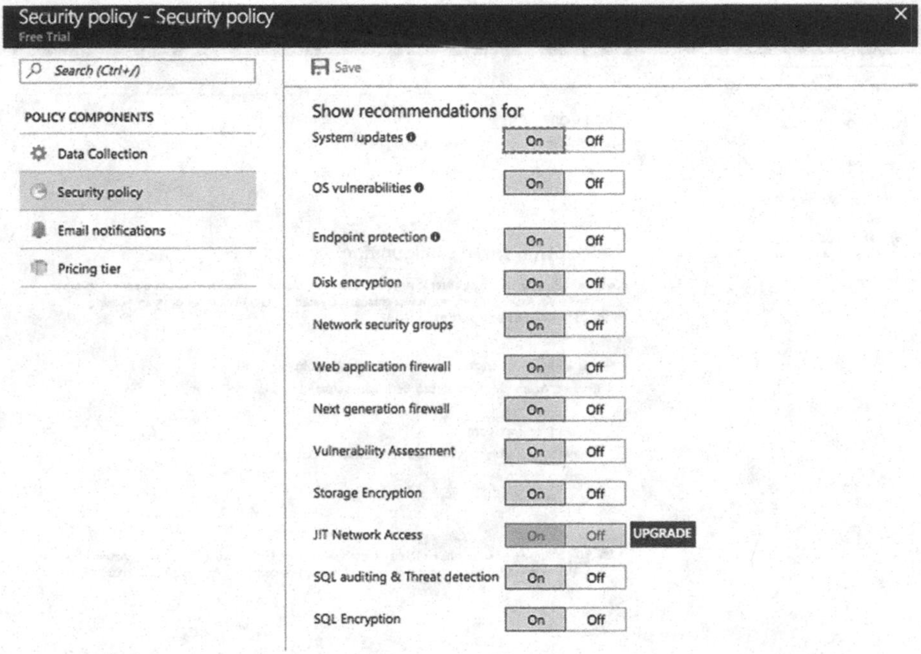

Figure 7-39. *Choosing Security Policy shows the recommendations*

You can also set email notifications so you are contacted in case the Azure security team finds that your resources have been compromised.

Security for SQL Database

This section covers the process of securing PostgreSQL databases on Azure.

There are two ways to do so:

- Create and manage firewall rules

- Configure SSL

To configure an SSL, you need a Azure Database for PostgreSQL instance. Once the instance has been created, follow these steps:

1. Click on the instance that you created.

2. On the left panel, you'll see Connection Security. Click on it to see the window shown in Figure 7-40.

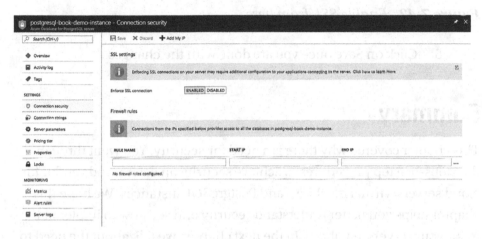

Figure 7-40. *Connection security window*

3. Fill the details under the Firewall Rules section, as shown in Figure 7-41.

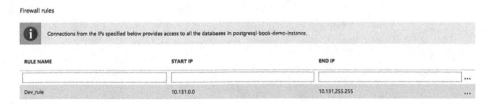

Figure 7-41. *Fill in the Firewall Rules section*

For this demo, we added a rule named `Dev_rule` with IP starting and ending ranges so that only requests from these IPs can be served.

4.   On the same page, you can enable SSL under the
     SSL Settings area, as shown in Figure 7-42.

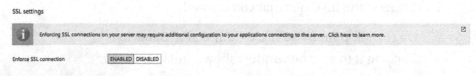

Figure 7-42. *Enable SSL from here*

5.   Click on Save once you are done with the changes.

Summary

This chapter covered why there is a need for security. You went through
the steps-by-step procedures to achieve security on each cloud vendor for
cloud servers/virtual machines and PostgreSQL instances. We hope this
chapter helps you better understand security and see how to implement
in for your servers/database. In the next chapter, we talk about the need to
back up your virtual machines and PostgreSQL instances, including how to
schedule machine backups using each vendor in detail.

CHAPTER 8

Backups on the Cloud

This chapter covers why we need backups for our machines and databases. The chapter talks about the backup options available with each cloud vendor and how to deal with them. Every cloud vendor is not the same when it comes to backup schedules and cost. We cover all the backup solutions available with each vendor.

Backups on the AWS Cloud

Amazon allows users to manage backups of RDS instances through a user-friendly console. These backups can also be encrypted and are easily recoverable. The AWS Console allows users to perform point in time recovery of their RDS instances with a few clicks. This makes it one of the easiest backup tools available on the cloud for users.

While creating an RDS instance, you can choose your backup policy. If you already have an RDS instance, you can easily modify and choose a backup strategy using the options covered here.

© Baji Shaik, Avinash Vallarapu 2018
B. Shaik and A. Vallarapu, *Beginning PostgreSQL on the Cloud*,
https://doi.org/10.1007/978-1-4842-3447-1_8

Backing Up an RDS Instance

Let's look at backing up an RDS instance:

1. Log in to the Amazon AWS Console and search for RDS. Click on it.

2. Click on Instances to view a list of Instances created using the account.

3. Choose the instance for which you want to modify the backup policy and click on Instance Actions, as shown in Figure 8-1. Click on Modify to proceed.

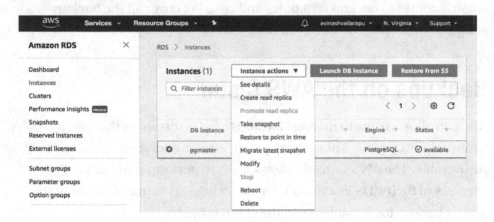

Figure 8-1. *Accessing the instance actions*

4. You can modify the backup retention period and the backup window, as shown in Figure 8-2.

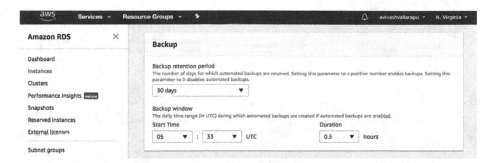

Figure 8-2. *Modifying the backup options*

5. Click on Continue and Modify DB Instance to make the changes, as shown in Figure 8-3.

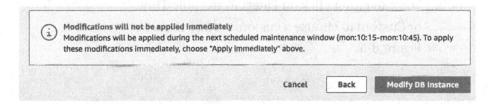

Figure 8-3. *Click on Modify DB Instance*

Restore an AWS RDS Instance from Backup

Using the AWS Console, users can easily restore a backup without needing to understand how PostgreSQL backup works in real time. The following steps perform a recovery using an existing backup of an RDS instance. You cannot restore a backup of an RDS instance to an EC2 instance or vice versa.

1. Choose the instance for recovery. Click on Instance Actions and choose Restore to Point in Time, as shown in Figure 8-4.

237

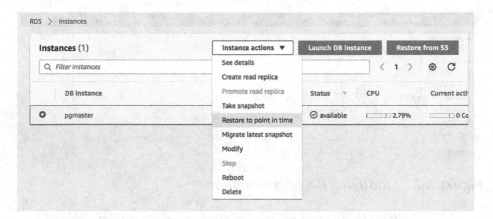

Figure 8-4. *Restoring an instance to a point in time*

2. You can either click on Latest Restorable Time
    or Custom to choose a custom restore time. See
    Figure 8-5.

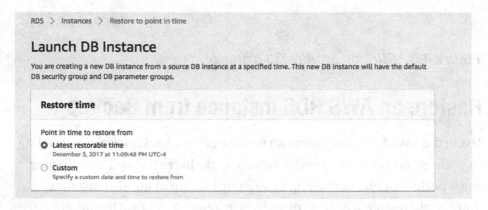

Figure 8-5. *Choose the restore options*

3. Now you can choose the DB Instance Identifier and
    click on Launch DB Instance to perform recovery of
    the database you selected. See Figure 8-6.

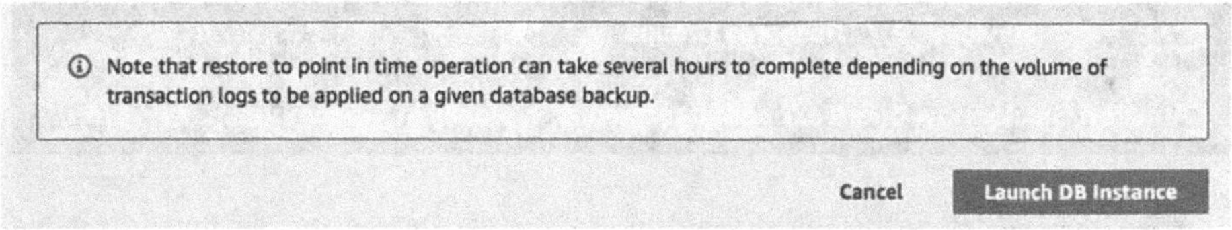

> (i) Note that restore to point in time operation can take several hours to complete depending on the volume of transaction logs to be applied on a given database backup.

Cancel   **Launch DB Instance**

Figure 8-6. *The restore operation can take several hours*

Backup of an EC2 Instance

The AWS Console does not give you an option to manage backup and recovery of a PostgreSQL database on an EC2 instance. You can use backup options such as pg_basebackup and pgbackrest or pgbarman to manage backups on an EC2 instance. However, these backups need not be stored locally.

Amazon allows you to create storage services on the cloud such as the following:

- S3 (Simple Storage Service). Object based storage.

- GLACIER. Used to archive S3 backups as it is very low cost. Takes more time to restore.

- EFS. Elastic File Service is block-based storage. This type of storage is good for DBs and apps.

- EBS. Elastic Block Store for EC2 instances.

Here are the steps involved in creating storage to store the DB backups.

1. On the AWS Cloud Console, search for S3 Service and click on it.

2. Click on Create Bucket, as shown in Figure 8-7.

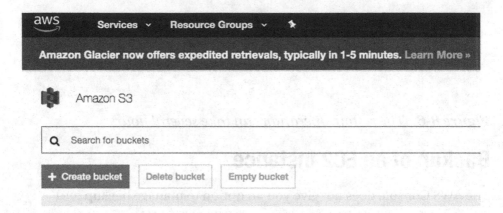

Figure 8-7. *Click on Create Bucket*

3. Choose a bucket name that can be uniquely
    identified for its purpose. Select the region where
    you want to create this bucket (see Figure 8-8).
    Click Next to continue. If you already have a bucket,
    you can copy the settings from that and skip the
    following steps.

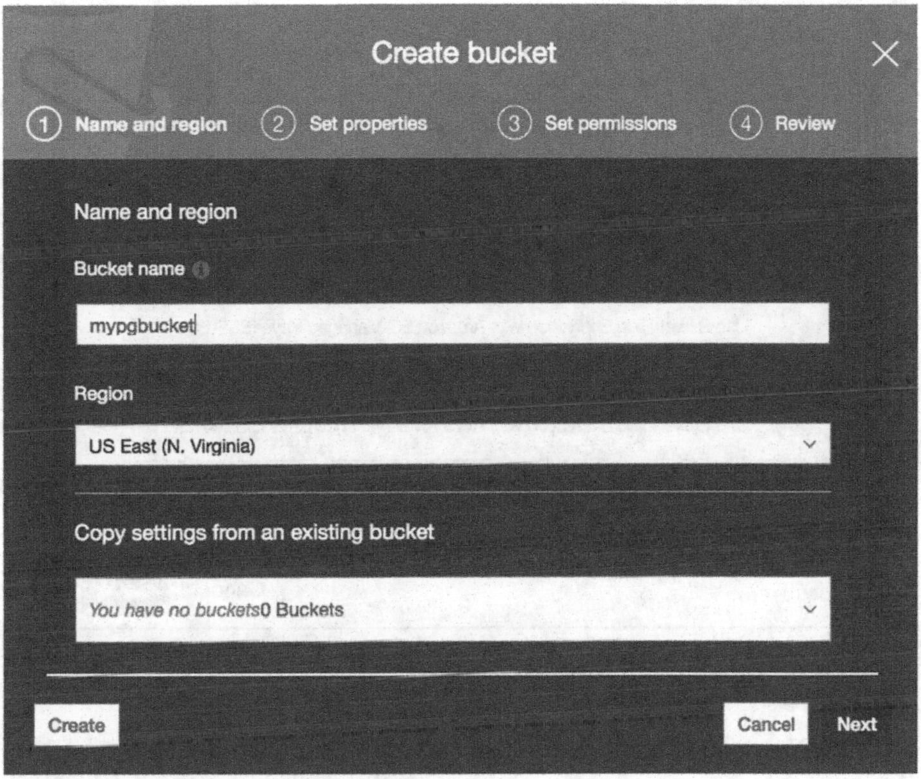

Figure 8-8. *Enter the bucket's settings*

4. You can now choose an encryption option. Choose the KMS key you want to use to encrypt the data in the S3 bucket, if needed. See Figure 8-9.

Click Next to proceed.

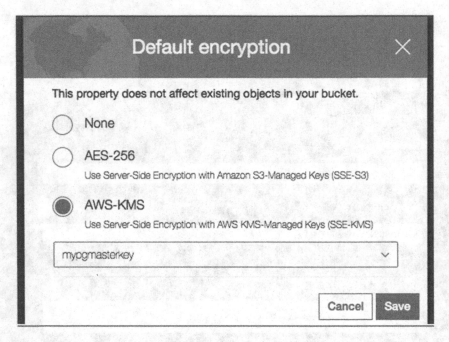

Figure 8-9. *Pick an encryption option*

5. Now you can choose all the accounts that can have read or read/write access to this S3 bucket. See Figure 8-10.

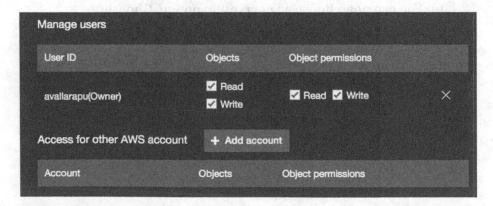

Figure 8-10. *Choose the accounts*

6. Click on Create Bucket. Now, the S3 Bucket you
    created should appear, as shown in Figure 8-11.

Figure 8-11.   *The new bucket is shown here*

Performing Backups on an EC2 Instance

As discussed earlier, you can connect to your EC2 instance and install the
AWS cli using the following steps.

1. If you do not have pip already installed on your OS,
    install it (see the commented section at the start of
    the following listing). Once you're done, you can
    proceed to install AWS cli using pip.

    ```
    # yum install python-setuptools -y
    # sudo easy_install pip
    # pip install --upgrade pip
    ```

    ```
    # Install awscli using pip and set PATH
    ```

    ```
    su - postgres
    pip install --upgrade --user awscli
    export PATH=~/.local/bin:$PATH
    aws --version
    ```

2. Now configure AWS using the following command.
    You need to know your AWS access key ID and AWS
    secret ID, which are generated while creating the
    user account set as the owner of the S3 bucket you
    need to access.

243

```
$ aws configure
```

```
AWS Access Key ID [None]: (Access Key)
AWS Secret Access Key [None]: (Secret Key)
Default region name [None]:
Default output format [None]:
```

3. See if you are able to list the S3 buckets created or
    accessible to your account.

    ```
    $ aws s3 ls
    ```

4. Back up the PostgreSQL instance using pg_basebackup.

    ```
    $ pg_basebackup -h localhost -p 5432 -D /tmp/
    backup -x -Ft -z -P
    ```

5. Now, push the backup to S3 using the following
    command.

    ```
    $ aws s3 cp /tmp/backup s3://yourbucketname/
    dbbackups
    ```

Restore Your Backup to an EC2 Instance

This section covers the process of restoring the backups:

1. You need to use the same cp command to copy the
    backup pushed to S3.

    ```
    $ aws s3 cp s3://yourbucketname/dbbackups/* /tmp/
    backup/*
    ```

2. Once it's copied, you can use tar to extract the
    backup and restore it to start PostgreSQL using the
    backup.

Backups on Rackspace Cloud

In Chapter 4, we talked about the solutions that Rackspace provides—Managed Hosting, Managed Cloud, and Cloud Block Storage. In this chapter, we talk about how to back up a Rackspace cloud server.

It is very simple to back up Rackspace cloud servers. While creating the cloud server, there is an option to enable backups of the machines. If you check the box for backups, your backups will be enabled (see Figure 8-12). Note that this option cost more.

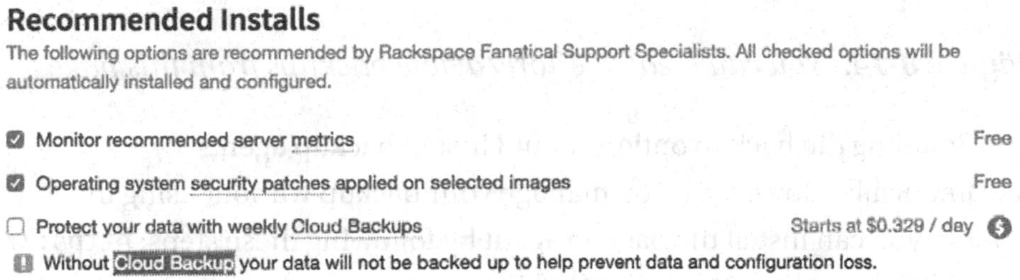

Recommended Installs

The following options are recommended by Rackspace Fanatical Support Specialists. All checked options will be automatically installed and configured.

☑ Monitor recommended server metrics   Free

☑ Operating system security patches applied on selected images   Free

☐ Protect your data with weekly Cloud Backups   Starts at $0.329 / day $

⊟ Without Cloud Backup your data will not be backed up to help prevent data and configuration loss.

Figure 8-12. *Check the box to enable backups*

You can also manage your backups by clicking on Manage Backups, as shown in Figure 8-13.

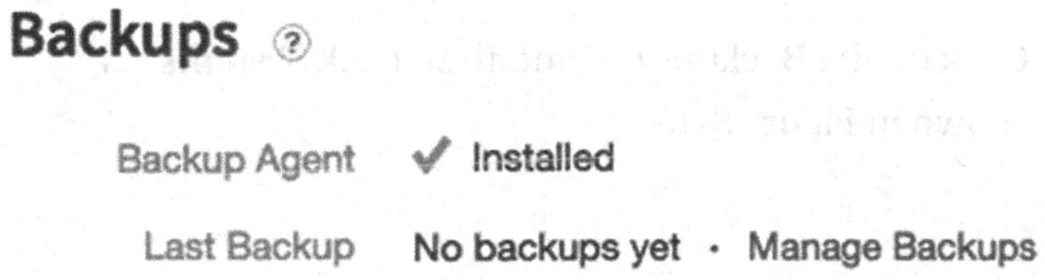

Backups ⑦

Backup Agent   ✓ Installed

Last Backup   **No backups yet** · Manage Backups

Figure 8-13. *Click the Manage Backups link*

You can create/restore/delete backups or enable encryption for your backups. You can also disable the backup option. See the options in Figure 8-14.

Cloud Backup Systems

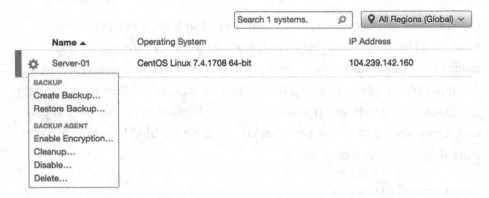

Figure 8-14. You can create/restore/delete backups from this page

Enabling the backup option should install backup agents automatically. However, if you manage your backup without using the option, you can install the backup agent by following these steps: `https://clouddrive.rackspace.com/installer`

If you want to schedule a backup other than the default one that we enabled, here are the steps:

1. Log in to the Rackspace Portal at `https://mycloud.rackspace.com/cloud/1042301/home`.

2. Click on the Backups tab and then click Systems, as shown in Figure 8-15.

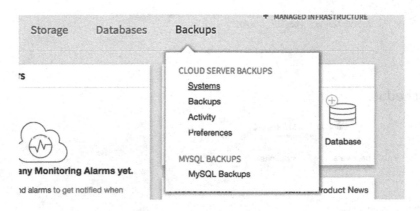

Figure 8-15. *Scheduling a backup*

3. On the Cloud Backup Systems page, click the name of the server for which you want to create a backup.

4. You will see the Configure Backups page, as shown in Figure 8-16.

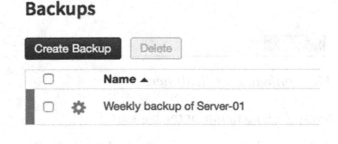

Figure 8-16. *The Configure Backups page*

5. On the Configure Backup page, configure the items shown in Figure 8-17 and then click Next Step.

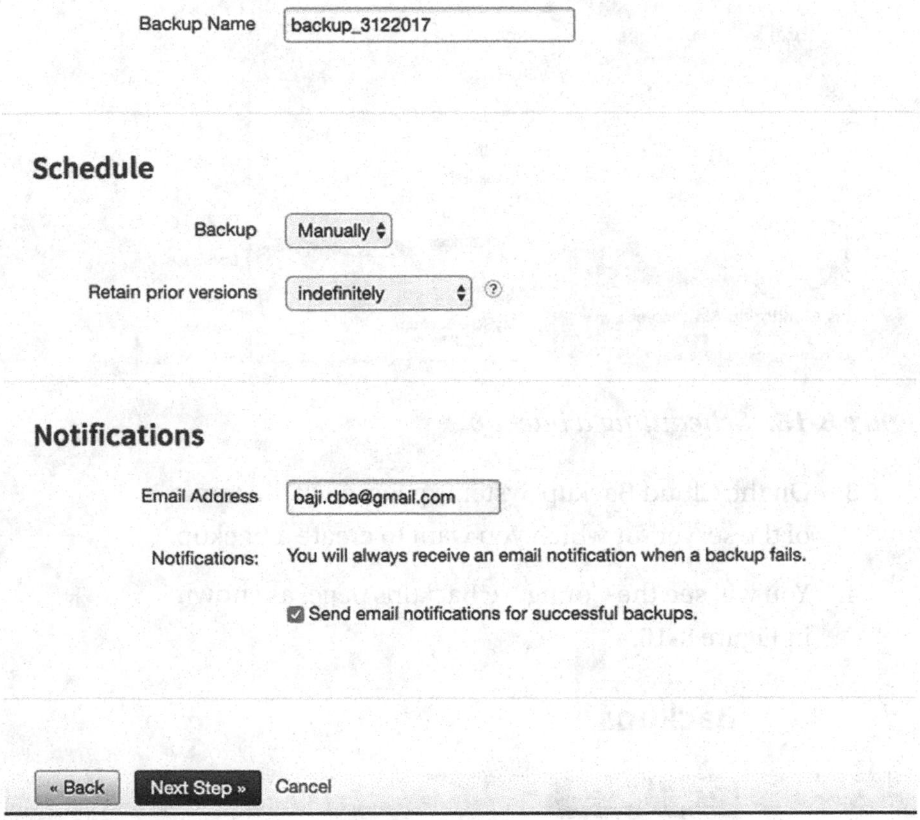

Backup Name   backup_3122017

Schedule

Backup   Manually ⟷

Retain prior versions   indefinitely   ⟷   ⑦

Notifications

Email Address   baji.dba@gmail.com

Notifications: You will always receive an email notification when a backup fails.

☑ Send email notifications for successful backups.

« Back   Next Step »   Cancel

Figure 8-17. *Configure the items here*

Name: Enter a name for the backup.

In the Schedule section, specify a schedule for the backup and select how many prior backup versions to retain.

In the Notifications section, specify the email address for notifications and select whether you want to receive notifications of successful backups.

6. Select the folder that you want to back up and click on Next Step, as shown in Figure 8-18.

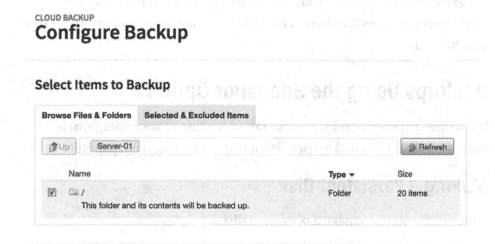

Figure 8-18. *Choose the folder you want to back up*

7. Check the backup details and click on Save. See Figure 8-19.

Figure 8-19. *Check the backup details before clicking Save*

249

Backups to Google Cloud

In Chapter 5, we saw how to create VM instances using the Compute Engine service. Now let's look at how you can take backup of instances that you created.

Backups Using the Snapshot Option

Using the snapshot option, you can take a backup of your data from a persistent disk. Let's make a persistent disk and create a snapshot for it.

Making a Persistent Disk

Here are the steps to make a persistent disk.

1. To make a persistent disk, connect your instance by adding SSH keys of your machine, as shown in Figure 8-20.

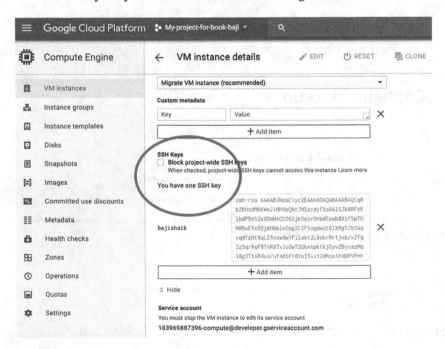

Figure 8-20. *Add the SSH keys*

2. You can connect through SSH using your private
   key, as shown in Figure 8-21.

```
C1MQV0FZDTY3:~ bajishaik$ ssh -i ~/.ssh/id_rsa bajishaik@35.193.7.102
[bajishaik@my-test-postgres ~]$
[bajishaik@my-test-postgres ~]$
[bajishaik@my-test-postgres ~]$
[bajishaik@my-test-postgres ~]$ hostname -I
10.128.0.2
[bajishaik@my-test-postgres ~]$ hostname
my-test-postgres
[bajishaik@my-test-postgres ~]$ df -h
Filesystem      Size  Used Avail Use% Mounted on
/dev/sda1        10G  1.7G  8.4G  17% /
devtmpfs        1.8G     0  1.8G   0% /dev
tmpfs           1.8G     0  1.8G   0% /dev/shm
tmpfs           1.8G  8.3M  1.8G   1% /run
tmpfs           1.8G     0  1.8G   0% /sys/fs/cgroup
tmpfs           354M     0  354M   0% /run/user/1000
[bajishaik@my-test-postgres ~]$
[bajishaik@my-test-postgres ~]$
```

Figure 8-21. *Connecting through SSH using your private key*

3. Just for demo purposes, we are installing
   PostgreSQL using the BigSQL package manager.
   See Figure 8-22.

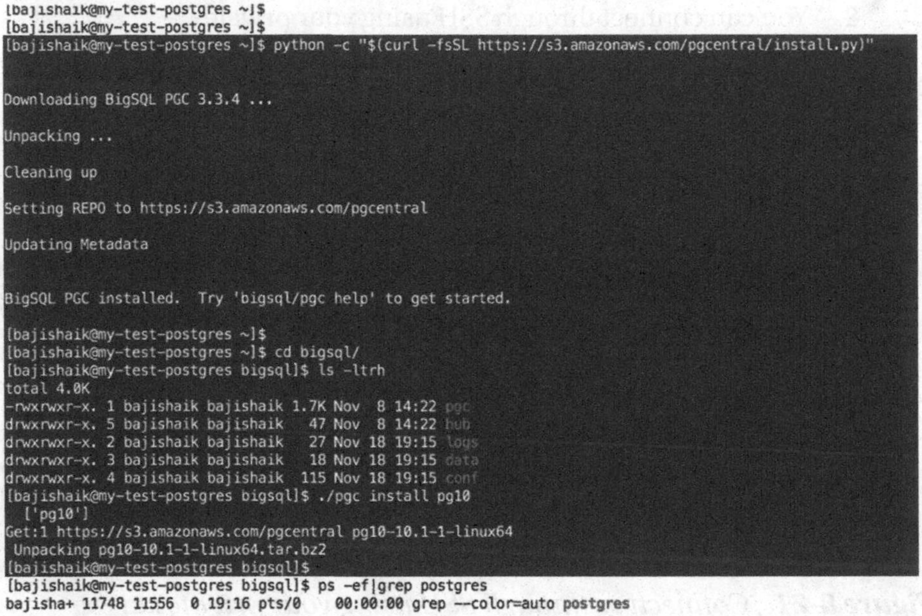
[bajishaik@my-test-postgres ~]$
[bajishaik@my-test-postgres ~]$
[bajishaik@my-test-postgres ~]$ python -c "$(curl -fsSL https://s3.amazonaws.com/pgcentral/install.py)"
Downloading BigSQL PGC 3.3.4 ...
Unpacking ...
Cleaning up
Setting REPO to https://s3.amazonaws.com/pgcentral
Updating Metadata
BigSQL PGC installed. Try 'bigsql/pgc help' to get started.
[bajishaik@my-test-postgres ~]$
[bajishaik@my-test-postgres ~]$ cd bigsql/
[bajishaik@my-test-postgres bigsql]$ ls -ltrh
total 4.0K
-rwxrwxr-x. 1 bajishaik bajishaik 1.7K Nov 8 14:22 pgc
drwxrwxr-x. 5 bajishaik bajishaik 47 Nov 8 14:22 hub
drwxrwxr-x. 2 bajishaik bajishaik 27 Nov 18 19:15 logs
drwxrwxr-x. 3 bajishaik bajishaik 18 Nov 18 19:15 data
drwxrwxr-x. 4 bajishaik bajishaik 115 Nov 18 19:15 conf
[bajishaik@my-test-postgres bigsql]$ ./pgc install pg10
['pg10']
Get:1 https://s3.amazonaws.com/pgcentral pg10-10.1-1-linux64
Unpacking pg10-10.1-1-linux64.tar.bz2
[bajishaik@my-test-postgres bigsql]$
[bajishaik@my-test-postgres bigsql]$ ps -ef|grep postgres
bajisha+ 11748 11556 0 19:16 pts/0 00:00:00 grep --color=auto postgres

***Figure 8-22.** Installing PostgreSQL using the BigSQL package manager*

4. Create a data directory on a mount point, as shown in Figure 8-23.

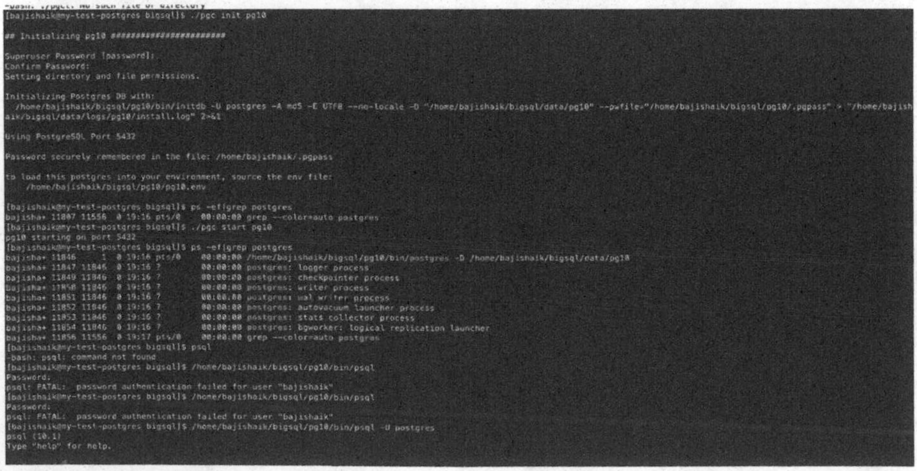
[bajishaik@my-test-postgres bigsql]$ ./pgc init pg10
Initializing pg10
Superuser Password [password]:
Confirm Password:
Setting directory and file permissions.
Initializing Postgres DB with:
/home/bajishaik/bigsql/pg10/bin/initdb -U postgres -A md5 -E UTF8 --no-locale -D "/home/bajishaik/bigsql/data/pg10" --pwfile="/home/bajishaik/bigsql/pg10/.pgpass" > "/home/bajish
aik/bigsql/data/logs/pg10/install.log" 2>&1
Using PostgreSQL Port 5432
Password securely remembered in the file: /home/bajishaik/.pgpass
to load this postgres into your environment, source the env file:
/home/bajishaik/bigsql/pg10/pg10.env
[bajishaik@my-test-postgres bigsql]$ ps -ef|grep postgres
bajisha+ 11807 11556 0 19:16 pts/0 00:00:00 grep --color=auto postgres
[bajishaik@my-test-postgres bigsql]$ ./pgc start pg10
pg10 starting on port 5432
[bajishaik@my-test-postgres bigsql]$ ps -ef|grep postgres
bajisha+ 11846 1 0 19:16 pts/0 00:00:00 /home/bajishaik/bigsql/pg10/bin/postgres -D /home/bajishaik/bigsql/data/pg10
bajisha+ 11847 11846 0 19:16 ? 00:00:00 postgres: logger process
bajisha+ 11849 11846 0 19:16 ? 00:00:00 postgres: checkpointer process
bajisha+ 11850 11846 0 19:16 ? 00:00:00 postgres: writer process
bajisha+ 11851 11846 0 19:16 ? 00:00:00 postgres: wal writer process
bajisha+ 11852 11846 0 19:16 ? 00:00:00 postgres: autovacuum launcher process
bajisha+ 11853 11846 0 19:16 ? 00:00:00 postgres: stats collector process
bajisha+ 11854 11846 0 19:16 ? 00:00:00 postgres: bgworker: logical replication launcher
bajisha+ 11856 11556 0 19:17 pts/0 00:00:00 grep --color=auto postgres
[bajishaik@my-test-postgres bigsql]$ psql
-bash: psql: command not found
[bajishaik@my-test-postgres bigsql]$ /home/bajishaik/bigsql/pg10/bin/psql
Password:
psql: FATAL: password authentication failed for user "bajishaik"
[bajishaik@my-test-postgres bigsql]$ /home/bajishaik/bigsql/pg10/bin/psql
Password:
psql: FATAL: password authentication failed for user "bajishaik"
[bajishaik@my-test-postgres bigsql]$ /home/bajishaik/bigsql/pg10/bin/psql -U postgres
psql (10.1)
Type "help" for help.

***Figure 8-23.** Creating a data directory on a mount point*

5. As you can see, this data is on a root mount point.

6. Execute a checkpoint in the database by connecting
    using psql. Your mount point is ready for a snapshot.

Take a Backup of a Persistent Disk

Here are the steps to take a backup of a persistent disk using the snapshot
option.

1. Connect to your console and select Compute Engine
    and then choose Storage from the left panel. Then
    you can see the Create Snapshot button, as shown in
    Figure 8-24.

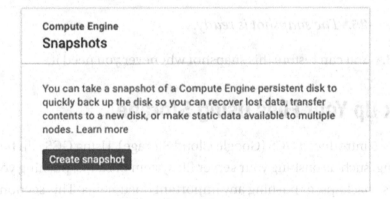

Figure 8-24. *The Create Snapshot button*

2. Give your snapshot a name and a source disk
    in order to create it. You can use instance name
    for your source disk. Then click on Create. Your
    snapshot will be ready, as shown in Figure 8-25.

253

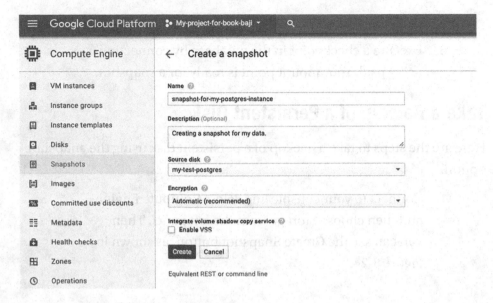

Figure 8-25. *The snapshot is ready*

3.   You can restore this snapshot whenever you need it.

Back Up Your Files Using Storage

Chapter 5 introduced GCS (Google Cloud Storage). Using GCS can be anything, such as pushing your server filesystem backups, pushing your database backups, or pushing any important documents. This section covers creating, configuring, and using the GCS.

Data (unstructured objects) will be stored in containers called *buckets*. If you want to push any kind of backups to GCS, you need to create a bucket. You can use buckets to store the data for other Google Cloud Platform services.

Create Buckets and Upload Files

This section covers creating a bucket and uploading files/folders to it:

1. You will see "Storage" in the left panel after you log in to the console. See `https://console.cloud.google.com/`, as shown in Figure 8-26.

Cloud Storage
Buckets

Cloud Storage lets you store unstructured objects in containers called buckets. You can serve static data directly from Cloud Storage, or you can use it to store data for other Google Cloud Platform services.

Create bucket   or   Take the quickstart

Figure 8-26. *Cloud storage*

2. You then enter the details shown in Figure 8-27.

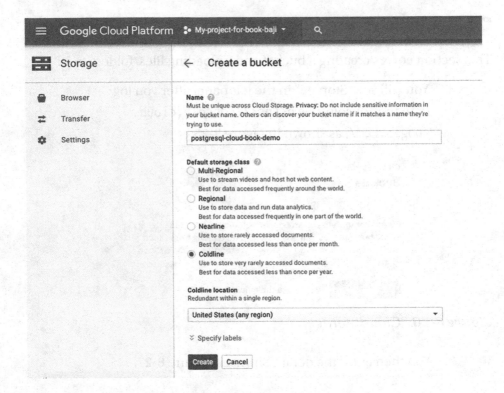

Figure 8-27. *Enter these details to create a bucket*

Name: Name of the bucket where you are going to store the data. It is not recommended to use any sensitive information in your bucket name, as it will be easy to figure out by others.

We used `postgresql-cloud-book-demo` for the name here.

Default storage class: As explained in Chapter 5, there are four types of storage classes. The storage class you choose depends on your data type, purpose, and how frequently you access data.

Region: The region where your bucket is created.

3. Click on Create.

4. As shown in Figure 8-28, you'll see options like
    Upload Files, Upload Folder, and Create Folder once
    you have created the bucket.

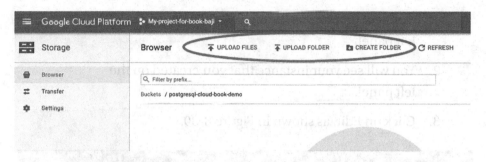

Figure 8-28. *Bucket options*

5. After the bucket has been created and selected,
    click on Upload Files to upload the files or click
    on Upload Folder to upload any directories. See
    Figure 8-29.

Figure 8-29. *Choose Upload Files or Upload Folder*

Back Up Your Cloud SQL for PostgreSQL

Chapter 5 discussed Cloud for PostgreSQL in detail. This section covers enabling backups for the PostgreSQL instances.

Here are the steps:

1. Connect to the console and select Cloud SQL on the left panel.

2. You will see your instance that you created on the left panel.

3. Click on Edit, as shown in Figure 8-30.

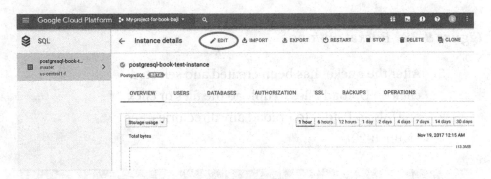

Figure 8-30. *Click Edit to edit the instance*

4. Scroll down to the Enable Auto Backups and High Availability section, where you can find the option to enable auto backups of your instance. You can provide a time to perform the backup. It is recommended to choose a window of time that's during off-peak hours of your application. See Figure 8-31.

258

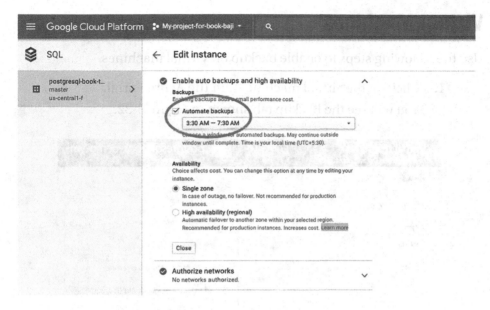

Figure 8-31. *Choose the time that the backups are performed*

Backups to Microsoft Azure

Chapter 6 talked about the services related to PostgreSQL that Microsoft Azure provides. This section discusses how you enable/take backups for the services that are created by Azure. The services that we talked about are:

- Virtual machines

- Storage

- Azure Database for PostgreSQL

The following sections cover enabling/taking backups of each service.

259

Virtual Machines

Use the following steps to enable backup on virtual machines.

1. Click on the virtual machine from the Azure Portal. You will see the Backup tab shown in Figure 8-32.

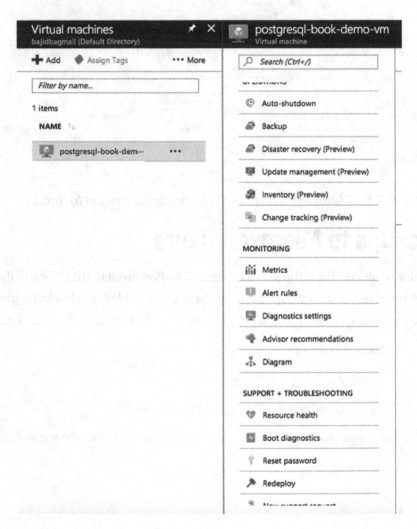

Figure 8-32. *The Backup tab*

2. Click on the Backup tab. You'll see the options for backing up the machine, as shown in Figure 8-33.

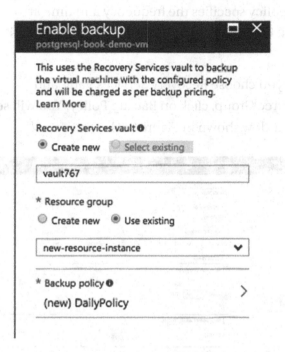

Figure 8-33. *Options for backing up your virtual machine*

The recovery services vault holds the backup copies and you can monitor backup using this vault. You can create a new vault or if you have an existing vault, you can use that.

The Azure Backup service has two types of vaults—the Backup vault and the Recovery Services vault. The Backup vault came first. Then the Recovery Services vault came along to support the expanded Resource Manager deployments. Microsoft recommends using Resource Manager deployments unless you specifically require a Classic deployment. Just to differentiate, Classic deployment is old portal and it's going to be retired soon (see https://manage.windowsazure.com). The new portal is https://portal.azure.com/.

For the resource group, you can create a new one or use an existing resource group to be backed up.

The backup policy specifies the frequency and time at which items will be backed up and how long backup copies are retained.

3.   After you choose Recovery Services Vault and Resource Group, click on Backup Policy. You will see the window shown in Figure 8-34.

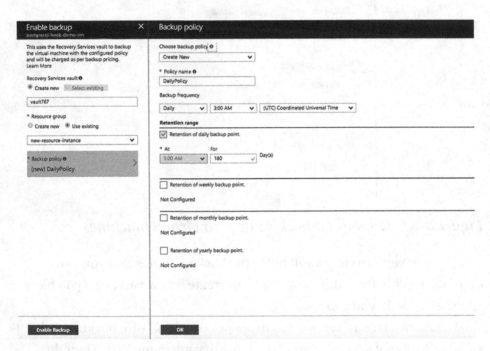

Figure 8-34. *Setting up the backup policy*

Choose backup policy: Specifies frequency and time at which items will be backed up, as well as how long backup copies are retained.

Policy name: Choose the name for the backup policy that you are going to create.

Backup frequency: You can set up daily or weekly backups with the time window.

You can set retention of policy in terms of days under the Retention Range option.

4. Once you are done, click on OK and then on Enable. Backup for your VM is enabled now. Click on Backup after it is configured to see the details shown in Figure 8-35.

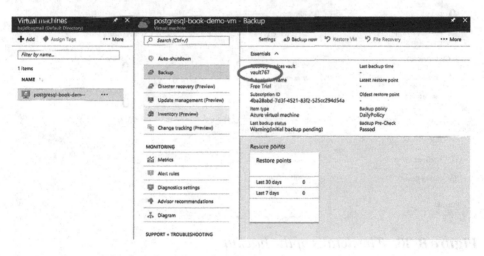

Figure 8-35. *The backup has been set up*

5. If you click on the vault as highlighted in Figure 8-35, you will see the backup alerts, backup pre-check status, site recovery health, etc. See Figure 8-36.

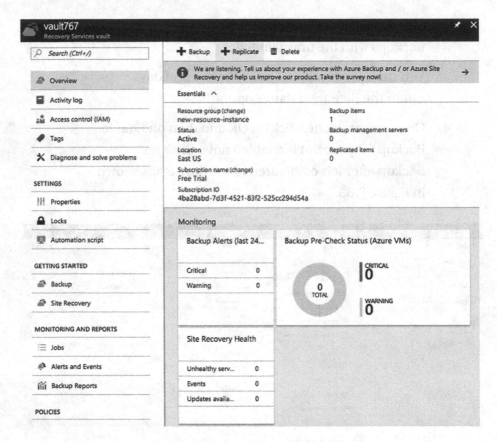

Figure 8-36.   *The details of the backup*

Storage

Azure Storage consists of three data services: blob storage, file storage, and queue storage. Blob storage supports standard and premium storage, with premium storage using only SSDs for the fastest performance possible. Another feature is cool storage, which allows you to store large amounts of rarely accessed data at a lower cost.

This section covers blob storage and how to create/manage it. Here are the steps to create it:

1. On the Azure Portal, select Storage Accounts on the left panel and click on Add to create storage. See Figure 8-37.

Figure 8-37. *Click Add to create storage*

2. When you click on Add, the program opens new options to be entered to create your storage, as shown in Figure 8-38.

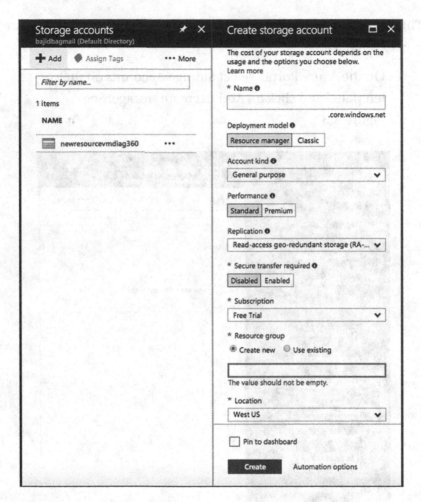

Figure 8-38. *Add details about the new storage*

Name: This name should be unique across all storage account names in Azure. It must be 3 to 24 characters long, and can contain only lowercase letters and numbers.

Deployment model: Use the Resource Manager for new applications and for the latest Azure features. Use Classic if you have any existing applications deployed in a Classic virtual network.

Account kind: General purpose storage accounts provide storage for files, blobs, tables, and queues in a unified account. Blobstore accounts are specialized for storing blob data and support choosing an access tier, which allows you to specify how frequently data in the account is accessed. Choose an access tier that matches your storage needs and optimizes cost.

Performance: Standard storage accounts are backed by magnetic drives and provide the lower cost per gigabyte. They are best for applications that require bulk storage or where data is being accessed infrequently. Premium storage accounts are backed by solid state drives and offer consistent low-latency performance. They can only be used with Azure virtual machine disks and are best for I/O intensive applications, like databases. Additionally, virtual machines that use Premium storage for all disks qualify for a 99.9% SLA, even when running outside of availability set. This setting can't be changed after the storage account is created.

Replication: The data in your Azure storage account is always replicated to ensure durability and high availability. Choose a replication strategy that matches your durability requirements. Some settings can't be changed after the storage account is created.

Secure transfer required: This option enhances the security of your storage account by only allowing requests to the storage account by secure connection. For example, when calling REST

APIs to access your storage accounts, you must connect using HTTPs. Any requests using HTTP will be rejected when Secure Transfer Required is enabled. When you are using the Azure files service, connection without encryption will fail.

Subscription: Choose the subscription in which you want to create the storage.

Resource group: Choose an existing Resource Group or create a new one.

Location: Choose the region in which you want to create your storage.

Configure virtual networks: Enabling this setting will grant exclusive access to this storage account from the specified virtual network and subnets. Additional virtual networks and subnets can be specified after storage account creation.

3. Click on Create once you fill in all the details.

   If you want to know more about the Azure storage services, the types of storage accounts, accessing your blobs/queues/files, encryption, replication, transferring data into or out of storage, and the many storage client libraries available, visit `https://docs.microsoft.com/en-us/azure/storage/common/storage-introduction` for more information.

Azure Database for PostgreSQL

When you create an Azure Database for PostgreSQL service, you are automatically set up with the default backup policy. This service automatically makes a back up of the database every five minutes. Retention of these backups depends on the pricing tier that you choose. If it is Basic, retention of backups is seven days, and if it is Standard, retention is 35 days. More information about pricing tiers is at `https://docs.microsoft.com/en-us/azure/postgresql/concepts-service-tiers`.

If you want to restore the database, the steps to do so are found at `https://docs.microsoft.com/en-us/azure/postgresql/howto-restore-server-portal#restore-in-the-azure-portal`.

The automatic backups, which are part of the service, cannot be altered. The service takes full backups every week, two incremental backups per day, and log backups every five minutes.

Summary

This chapter talked about why backing up a server or a database is important. We covered all backup solutions available by default from each cloud vendor and how you can modify the default schedules or retentions. There are lot of differences in backups from each vendor. We hope this chapter helps you understand the differences and choose the correct backup policy for your setup and requirements. The next chapter covers the need for data replication and high availability in the current world, including what solution each vendor provides for replication and high availability.

CHAPTER 9

Replication and High Availability on the Cloud

In this chapter, we talk about the purpose of replicating data or databases and why we need high availability. Some cloud vendors provide replication for the disks of virtual machines or databases and some do not. Similarly, some vendors provide high availability of servers and database instances by default and some do not. We talk about replication and high availability for every cloud vendor in detail.

The Purpose of Replication and High Availability

High availability is represented by the letter "D" in the ACID properties (for durability). Database servers are prone to single points of failure. In order to avoid such single point of failures, we have a feature called *replication* in the database world. If the master DB server goes down due to environmental or hardware level damages, we have a slave that can take the role of its master.

B. Shaik and A. Vallarapu, *Beginning PostgreSQL on the Cloud*,
https://doi.org/10.1007/978-1-4842-3447-1_9

271

Achieving high availability in PostgreSQL has been easy since streaming replication was introduced. We can build slaves (aka, replicas or DRs) to a master (primary) PostgreSQL database server, and these slaves are in a continuous replication with their master at any given time. Replication in the database language is a process in which a DB server can ship its changes to another DB server. It can be achievable using several solutions in the RDBMS world.

We have two types of replication in PostgreSQL:

- Streaming replication

- Logical replication

Streaming replication deals with the blocks that have been modified by the processes writing to the master. These blocks are shipped over the network to the slave and replayed on the slave continuously. This replication can be both synchronous and asynchronous.

Logical replication helps users configure replication between multiple versions of PostgreSQL and have a selected list of tables or databases replicated to slaves and cascaded slaves. However, this may not serve the purpose of a true high-availability cluster unless every database object is in the replication set, which may not be possible unless every object has a primary or a unique key and a NOT NULL column.

Thus, to achieve high availability, you may want to have at least one slave server that is in replication (preferably streaming replication) with its master. PostgreSQL allows us to use cascaded replication. This way, a slave can ship its changes to another slave. In this case, the first slave is treated as a master by the second slave.

A few important factors to be considered while building replication in a PostgreSQL environment.

- Ensure you have the same server configurations on both the master and the slave DB servers. In the event of failure, the slave should be able to take the load that would usually hit the master.

- Ensure you have a common mount point, such as a NAS mount point, accessible by the master and slave. This mount point can be used to archive the WALs (write-ahead logs or transaction logs). If you subscribed to a DBaaS such as an Amazon RDS, you may not have to worry about archiving WALs. However, if you selected an EC2 Instance (IaaS) or a virtual machine on Azure or GCP or Rackspace, you may subscribe to the vendor-specific cloud storage service for archiving. Vendors provide several APIs that use WALs that can either be sent to or pulled from storage as needed.

- Load-balance your reads. When the wal_level has been set to hot_standby, an application can send its read queries to the slave. Slaves are open for read-only queries. Thus, you can have your application logic rewritten in such a way that your writes go to one connection string that connects to the master and the reads go to another connection string that redirects the connections to the slave. You may also have a load balancer service that can redirect your reads to multiple slaves or to the master and the slave in an even manner. This way, you let the idle computing resources on the slave become busy with reporting or read queries.

Consider high availability a key to avoiding single point of failures and an enabler for developing always-on database systems.

Replication and High Availability in AWS

AWS allows you to build replication for RDS and EC2 services. AWS console allow users to achieve replication in RDS instances in very few clicks.

Read Replicas for RDS

This section shows the steps involved in building a read replica for an AWS RDS instance. In the previous chapters, we saw the steps involved in creating an RDS instance. While creating an RDS instance, you have an option to automatically create a read replica, as shown in Figure 9-1.

Figure 9-1. *Automatically create a read replica*

If you did not create a read replica at the time of instance creation, follow these steps, which allow you to add a read replica to an existing RDS instance.

1. Search for RDS in the AWS Console and click on it to proceed, as shown in Figure 9-2.

Figure 9-2. *Choose RDS from the AWS Console*

2. Click on Instances to view the list of your RDS
    instances. You may find one or more depending
    on the number of RDS instances you have already
    created. See Figure 9-3.

Figure 9-3. *View the list of RDS instances*

3. Select the instance for which you need to create
    the read replica. Once it's selected, click on the
    dropdown for Instance Actions. You see an option
    that says Create Read Replica, as shown in Figure 9-4.
    Click on it.

Figure 9-4. *The Create Read Replica option*

4. Now you should see the options to choose the region and availability zone in which you want to create your read replica. You may choose any region and availability zone depending on your business requirements. See Figure 9-5.

Create read replica DB instance

You are creating a replica DB instance from a source DB instance. This new DB instance will have the source DB instance's DB security groups and DB parameter groups.

Network & Security

Destination region
The region in which the replica will be launched

US East (N. Virginia) ▼

Destination DB subnet group

default ▼

Availability zone
The EC2 Availability Zone that the database instance will be created in.

us-east-1d ▼

Publicly accessible

🔘 Yes
EC2 instances and devices outside of the VPC hosting the DB instance will connect to the DB instances. You must also select one or more VPC security groups that specify which EC2 instances and devices can connect to the DB instance.

Figure 9-5. *Read replica options*

5. On the same page, scroll down to choose the
    instance type and storage. You may choose any
    configuration for the read replica that supports your
    business needs. Once you choose the instance type,
    choose the DB instance identifier that will help
    you uniquely identify this read replica, as shown in
    Figure 9-6.

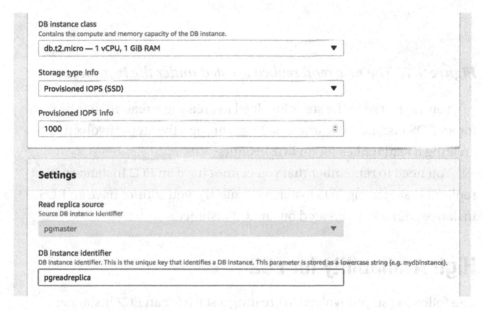

Figure 9-6. *Choose a DB instance identifier*

6. Click on Create Replica to proceed further. Now
    you should see the read replica listed under the
    Instances, as shown in Figure 9-7.

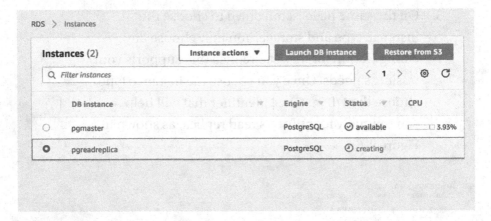

Figure 9-7. *The new read replica is listed under the Instances*

You've now seen the steps involved in creating a read replica or slave for an RDS instance. It's now time to go through the steps involved in creating a read replica for an EC2 instance.

You need to remember that you cannot have an EC2 instance with a replica created using RDS instance. Similarly, you cannot have an RDS instance with a slave created on an EC2 instance.

High Availability for EC2

The following steps involved in creating a slave for an EC2 instance:

1. An EC2 instance master needs a slave to be created on an EC2 instance or any cloud virtual machine or a physical server in your data center. The server being created as a replica for the EC2 Instance should be using the same OS and PostgreSQL version as the master. The master and slave server should be able to connect between each other over the network. Create a new EC2 instance or a server that can be used as a slave and proceed to the next step.

2. Connect to the new server that has been created as a slave and install PostgreSQL as a root user. Install the latest pgdg repo that suits the PostgreSQL version. See Figure 9-8.

```
$ yum install https://yum.postgresql.org/9.6/redhat/
rhel-7.3-x86_64/pgdg-centos96-9.6-3.noarch.rpm -y
```

```
[ec2-user@ip-172-31-20-217 ~]$yum install https://yum.postgresql.org/9.6/redhat/rhel-7.3-x86_64/pgdg-centos96-9.6-3.noarch.rpm -y
Loaded plugins: fastestmirror
pgdg-centos96-9.6-3.noarch.rpm                                                                          | 4.7 kB  00:00:00
Examining /var/tmp/yum-root-EF5wV0/pgdg-centos96-9.6-3.noarch.rpm: pgdg-centos96-9.6-3.noarch
Marking /var/tmp/yum-root-EF5wV0/pgdg-centos96-9.6-3.noarch.rpm to be installed
Resolving Dependencies
--> Running transaction check
---> Package pgdg-centos96.noarch 0:9.6-3 will be installed
--> Finished Dependency Resolution

Dependencies Resolved

===============================================================================================================================
 Package                    Arch              Version              Repository                              Size
===============================================================================================================================
Installing:
 pgdg-centos96              noarch            9.6-3                /pgdg-centos96-9.6-3.noarch             2.7 k

Transaction Summary
===============================================================================================================================
Install  1 Package

Total size: 2.7 k
Installed size: 2.7 k
Downloading packages:
Running transaction check
Running transaction test
Transaction test succeeded
Running transaction
  Installing : pgdg-centos96-9.6-3.noarch                                                                        1/1
  Verifying  : pgdg-centos96-9.6-3.noarch                                                                        1/1

Installed:
  pgdg-centos96.noarch 0:9.6-3

Complete!
[ec2-user@ip-172-31-20-217 ~]$
```

Figure 9-8. *Install the pgdg repo that suits the PostgreSQL version*

3. Install PostgreSQL using the following code. The following example in Figure 9-9 installs PostgreSQL 9.6.

```
$ yum install postgresql96* -y
```

```
[ec2-user@ip-172-31-20-217 ~]$yum install postgresql96* -y
Loaded plugins: fastestmirror
Loading mirror speeds from cached hostfile
 * base: mirror.its.dal.ca
 * extras: centos.mirror.netelligent.ca
 * updates: centos.mirror.netelligent.ca
Resolving Dependencies
--> Running transaction check
---> Package postgresql96.x86_64 0:9.6.6-1PGDG.rhel7 will be installed
---> Package postgresql96-contrib.x86_64 0:9.6.6-1PGDG.rhel7 will be installed
```

Figure 9-9. *Installing PostgreSQL 9.6*

4. Be sure to set the appropriate parameters on the
    master EC2 instance if this has not been done
    already.

    The parameters shown in Figure 9-10 are set as an
    example. However, you may need to set different
    parameters as appropriate for your environment on
    your master EC2 instance.

```
postgres=# ALTER SYSTEM SET listen_addresses = '*';
ALTER SYSTEM
postgres=# ALTER SYSTEM SET max_wal_senders = 5;
ALTER SYSTEM
postgres=# ALTER SYSTEM SET wal_level = hot_standby;
ALTER SYSTEM
postgres=# ALTER SYSTEM SET hot_standby = ON;
ALTER SYSTEM
postgres=# ALTER SYSTEM SET archive_mode = ON;
ALTER SYSTEM
postgres=# ALTER SYSTEM SET logging_collector = ON;
ALTER SYSTEM
postgres=# ALTER SYSTEM SET wal_keep_segments = 200;
ALTER SYSTEM
postgres=# ALTER SYSTEM SET archive_command = '/bin/true';
ALTER SYSTEM
```

Figure 9-10. *Parameters for the master EC2 instance*

5. Create a replication user on the master server that
    can be used by the slave EC2 instance. Add the
    slave server IP to pg_hba.conf to allow replication
    connections from the new slave, as shown in
    Figure 9-11.

```
postgres=# CREATE USER REPLICATOR WITH REPLICATION PASSWORD 'replicator';
CREATE ROLE
postgres=# \q
-bash-4.2$ echo "host    replication    replicator    172.31.20.216/32    md5" >> $PGDATA/pg_hba.conf
-bash-4.2$ /usr/pgsql-9.6/bin/pg_ctl -D $PGDATA reload
server signaled
```

Figure 9-11. *Create a replication user on the master server*

6. Take a backup of the master using pg_basebackup
    and start the slave. Run the following command on
    the slave to directly copy the data directory to the
    network. You may choose a different method to copy
    the data directory to the network.

    ```
    $ pg_basebackup -h 172.31.20.216 -p 5432 -U replicator
    -D $PGDATA -Fp -P -Xs -R
    ```

7. Start the slave using hot_standby = ON.

    ```
    $ echo "hot_standby = 'ON'" >> $PGDATA/postgresql.conf
    $ pg_ctl -D $PGDATA start
    ```

8. Setting up a high availability replica on an EC2
    instance uses exactly same approach as setting up
    the slave on any other virtual machine or dedicated
    server. As hot_standby is ON, this slave is now open
    for read connections, making it a read replica.

Replication and High Availability of Rackspace Cloud

Rackspace has no built-in mechanism for high availability of cloud servers,
but you can always schedule or manually take backups of your filesystems,
as explained in Chapter 8. See Figure 9-12.

Figure 9-12. The Backups menu

And for PostgreSQL installed on Rackspace cloud servers, you can follow the same HA solution that you follow for PostgreSQL with on-premises servers by following the steps mentioned in the "High Availability for EC2" section.

Replication and High Availability of Google Cloud Instances

Like other cloud providers, Google Cloud also provides read replicas and high availability options for PostgreSQL instances. If a PostgreSQL instance is configured for high availability, we call it a "regional instance". A regional instance is located in two zones in the configured region, so if it cannot serve data from its primary zone, it fails over and continues to serve data from its secondary zone.

This high availability configuration provides an auto-failover to a secondary zone if an instance experiences outage or is unresponsive. Highly-available PostgreSQL instances do not have a separate failover instance the way MySQL instances do.

Configure an Instance for High Availability

There is a two-step process for an already created instance to configure high availability.

1. Select the instance that you want to configure for high availability after logging in to the console and selecting Cloud SQL from the left panel and instance from the right panel, as shown in Figure 9-13.

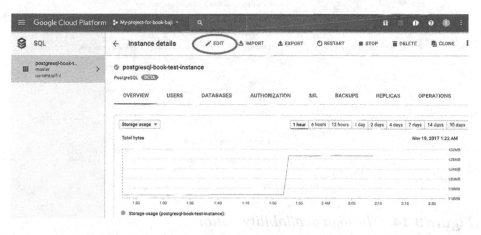

Figure 9-13. *Select an instance to configure for high availability*

2. Once you click on the Edit instance option, scroll down to the Enable Auto Backups And High Availability section. Then you'll find the High Availability option under the Availability sub-section. See Figure 9-14.

    Single zone: By selecting this, there will not be any failover in case of outage. So it is not recommended for production instances.

283

High availability (regional): This will enable auto-failover to another zone within the selected region. So it is recommended for production instances.

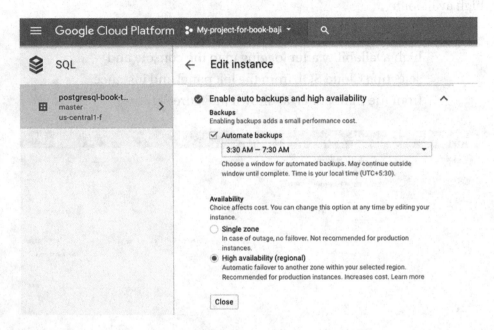

Figure 9-14. The high availability option

Configuring for high availability does not affect your backups and does not change the backup/restore procedures. You can follow the same procedures for backup/restore that you followed before configuring the high availability.

How Failover Works

Auto-failover happens when one of the following scenarios occurs:

- The zone where the regional instance is located experiences an outage.

- The regional instance is unresponsive for approximately 60 seconds.

There is no concept of a replication lag; as as long as the secondary zone is healthy, failover can occur. When failover occurs, all the connections to the primary will be dropped and any new connections will be connected to the promoted instance. There is no need to change anything in the application end for connectivity.

You can manually initiate a failover to check how your application behaves in failover situations. For that, you just need to click the Failover button on the Instance Details tab, as shown in Figure 9-15.

Figure 9-15. *Click the Failover button on the Instance Details tab*

Read Replicas

A read replica is just a copy of the master. It is used to offload read requests or analytics traffic from the master. It does not provide failover capability.

Here are the steps to create a read replica:

1.   Go to the console and select Cloud SQL from the left panel.

2.   Choose the instance that you want to create a replica for and open its More Actions menu at the far right of its listing, as shown in Figure 9-16. Select a zone in which to create the replica.

Figure 9-16.   *Choose Create Read Replica from the more actions menu*

3.   Click on Create Read Replica.

4.   From the Replicas tab, as shown in Figure 9-17, you can see the replica.

Figure 9-17.   *The new read replica on the Replicas tab*

5. If the replica is created, the master instance will
    have the details of its replica. You can check the
    pg_stat_replication view for the replica details.
    It will show the ID of the process responsible for
    sending data to the replica from the master and
    the user through which replication was set up. To
    check the replica from the psql terminal, click on
    Connect Using Cloud Shell from the Overview tab of
    the primary instance. You will be connected to the
    primary instance, as shown in Figure 9-18.

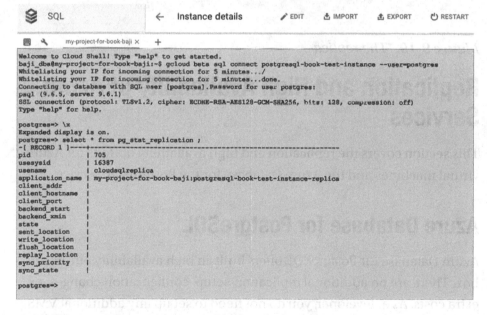

Figure 9-18. *The primary instance*

6. Connect to the replica using the Connect Using
    Cloud Shell option from the Overview tab of the
    replica instance. Now you will be connected to the
    replica, as shown in Figure 9-19.

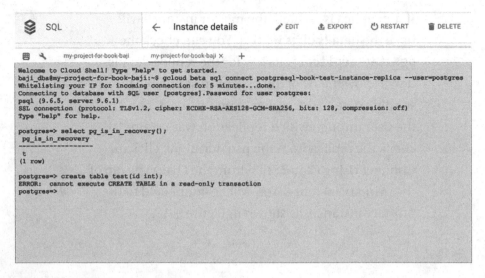

Figure 9-19. *The replica*

Replication and High Availability of Azure Services

This section covers the replication and high availability options for Azure virtual machines and the Azure Database for the PostgreSQL service.

Azure Database for PostgreSQL

Azure Database for PostgreSQL offers built-in high availability out-of-the-box. There are no additional replication setup, configuration changes, or extra costs. As a developer, you do not need to set up any additional VMS or manually configure any replication to achieve high availability. While in preview, the service is not backed up with a specific SLA. However, all databases will have an SLA of 99.99% availability.

This high availability mechanism is based on a built-in fail-over mechanism. It fails over only when node-level interruption occurs, which means if any hardware fails on any node, the total node is shut down.

Every time changes are made to an Azure database for PostgreSQL database server, they will be recorded synchronously in Azure storage. This works on a transaction basis. When a transaction is committed, changes will be recorded to the storage. During the time of failover, it creates a new node and attaches data storage where changes being recorded are attached to the node. However, any active connections during the failover will be dropped.

This service is fairly new, so they are still trying to implement lots of features that other vendors in the market have. Azure continuously allows customers to provide feedback about the service and improve according to the customer requests. There are a lot of feature requests being taken care by the Azure development team to improve the service and make it more reliable when compared to other venders.

As an example, many customers want to create a streaming replica in an Azure service database for many unsupported use cases. However, this has been raised as feature request for the Azure development team. See `https://feedback.azure.com/forums/597976-azure-database-for-postgresql/suggestions/19418071-replication-support-or-is-that-built-in` for more information.

Replication for read-only replicas is not supported yet in the Azure database for PostgreSQL service. Read replicas are currently in the Azure plan to announce early next year. They are also going to add replication from on-premises to Azure Postgres services. High availability is built into the service using Azure Service Fabric.

You can find feature requests for Azure service at `https://feedback.azure.com/forums/597976-azure-database-for-postgresql`.

Virtual Machines

While creating the virtual machine during on Step 3 (Settings, Configure Optional Features), select High Availability, as shown in Figure 9-20.

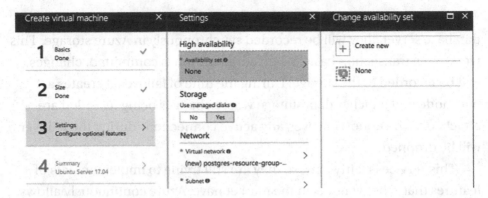

Figure 9-20. *Choose high availability*

To provide redundancy to your application, we recommend that you group two or more virtual machines in an availability set (see Figure 9-21). This configuration ensures that, during a planned or unplanned maintenance event, at least one virtual machine will be available and meet the 99.9% Azure SLA. The availability set of a virtual machine can't be changed after it has been created.

Figure 9-21. *Group virtual machines in an availability set*

Summary

The chapter explored how replication and high availability help you when something goes wrong or in disaster situations. We covered details about which cloud vendor provides what kind of replication and which types of high availability solutions. We hope this helps readers proceed with setting up replication and high availability for their cloud instances. The next chapter covers the need of encryption and how to implement it. It also discusses what kind of encryption each cloud vendor provides for its servers and instances by default.

CHAPTER 10

Encryption on the Cloud

This chapter explains encryption and how it helps you secure your data. We cover encryption at rest and in motion. Each cloud vendor provides default encryption for virtual machines at the disk level and for PostgreSQL at the disk level and in motion. The chapter also covers how to manage your encryption keys.

A database system is considered a store for application data. An application may refer to a website that has static data that almost never changes. Or an application may refer to a critical transactional that always has over several thousands of write transactions sending or retrieving data from the DB server. For example, see `www.postgresql.org/docs` for versions 9.1 or 9.2. As these are currently unsupported versions, you would find no new patches of PostgreSQL. Thus, you would not find any updates happening to the pages that refer to the 9.1 or 9.2 versions of PostgreSQL database software.

However, users who have implemented PostgreSQL 9.1 or 9.2 may still retrieve such pages from the website. Several organizations might archive their data up to several years. Such data may not be accessed (read or written) by any of the application logic, but need to be stored for archiving purposes. Such data that is stored for the purpose of archiving, but not read or updated, can be considered *data at rest*. Also, any database that is not being written frequently can be considered static but cannot be

© Baji Shaik, Avinash Vallarapu 2018
B. Shaik and A. Vallarapu, *Beginning PostgreSQL on the Cloud*,
https://doi.org/10.1007/978-1-4842-3447-1_10

considered at rest. For example, we discussed that the older version of the PostgreSQL docs are not being updated but are being read by users. Thus, this data cannot be treated as data at rest. Any data that is being read or written to or frequently being moved via network packets from one server to another is considered data at rest.

Encryption for Amazon Cloud Servers

AWS offers KMS (Key Management Services) to manage the encryption of data on RDS and EC2 instances. Using KMS, we can create encryption keys that help us encrypt data. KMS is integrated with several other services such as RDS and EC2. KMS enables you to access the logs that help you understand the key usage. KMS provides a centralized key management system that gives you a centralized view of keys created for the organization and a view of the usage details over the AWS command-line interface, etc.

The following steps are involved in creating a master key.

1. In the AWS Services Console, search for IAM and click it to proceed. See Figure 10-1.

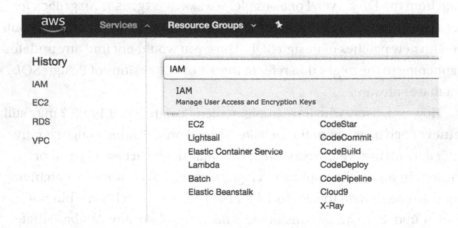

Figure 10-1. *Find IAM on the AWS Services Console*

2. Click on Encryption Keys (see Figure 10-2). You'll
    then see a list of encryption keys already created or
    available for use for the account.

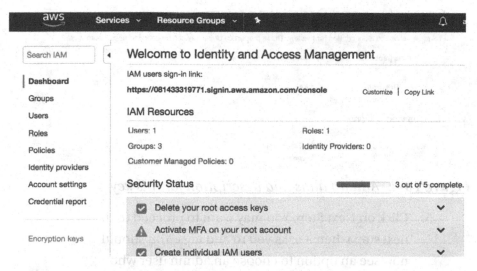

Figure 10-2. *Click on Encryption Keys on the left*

3. Click on the Create Key button to begin creating a
    key, as shown in Figure 10-3.

Figure 10-3. *Click Create Key*

4.   Choose an alias name to identify the key. Add a description that helps you uniquely identify and understand the purpose of this key. See Figure 10-4.

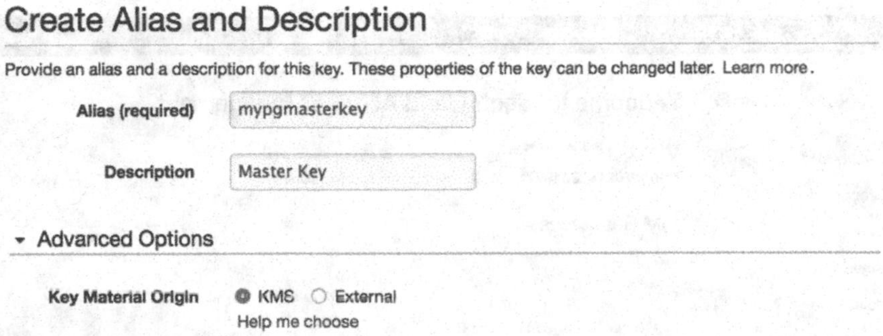

Create Alias and Description

Provide an alias and a description for this key. These properties of the key can be changed later. Learn more .

| Alias (required) | mypgmasterkey |
| Description | Master Key |

▾ Advanced Options

Key Material Origin   ⦿ KMS   ○ External
Help me choose

Figure 10-4.   *Add an alias and description for this key*

5.   Click on Next Step. You may want to proceed to the next step when it asks you to add tags. You should now see an option to choose an admin user who can manage the key being created (see Figure 10-5). Click Next Step once you have chosen the user.

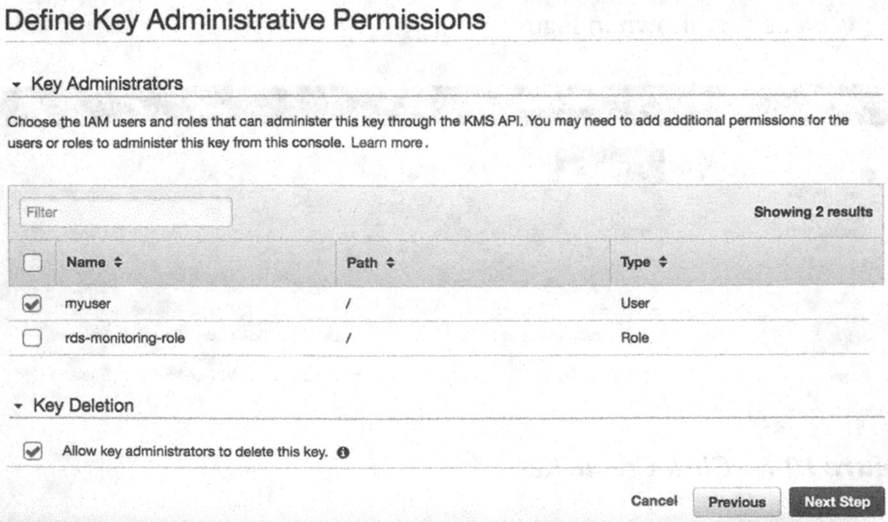

Define Key Administrative Permissions

▾ Key Administrators

Choose the IAM users and roles that can administer this key through the KMS API. You may need to add additional permissions for the users or roles to administer this key from this console. Learn more .

	Name ⬍	Path ⬍	Type ⬍
☑	myuser	/	User
☐	rds-monitoring-role	/	Role

Filter   Showing 2 results

▾ Key Deletion

☑ Allow key administrators to delete this key. ➊

Cancel   Previous   Next Step

Figure 10-5.   *Choose the admin user*

6. Now you can choose the user or role that will use this key to encrypt or decrypt data from applications, as shown in Figure 10-6. Click Next Step to proceed.

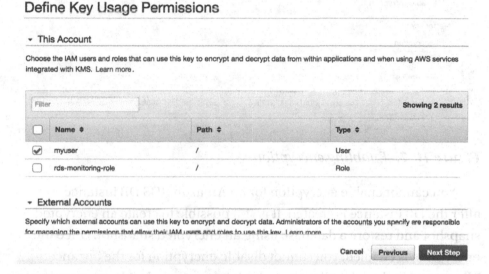

Figure 10-6. *Choose the IAM users and roles*

7. Click Finish to complete creating the key.

Enable Encryption for an RDS Instance

It is not possible to enable encryption for all the RDS instance types during instance creation. You have a list of instances that use encryption at the time of instance creation, as shown in Figure 10-7. You can choose the master key that you created in advance, before creating an RDS instance that needs to be encrypted (we are talking about data at rest).

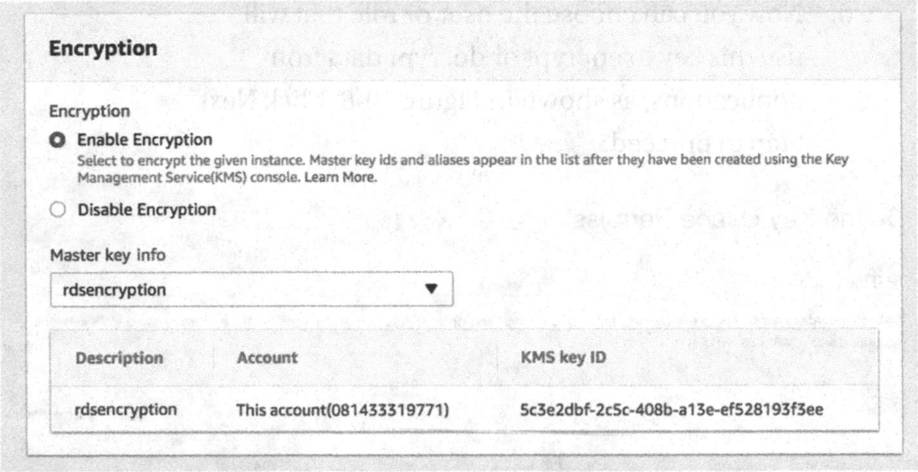

Figure 10-7. *Enabling encryption*

You cannot enable encryption for an Amazon RDS DB instance after the DB instance is created. It is still possible to create an encrypted snapshot and restore a database using an encrypted snapshot. Once the encryption is enabled, you cannot disable encryption for the instance. The master and read replicas must both be encrypted with the same key and you cannot have a master or read replica with only one of them being encrypted.

Amazon also supports SSL encryption for PostgreSQL DB instances. SSL is the preferred mode of encryption for data in motion, while KMS can be used for encrypting data at rest.

To connect to a PostgreSQL instance using SSL, you can use the following steps.

1. Download the certificate stored at `https://s3.amazonaws.com/rds-downloads/rds-combined-ca-bundle.pem`.

2. Import the certificate.

3.   Force connections over SSL by setting the
rds.force_ssl parameter to 1. It is set to 0 by default.
A value of 1 would set SSL encryption to ON forcefully.

Once you set the parameter to ON in the parameter group, this is how
the connection output looks.

```
$ psql postgres -h $hostname -p 5432 -U myuser
psql (9.6.4, server 9.6.4)
SSL connection (cipher: DHE-RSA-AES256-SHA, bits: 256)
Type "help" for help.
postgres=>
```

Encryption on an Amazon EC2 Instance

Amazon supports encryption of EBS volumes, making it possible to
encrypt data at rest. Encryption is supported by all EBS volume types of
an EC2 instance such as General Purpose, Provisioned IOPS, Throughput
Optimized HDD, Cold HDD, and Magnetic. Encrypted volumes come with
a performance cost, although it's negligible for several workloads. EBS
volume encryption is available by default for only a selected list of EC2
instances, as shown in the list in Figure 10-8.

Instance family	Instance types that support Amazon EBS encryption
General purpose	t2.nano | t2.micro | t2.small | t2.medium | t2.large | t2.xlarge | t2.2xlarge | m3.medium | m3.large | m3.xlarge | m3.2xlarge | m4.large | m4.xlarge | m4.2xlarge | m4.4xlarge | m4.10xlarge | m4.16xlarge | m5.large | m5.xlarge | m5.2xlarge | m5.4xlarge | m5.12xlarge | m5.24xlarge
Compute optimized	c3.large | c3.xlarge | c3.2xlarge | c3.4xlarge | c3.8xlarge | c4.large | c4.xlarge | c4.2xlarge | c4.4xlarge | c4.8xlarge | c5.large | c5.xlarge | c5.2xlarge | c5.4xlarge | c5.9xlarge | c5.18xlarge
Memory optimized	r3.large | r3.xlarge | r3.2xlarge | r3.4xlarge | r3.8xlarge | r4.large | r4.xlarge | r4.2xlarge | r4.4xlarge | r4.8xlarge | r4.16xlarge | x1.16xlarge | x1.32xlarge | x1e.xlarge | x1e.2xlarge | x1e.4xlarge | x1e.8xlarge | x1e.16xlarge | x1e.32xlarge | cr1.8xlarge
Storage optimized	d2.xlarge | d2.2xlarge | d2.4xlarge | d2.8xlarge | h1.2xlarge | h1.4xlarge | h1.8xlarge | h1.16xlarge | i2.xlarge | i2.2xlarge | i2.4xlarge | i2.8xlarge | i3.large | i3.xlarge | i3.2xlarge | i3.4xlarge | i3.8xlarge | i3.16xlarge
Accelerated computing	f1.2xlarge | f1.16xlarge | g2.2xlarge | g2.8xlarge | g3.4xlarge | g3.8xlarge | g3.16xlarge | p2.xlarge | p2.8xlarge | p2.16xlarge | p3.2xlarge | p3.8xlarge | p3.16xlarge

Figure 10-8. *Instance types that support Amazon EBS encryption*

You can choose to enable encryption for your EC2 instances at the time of creation. As shown in Figure 10-9, while creating your EC2 instance, under the Storage section, choose the EBS volume of any type and click on the checkbox that allows you to enable encryption.

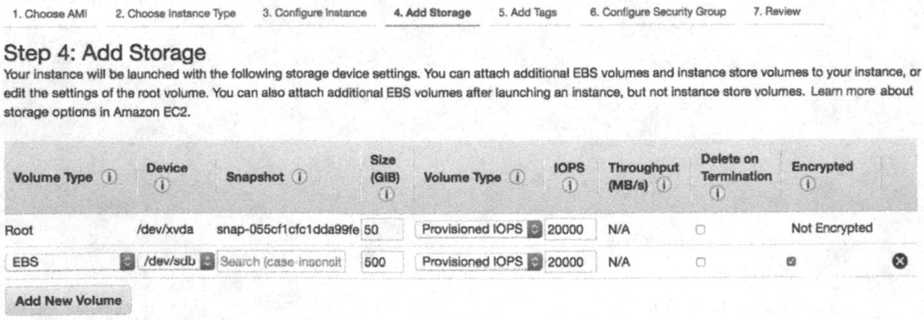

1. Choose AMI	2. Choose Instance Type	3. Configure Instance	4. Add Storage	5. Add Tags	6. Configure Security Group	7. Review

Step 4: Add Storage

Your instance will be launched with the following storage device settings. You can attach additional EBS volumes and instance store volumes to your instance, or edit the settings of the root volume. You can also attach additional EBS volumes after launching an instance, but not instance store volumes. Learn more about storage options in Amazon EC2.

Volume Type ⓘ	Device ⓘ	Snapshot ⓘ	Size (GIB) ⓘ	Volume Type ⓘ	IOPS ⓘ	Throughput (MB/s) ⓘ	Delete on Termination ⓘ	Encrypted ⓘ	
Root	/dev/xvda	snap-055cf1cfc1dda99fe	50	Provisioned IOPS ◌	20000	N/A	☐	Not Encrypted	
EBS ◌	/dev/sdb ◌	Search (case-insensit	500	Provisioned IOPS ◌	20000	N/A	☐	☑	⊗

Add New Volume

Figure 10-9. *Enabling encryption for EC2 instances at the time of creation*

Encryption for Rackspace Cloud Servers

The purpose of encryption is to secure your data. However, encrypting data may involve some overhead, which means that backing up and restoring encrypted data takes significantly longer. If you really want encryption for your data, go for it, but don't forgot the overhead costs.

Rackspace provides encryption for your backups using AES-356 encryption. You need to create a key or a passphrase that's known only to you. Without the key or passphrase you will not be able to recover your backups. Once you choose to encrypt the backups, you cannot disable encryption. However, you can change your passphrase when you want.

To encrypt your backups, perform the following steps:

1. Click on the Backups tab and then on Systems in the Rackspace portal, as shown in Figure 10-10.

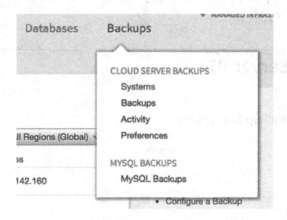

Figure 10-10. *Choose backup systems*

2. From the backup settings, click on the Enable
    Encryption option.

Cloud Backup Systems

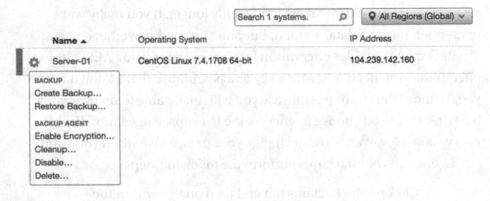

3. Enter a passphrase for encryption, as shown in
    Figure 10-11.

Figure 10-11. *Choose a passphrase for encryption*

Encrypting the data contained in your backups from
this system provides an additional level of security.
Without having the passphrase, the contents of
your backup are unreadable. Thus, be sure to use
a passphrase that you will remember. If you forget
your passphrase, you will not be able to recover the
data from your backups.

Once encryption has been enabled, you will not be
able to disable it.

4. Once you encrypt it, you can see in the backup
    configuration details that your backup is encrypted,
    as shown in Figure 10-12.

CLOUD BACKUP CONFIGURATION

backup_3122017

⚙ Actions ∨

Configuration Details

Status	Configured
System	Server-01 ☑ Backup agent is connected.
Schedule	This backup is **not scheduled** and must be run **manually**.
Version Retention	**Modifications** since the last backup are kept **indefinitely**.
Notification	Inform **baji.dba@gmail.com** when a backup **completes successfully** or **fails to complete**.
Encryption	This backup is **encrypted**.

Figure 10-12. *The backup has been encrypted*

Encryption for Google Cloud Instances

In previous chapters, we discussed creating instances, cloud storages,
cloud SQL instances, and how to back up instances and replication/high
availability of instances. Now, let's look at encrypting the data when we use
Google cloud.

303

Encrypting Cloud Storage

Encryption of data for Google cloud storage is on the server side by default. It will be encrypted before it is written to disk and needs no extra charges. This encryption is data at rest using AES-256 encryption. Server-side encryption keys will be managed by Google cloud storage, so you do not need to worry about the keys. To enable encryption, you don't need to perform any additional configuration. The overhead is very small so there is no visible performance impact.

If you don't want to use default encryption, you can choose your own encryption option when you provide your own encryption keys for server-side encryption. It will replace the default encryption keys. However, you are responsible for your keys. If you lose your keys, you will not be able to use your backups.

The steps to set up encryption using the Customer-Supplied Encryption Keys are at `https://cloud.google.com/storage/docs/using-encryption-keys`.

More options to encrypt data at rest are at `https://cloud.google.com/security/encryption-at-rest/`.

Cloud SQL Encryption

Encryption for cloud SQL can be done in two ways.

- Using SSL
- Using Proxy

Using SSL

Cloud SQL supports connecting to your PostgreSQL instances using SSL. It works on certificates. Server-side certificates are self-signed and need a certificate at the client side. These certificates work together to enable the server (instance) and client (application) to encrypt their communication.

You can manage your certificate through the console. Select Cloud SQL on left panel of the console and then click on the instance and use the SSL tab to see/manage your certificates. See Figure 10-13.

Figure 10-13. *Managing SSL configuration*

Using Cloud Proxy

Another way to secure your connection is using cloud proxy. That way, you need not whitelist your IP addresses or configure SSL. More information on Cloud Proxy is at `https://cloud.google.com/sql/docs/postgres/sql-proxy`.

Encryption for Azure Cloud Services

When it comes to data security, Azure Database for PostgreSQL has features that protect data at rest and in motion, limit access, and help you monitor activity. If you want to know more about Azure's platform security, visit the Azure Trust Center at `https://www.microsoft.com/en-us/trustcenter`.

This section covers encryption for PostgreSQL services on Azure. There are two ways to secure the data—one is to encrypt the data at rest or in motion and the other is to secure the connection.

This service uses storage encryption for data at rest. Except temporary files created by the engine while running the queries, all the data, including backups, are encrypted on disks. The encryption type that the service uses is AES 256-bit, which is included in Azure storage encryption. You do not need to manage keys, as they are system managed. Encryption for storage is ON by default and you cannot disable it.

When it comes to data in motion, the Azure Database for PostgreSQL service is configured to require SSL connection security. Enforcing SSL connections between your database server and your client applications helps protect against "man in the middle" attacks by encrypting the data stream between the server and your application. Optionally, you can disable requiring SSL for connecting to your database service if your client application does not support SSL connectivity.

As storage encryption is ON by default and we do not have any option to change it, let's look at enabling SSL for PostgreSQL connections.

1. Select your PostgreSQL instance from your resources, as shown in Figure 10-14.

Figure 10-14. *Select the PostgreSQL instance from the resources*

2. Click on Connection Security and you will see the
    ENABLED/DISABLED option under SSL settings on
    the right panel, as shown in Figure 10-15.

Figure 10-15. *Enabling SSL for PostgreSQL connections*

Many applications that use PostgreSQL for their database services—such as Drupal and Django—do not enable SSL by default during installation. So, make sure your application supports SSL before you enable it for database service.

For applications that require certificate verification for SSL connectivity, see the steps at `https://docs.microsoft.com/en-us/azure/postgresql/concepts-ssl-connection-security#applications-that-require-certificate-verification-for-ssl-connectivity`.

Summary

This chapter covered encrypting data and how doing so helps in terms of security. We also talked about encryption of virtual machines and PostgreSQL service data at rest and in motion. We hope that this chapter has helped readers understand the need for encryption and how to do that in the cloud for each vendor. In the next chapter, we cover connection pooling in detail—what is it, how it works, and what solutions are available for each cloud vendor in terms of it.

CHAPTER 11

Connection Pooling on the Cloud

This chapter covers what a connection pooler is and how it helps database connections. We include installation and configuration of external connection poolers like pgBouncer on each cloud vendor, as well as external connection poolers like DBCP on all cloud venders. Apart from learning about the external tools, you'll learn how to set up connection poolers at the application level.

Connection Pooling

To get started with connection pooling, you learn how connections are handled in PostgreSQL. When an application or an application server (aka, a client) sends a request to PostgreSQL database for a connection, the postmaster listens to it first.

It is similar to a listener for Oracle. The postmaster listens to the connection and forks another backend process for it. The client connection now has a process in the operating system.

© Baji Shaik, Avinash Vallarapu 2018
B. Shaik and A. Vallarapu, *Beginning PostgreSQL on the Cloud*,
https://doi.org/10.1007/978-1-4842-3447-1_11

What Is Forking?

Forking is the process of creating a child process that looks identical to the parent process that created it. This child process is also called a fork. Both the parent and the child process have the same code segment, but with a different address space. The child process has a different process ID. In a multiprogramming operating system, semaphores are used to control access to a common resource. The same semaphores as parent processes will be open in child process.

Figure 11-1 shows a good example of forking in Linux.

```
[avinash@OpenSCG$ps -eaf | grep postgres
postgres  2236     1  0 22:46 pts/0    00:00:00 /usr/pgsql-9.5/bin/postgres -D /var/lib/pgsql/9.5/data
postgres  2237  2236  0 22:46 ?        00:00:00 postgres: logger process
postgres  2239  2236  0 22:46 ?        00:00:00 postgres: checkpointer process
postgres  2240  2236  0 22:46 ?        00:00:00 postgres: writer process
postgres  2241  2236  0 22:46 ?        00:00:00 postgres: wal writer process
postgres  2242  2236  0 22:46 ?        00:00:00 postgres: autovacuum launcher process
postgres  2243  2236  0 22:46 ?        00:00:00 postgres: stats collector process
root      2291  2187  0 22:49 pts/0    00:00:00 su - postgres
postgres  2292  2291  0 22:49 pts/0    00:00:00 -bash
postgres  2324  2236  0 22:49 ?        00:00:00 postgres: postgres postgres 192.168.0.9(58606) idle
postgres  2329  2236  0 22:49 ?        00:00:00 postgres: postgres postgres 192.168.0.9(58612) idle
postgres  2355  2292  0 22:51 pts/0    00:00:00 ps -eaf
postgres  2356  2292  0 22:51 pts/0    00:00:00 grep --color=auto postgres
[avinash@OpenSCG$
```

Figure 11-1. *An example of forking in Linux*

In Figure 11-1, note that the process ID of the parent postgres process is 2236.

As discussed in the PostgreSQL architecture, there are several backend utility process started by Postgres, such as the writer process, the logger process, the checkpointer, the WAL writer, etc. All these processes are created or forked by the postmaster as child processes. If you observe carefully, you see a different process ID for each of these child processes, but with the same parent process ID (2236) as the parent process. In the last four lines of the output in Figure 11-2, you can see idle connections from 192.168.0.9. These are two client connections for which two child processes have been created by the Postgres parent process.

```
postgres   2324   2236   0 22:49 ?        00:00:00 postgres: postgres postgres 192.168.0.9(58606) idle
postgres   2329   2236   0 22:49 ?        00:00:00 postgres: postgres postgres 192.168.0.9(58612) idle
postgres   2355   2292   0 22:51 pts/0    00:00:00 ps -eaf
postgres   2356   2292   0 22:51 pts/0    00:00:00 grep --color=auto postgres
[avinash@OpenSCG$
[avinash@OpenSCG$
[avinash@OpenSCG$psql
psql (9.5.7)
Type "help" for help.

[postgres=# select pid, state from pg_stat_activity ;
  pid  | state
-------+---------
  2324 | idle
  2329 | idle
  2397 | active
(3 rows)
```

Figure 11-2. *Child processes created for the client connections*

Every child process created for the client connections can be observed in pg_stat_activity, as shown in Figure 11-2.

Understanding Why Process Creation Is Costly

Several system resources are involved in creating a process in the operating system. Likewise, once a client connection is closed or terminated, it involves several system resources in closing a child process. Consider a critical production database server that takes over 1000 transactions per second. For every client request, a process needs to be opened and closed by the server. Creating or forking a process for every client connection in such a production database system is very costly and time consuming. More time is consumed while creating address space, file descriptors the same as parent processes, and semaphores for the child process.

What Is Connection Pooling and How Can It Help?

Connection pooling is a mechanism that uses a cache of connections that are maintained on the database server. This helps applications reuse the already established connections on a database.

Reusing the already existing connections avoids the time consumption involved in starting and stopping processes for every client request. Applications either use a built-in connecting pooling mechanism or external connection poolers. These connections poolers establish a pool of connections to the database and keep them persistent until a timeout. Applications can configure the minimum number of connections that always exist in the pool and the maximum number of connections that a pool of connections can reach up to. A connection pooler provides better performance between an application and a database when compared to an application without an connection pooler.

PgBouncer

PgBouncer is an open source, lightweight connection pooler that is designed and built for PostgreSQL databases. Applications that do not support native connection pooling can implement pgBouncer-like external connection poolers to achieve better performance results. Just as with the definition of connection pooling, pgBouncer establishes a pool of connections upon client requests, having all the established connections placed back into the pool when the client disconnects. This pool of connections can be reused by further client requests.

PgBouncer can understand the startup parameters on the PostgreSQL database. It also detects changes to the startup parameters and ensure that the parameters remain consistent for clients. The startup parameters include timezone, datestyle, client_encoding, application_name, and standard_conforming_strings.

PgBouncer supports three modes of connection pooling:

- Session pooling

- Transaction pooling

- Statement pooling

Let's begin by understanding what mode you should use while using pgBouncer.

Session Pooling

This is one of the most widely used modes, as it is a polite method. When a client connects, a server connection is created on the DB server and it is assigned to the client connection. That server connection or child process stays with the client for the entire duration until the client disconnects. This mode supports all PostgreSQL features.

Transaction Pooling

We have seen PgBouncer performing better with transaction pooling. In Transaction pooling, a server connection is assigned to the client only during a transaction. If the transaction is over, the server connection will be placed back into the pool. Unlike session mode, transaction mode does not let a client connection stay until the client is disconnected. A server connection will be assigned for every transaction and taken back once it is over.

There are a few features that could break if the application does not cooperate. For example, transaction mode does not support prepared statements. Prepared statements reuse the execution plan and the cache of the first SQL. In this mode, the client connection is disconnected once the first transaction is over. The next SQLs cannot take the advantage of an SQL being prepared. If your application logic does not support all of its logic to be completed within a single transaction but depends on the entire session that got established, transaction pooling is not a good choice. You should instead look for session pooling.

Statement Pooling

Statement pooling is the most aggressive. It does not support transactions with multiple statements. For every statement, a server connection is assigned and the connection is placed back into pool when the statement is finished. This is mainly used for auto-commit of every statement of the client. If you are using transactions with multiple SQLs or sessions with multiple transactions, this pool may not be the right choice for you.

When Should You Think About a PgBouncer?

PostgreSQL is observed to have scaling issues with connections if the native application pooler is not configured properly or if there is no application pooler. There is a general rule that PostgreSQL scales up to 350 transactions per second without any connection pooler and the performance is optimal. This number may be higher or lower depending on your application logic, server configuration, and other reasons. There is no such hard limit as to when you should implement a connection pooler. However, with increasing demand of connection traffic from an application, we must think about introducing the correct connection pooler. This is because every connection established directly is a process fork with a resident memory of up to 10 MB or more. If you have 1000 connections, you should be able to save around 9 to 10GB of RAM.

Most of the production database environments deal with several tens of application servers. Each individual application server may have either built-in connection poolers or external connection poolers. Consider an example where 20 app servers establish over 10 connections every second to the database on an average. You may need to have a connection pooler on every app that establishes a minimum of 10 connections to the database, which can go up to 20 or 30 assuming the highest transaction peak. If you observe that the active connections on the database at any given time are not more than 50, this is because not all app servers are expected to get the same load. You may still need to have several idle connections opened on the database. There is a cost to maintaining those idle connections.

We have observed several situations in real-time scenarios where the application pooler fails to terminate the maximum pool of connections established during a huge peak due to the timeout settings. There are also situations where the process memory area created by the previous statement is held in memory but not released. This is mostly useful in prepared transactions or prepared statements. The prepared transactions require the SQL to be pre-cached so that further SQLs reuse the cached buffers. This has been observed to be a pain point. If the memory used by the previous transaction is not released, you would always see a lot of memory being used even when you have 3 to 10 active connections on the database. There could be some settings on the application pooler that allow you to reset the cache created by the transaction upon its disconnect. This is configurable with a few poolers and may not be configurable across the board. PgBouncer allows you to have parameters in place that take care of resetting the memory used by the previous SQLs.

One of the most difficult tasks with connection poolers on application servers is high availability. When a master or primary database is down, you need to promote its slave to the master and ensure that all the app servers connect to the newly promoted master. This involves modification of the connection strings on all application servers with great downtime.

If your application servers connect to a pgBouncer, it just involves modification of one connection string. That redirects all connections to the newly promoted master. We discuss the steps involved in setting up a high availability cluster using pgBouncer that also serves the purpose of connection pooler in this chapter.

Installing PgBouncer

If you have very few application servers, you may want to build pgBouncer on all of them. However, in an environment that has several tens of application servers, you may need to build pgBouncer externally and have all the application servers connect to it. See the following instructions on how to install and configure pgBouncer in a Linux environment.

These steps were performed on a CentOS 7.3 operating system:

1. Have the latest pgdg repo installed on your virtual machine. Pgdg repo contains a list of Postgres software being used by users in their production environments. You have to install the pgdg repo that suits your operating system and the PostgreSQL database version.

   Say that you need PostgreSQL 9.6 on CentOS 7.3 OS. In that case, you would use the following link and click on the PostgreSQL version that suits your needs.

   https://yum.postgresql.org/

   Figure 11-3 should help you understand how you can choose the pgdg repo that has all the software that's built and tested for the PostgreSQL version you choose.

   Let's assume that you need PostgreSQL 9.6. Click on it to proceed.

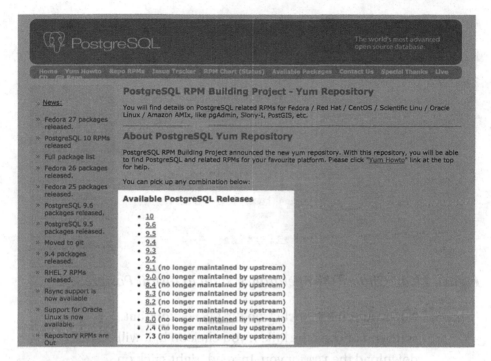

Figure 11-3. *Click on PostgreSQL 9.6 to proceed*

2. Now you get an option to choose the operating system on which you want PostgreSQL or its tools to be installed (see Figure 11-4). Select the OS on which you need to install pgBouncer (same as with the PostgreSQL database OS).

317

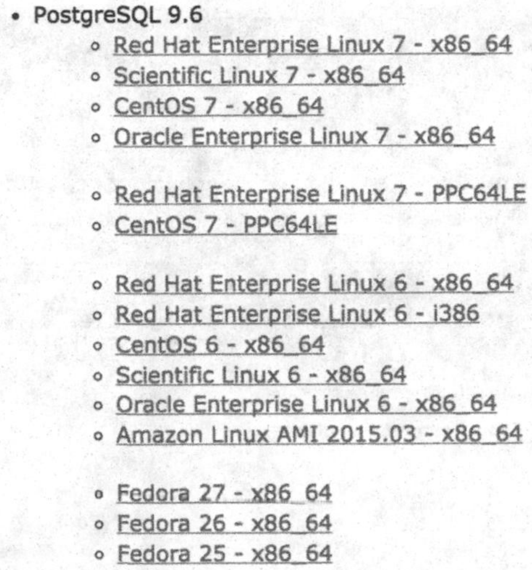

- PostgreSQL 9.6
  - Red Hat Enterprise Linux 7 - x86_64
  - Scientific Linux 7 - x86_64
  - CentOS 7 - x86_64
  - Oracle Enterprise Linux 7 - x86_64

  - Red Hat Enterprise Linux 7 - PPC64LE
  - CentOS 7 - PPC64LE

  - Red Hat Enterprise Linux 6 - x86_64
  - Red Hat Enterprise Linux 6 - i386
  - CentOS 6 - x86_64
  - Scientific Linux 6 - x86_64
  - Oracle Enterprise Linux 6 - x86_64
  - Amazon Linux AMI 2015.03 - x86_64

  - Fedora 27 - x86_64
  - Fedora 26 - x86_64
  - Fedora 25 - x86_64

Figure 11-4. *Choose the operating system to install PostgreSQL*

3. Now you can either click on the OS version that suits you or copy the link. If you click on it, it will download the rpm for you. Instead, right-click on CentOS 7 - x86_64 and choose Copy Link Address. This link can be directly used in the pgBouncer server.

   This is how the link appears when you copy it for CentOS 7:

   ```
   https://download.postgresql.org/pub/
   repos/yum/9.6/redhat/rhel-7-x86_64/pgdg-
   centos96-9.6-3.noarch.rpm
   ```

4. Get the pgBouncer ready with a hard disk of at least 30GB. As we do not want to store several days or years of pgBouncer logs, we may need very small storage. pgBouncer is a single process. Thus, you may not need a very huge server configuration to set

it up. A server configuration with 8GB RAM and four CPUs may be good for a database that takes over 1000 to 2000 or more transactions per second.

5. As a root user, install the `pgdg repo rpm` on the pgBouncer server.

    Here is the command to install it. As you can see in the command, we can directly use the link to download the `pgdg repo rpm` and yum will download and install it automatically.

```
# yum install https://download.postgresql.
org/pub/repos/yum/9.6/redhat/rhel-7-x86_64/
pgdg-centos96-9.6-3.noarch.rpm
```

You may press Y when asked for confirmation to install the `pgdg repo`. Once it's installed, you should be able to see a new repo file created in the `/etc/yum.repos.d` directory. See Figure 11-5.

```
[root@localhost yum.repos.d]# ls -alrth | head -4
total 44K
-rw-r--r--.  1 root root 1012 Sep 20  2016 pgdg-96-
centos.repo
-rw-r--r--.  1 root root 2.9K Nov 29  2016 CentOS-
Vault.repo
-rw-r--r--.  1 root root 1.3K Nov 29  2016 CentOS-
Sources.repo
```

```
[root@localhost ~]# yum install https://download.postgresql.org/pub/repos/yum/9.6/redhat/rhel-7-x86_64/pgdg-centos96-9.6-3.noarch.rpm
Loaded plugins: fastestmirror
pgdg-centos96-9.6-3.noarch.rpm                                                                                      | 4.7 kB  00:00:00
Examining /var/tmp/yum-root-D7cdA0/pgdg-centos96-9.6-3.noarch.rpm: pgdg-centos96-9.6-3.noarch
Marking /var/tmp/yum-root-D7cdA0/pgdg-centos96-9.6-3.noarch.rpm to be installed
Resolving Dependencies
--> Running transaction check
---> Package pgdg-centos96.noarch 0:9.6-3 will be installed
--> Finished Dependency Resolution

Dependencies Resolved

================================================================================================================
 Package                  Arch              Version              Repository                              Size
================================================================================================================
Installing:
 pgdg-centos96            noarch            9.6-3                /pgdg-centos96-9.6-3.noarch            2.7 k

Transaction Summary
================================================================================================================
Install  1 Package

Total size: 2.7 k
Installed size: 2.7 k
Is this ok [y/d/N]: y
Downloading packages:
Running transaction check
Running transaction test
Transaction test succeeded
Running transaction
  Installing : pgdg-centos96-9.6-3.noarch                                                                 1/1
  Verifying  : pgdg-centos96-9.6-3.noarch                                                                 1/1

Installed:
  pgdg-centos96.noarch 0:9.6-3

Complete!
```

Figure 11-5. *The new repo file created in the /etc/yum.repos.d*
directory

6. Now search for the pgBouncer software and install
    it. These commands help you list the package
    named pgbouncer and install it. See Figure 11-6.

    ```
    # yum list pgbouncer
    # yum install pgbouncer -y
    ```

```
[root@localhost ~]# yum list pgbouncer
Loaded plugins: fastestmirror
Loading mirror speeds from cached hostfile
 * base: mirror.its.dal.ca
 * extras: centos.mirror.ca.planethoster.net
 * updates: mirror2.evolution-host.com
Available Packages
pgbouncer.x86_64                      1.7.2-7.rhel7                      pgdg96
[root@localhost ~]#
[root@localhost ~]#
[root@localhost ~]#
[root@localhost ~]# yum install pgbouncer -y
Loaded plugins: fastestmirror
Loading mirror speeds from cached hostfile
 * base: mirror.its.dal.ca
 * extras: centos.mirror.ca.planethoster.net
 * updates: mirror2.evolution-host.com
Resolving Dependencies
--> Running transaction check
---> Package pgbouncer.x86_64 0:1.7.2-7.rhel7 will be installed
```

***Figure 11-6.** Finding and installing the pgBouncer software*

7. If you observe Figure 11-7 closely, you can see that a
    user by the name pgbouncer has been automatically
    created for pgbouncer.

    Verify that pgBouncer is installed. The following
    command verifies the version of pgBouncer
    installed.

    # su - pgbouncer
    $ pgbouncer --version

321

```
[root@localhost ~]# whoami
root
[root@localhost ~]# su - pgbouncer
Last login: Sun Dec  3 10:42:44 EST 2017 on pts/0
[pgbouncer@localhost ~]$ pgbouncer --version
pgbouncer version 1.7.2
[pgbouncer@localhost ~]$ ls -l /etc/pgbouncer/
total 24
-rwx------. 1 root root  798 Dec  6  2012 mkauth.py
-rw-r--r--. 2 root root 1126 Jul 18 09:43 mkauth.pyc
-rw-r--r--. 2 root root 1126 Jul 18 09:43 mkauth.pyo
-rw-r--r--. 1 root root 8580 Jul 18 09:42 pgbouncer.ini
[pgbouncer@localhost ~]$ 
```

Figure 11-7. *The user pgbouncer has been automatically created for pgbouncer*

All the configuration files of pgBouncer are located by default in the /etc/pgbouncer directory.

8. Create all the required directories needed by pgBouncer, if they don't already exist. Here are the directories needed to log pgBouncer error logs and messages and the directories to create the socket files or lock files of pgBouncer:

    mkdir -p /var/log/pgbouncer/
    mkdir -p /var/run/pgbouncer/
    chown -R pgbouncer:pgbouncer /etc/pgbouncer/
    chown -R pgbouncer:pgbouncer /var/log/pgbouncer/
    chown -R pgbouncer:pgbouncer /var/run/pgbouncer/

9. Change the configuration file to let your application connect through pgBouncer to master or slave PostgreSQL servers. The following example pgBouncer file should help you build a better

pgBouncer setup the first time. However, you may still need to make modifications depending on your application requirements.

```
$ cat /etc/pgbouncer/pgbouncer.ini

[databases]
master = host=MasterServerIP port=5432
dbname=testing
slave = host=SlaveServerIP port=5432
dbname=testing
listen_addresses = *
[pgbouncer]
logfile = /var/log/pgbouncer/pgbouncer.log
pidfile = /var/run/pgbouncer/pgbouncer.pid
listen_addr = *
listen_port = 6432
auth_type = md5
auth_file = /etc/pgbouncer/cfg/pg_auth
admin_users = postgres
stats_users = postgres
pool_mode = session
server_reset_query = DISCARD ALL
ignore_startup_parameters = extra_float_digits
server_check_query = select 1
max_client_conn = 200
default_pool_size = 10
log_connections = 1
log_disconnections = 1
log_pooler_errors = 1
server_lifetime = 600
server_idle_timeout = 60
autodb_idle_timeout = 3600
```

Let's try to understand all these parameters to understand and build it better.

Under the [databases] section, you need to give the alias names to your master and slave DB servers. I refer to my master DB server as master and the slave DB Server as slave. You can give an alias of my choice that helps you identify the name and determine if it is a master or a slave.

- listen_addresses: Same as with PostgreSQL, you see a parameter that allows you to let only a fixed range of IPs or all IPs connect through pgBouncer to your DB Server. However, this does not bypass the pg_hba.conf file on your DB server. Restricting IPs through this setting may allow you to avoid pgBouncer, by allocating a connection from the pool for an IP that is not allowed to connect a master or slave DB server.

- listen_port: This is the port on which your pgBouncer should listen for connections. The default port of pgBouncer is 6432. You can always modify it and choose a port that is not being used by any other service on the pgBouncer server.

- logfile: You pass the log file name where pgBouncer can log errors and messages.

- pidfile: This is the location/filename where pgBouncer creates a file that contains the process ID of the pgBouncer service. This file will be updated upon restart with a new pid.

- auth_type: Defaults to md5. This can be modified
  if needed. Encrypted passwords are sent over the
  wire.

- auth_file: This is the name of the file used to load
  the usernames and passwords. This contains the list
  of users who can connect to the database through
  pgBouncer. This file contains two fields—username
  and password—surrounded by double quotes.

  For example:

  ```
  "app_user_reads" "md5abcd1234efgh5678"
  "app_user_writes" "md5abcd5678efgh1234"
  ```

  To get the list of users and md5 passwords of
  database users, you can run the following SQL in
  the database and store the output in this file.

  ```
  select '"'||usename||'" "'||passwd||
  '"' from pg_shadow;
  ```

- admin_users: Defaults to null. This is the list of
  users who can run all commands on the console.

- stats_users: List of DB users who can run read only
  queries on the console, such as SHOW commands.

- pool_mode: This is the parameter that lets you
  choose the mode from the list of three modes
  possible for pgBouncer, as discussed earlier.

- server_reset_query: This cleans the changes made
  to a database session leaving the session in a no
  cached state. DISCARD ALL cleans all the cache.
  DEALLOCATE ALL simply drops prepared statements.
  This parameter is not needed for transaction mode.

- `max_client_conn`: The maximum number of client connections allowed, including all the pools that can be created.

- `default_pool_size`: A pool is created for every combination of user/database. The number of connections to be allowed per such pool can be configured using this parameter. The default is 20.

- `min_pool_size`: The number of connections to be always maintained in the pool considering peak loads that could request more connections.

- `log_connections`: Log all successful connections. Default is 1.

- `log_disconnections`: Log all connection disconnections. Default is 1.

- `server_lifetime`: This is the time after which the pooler closes the server connections that have connected longer than this.

- `server_idle_timeout`: Drops all the connections that have been idle since these many seconds.

- `autodb_idle_timeout`: If database pools are unused for these many seconds, they are freed.

10. Now start pgBouncer using `service` or do so directly.

    `# service pgbouncer start`

    Or

    `$ pgbouncer -d /etc/pgbouncer/pgbouncer.ini`

How Does PgBouncer Work?

Let's say a user with the username abc established a connection for the first time to the pgBouncer from an application. PgBouncer would check if this user authentication was successful by reading its auth file. Once the user is authenticated successfully, pgBouncer establishes a pool of connections to the database. It would not just open one connection to the database. It would opens a `default_pool_size` number of connections.

If the application sends another session using the same user, the pool of connections will be used and one connection from the pool will be assigned to the application again. If the first connection is completed from the application, it disconnects from pgBouncer. But pgBouncer would not disconnect from the database until a timeout occurs. So, if application establishes another connection from the same user, the connection the from pool would be reused.

High Availability While Using PgBouncer

One of the major concerns in any environment is ensuring high availability. Adding a component or service may add more single point of failures. To ensure high availability in an environment where pgBouncer is used as an external connection pooler, you can use the design shown in Figure 11-8.

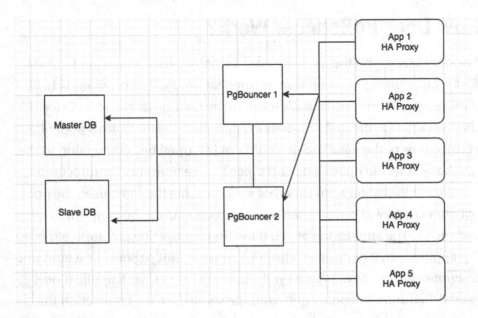

Figure 11-8. *Design for high availability with pgBouncer*

As you can see in Figure 11-8, you can configure two pgBouncer servers and install HAProxy on all the app servers. Choose two servers that belong to two different regions and that have pgBouncers installed in them. Now, HAProxy should connect to any of the available pgBouncer servers. This way, application connections are always redirected to the master or slave DB via at least one of the available pgBouncers, thus ensuring high availability.

Connection Pooling on AWS

PostgreSQL can be installed on AWS either by choosing RDS or an EC2 instance. It is much easier to configure and set up a secured and high performance PostgreSQL instance on AWS. Similarly, you may choose to build your application servers on EC2 instances or your own data centers.

While using your PostgreSQL instance that is being hit with several hundreds or thousands of transactions per second, you may choose to involve an external connection pooler such as pgBouncer. This is because the connection pooler would reuse the connections established to the database and avoid the time and resource costs involved in starting and stopping processes. For more details on the need for connection pooling, see the "Connection Pooling" section of this chapter.

There is no such service for PostgreSQL connection pooling on AWS. Instead, you may choose to install pgBouncer like external connection poolers on either the DB servers or on a separate EC2 instance. It is very easy to install pgBouncer on an EC2 instance.

Here are the steps that you need to follow to install pgBouncer.

1. Create an EC2 instance that is in the same region as the DB server. To ensure high availability, create multiple (two) pgBouncer instances.

2. Download and install the latest pgdg repo from yum.postgresql.org.

   ```
   # yum install https://download.postgresql.org/
   pub/repos/yum/9.6/redhat/rhel-7-x86_64/pgdg-
   centos96-9.6-3.noarch.rpm
   ```

3. Search for the pgBouncer package and install it.

   ```
   # yum list pgbouncer
   # yum install pgbouncer -y
   ```

   These are the steps that you need to follow to install pgBouncer on an EC2 instance. The step-by-step process of installing pgBouncer is explained in this chapter in the "Installing pgBouncer" section.

Connection Pooling for Rackspace Cloud Servers

There is no separate connection pooler from Rackspace for their cloud or dedicated servers.

You can use external poolers like pgBouncer for PostgreSQL installed on Rackspace cloud machines. The steps to install and configure pgBouncer are already described in this chapter in the "Installing PgBouncer" section.

You can also use an application level pooling for the PostgreSQL database. If you are using applications based on Java, widely used ORM frameworks like Hibernate provide built-in as well as pluggable connection pooler interfaces. The Postgres JDBC driver supports connection pooling as a DataSource Implementation. Documentation is available at `https://jdbc.postgresql.org/documentation/head/ds-ds.html`.

However, neither JDBC driver-provided pools or Hibernate-provided pools are recommended for production use. Instead, the most widely used and advanced connection poolers like C3P0 or DBCP are recommended for production use. See `http://commons.apache.org/proper/commons-dbcp/`.

Connection Pooling for Google Cloud Instances

There have been many discussions about implementing or using a connection pooler against Google cloud SQL instances. However, they never end up with a solution. The whole concept is that database connections in a cloud-hosted environment should be managed differently than those on a conventional server. In particular, be aware that your database instance may be taken offline while not in use, and any pooled connections would be closed. We recommend that you create a new connection to service each HTTP request, and then you reuse it for the duration of that request (since the time to create a new connection is similar to that required to test the liveness of an existing connection).

However, Google cloud is still open for discussions around connection pooling. They are really interested to know about requirements or use cases that help to understand the need of connection pooling to implement it.

One option is the commons DBCP pool (with straight JDBC, no JDO/JPA). It has a facility for testing a connection before returning from the pool, which prevents any errors if the database instance goes "to sleep". The test query adds 10-15ms seconds before every query, which is acceptable to most of the requirements. DBCP has more efficient ways to check for dead connections (e.g., every x seconds while sitting in the pool), but these can't be used because they involve starting up new maintenance threads that are not allowed in AppEngine.

Of course, this will prevent any errors, but it will not keep some requests from taking upward of 15 seconds while they wait for the database instance to come up. You can deal with that by having your monitoring server hit an URL every five minutes that involves a database call, so even in periods of very low activity, the database should stay on.

See more at http://commons.apache.org/dbcp/configuration.html.

Here's how we wire up our data source and transaction manager in Spring:

```
<bean id="dsSearchIndex" class="org.apache.commons.dbcp.
BasicDataSource" destroy-method="close">
    <property name="driverClassName" value="com.google.
    appengine.api.rdbms.AppEngineDriver"/>
    <property name="url" value="jdbc:google:rdbms://xxxx.
    com:web-prod:searchindex/ctssearchidx"/>
    <property name="username" value="xxx"/>
    <property name="password" value="xxx"/>
```

```
    <property name="testOnBorrow" value="true"/>
    <property name="validationQuery" value="select 1"/>
</bean>
    <bean id="tmSearchIndex" class="org.springframework.
    jdbc.datasource.DataSourceTransactionManager">
        <property name="dataSource" ref="dsSearchIndex"/>
        <qualifier value="searchIndex"/>
    </bean>
    <tx:annotation-driven mode="aspectj" transaction-
    manager="tmSearchIndex" />
<bean id="daoSearchIndex" class="com.commentous.
searchindex.SearchIndexJdbcDao">
    <property name="dataSource" ref="dsSearchIndex"/>
</bean>
```

If you want to install PgBouncer on Google cloud virtual machines, follow the steps explained in the "Installation of pgBouncer" section after you create the machine and connect to it.

Connection Pooling for Azure Cloud Instances

Like some of the other venders, there is no special connection pooler implemented for Azure database for PostgreSQL instances or PostgreSQL installed on virtual machines. You need to use external pooling software like pgBouncer or pool the connections at the application level. Since you have learned about pgBouncer in this chapter, can consider implementing it in this case.

Once you have connected to your Azure cloud virtual machine, you can follow the steps explained in the "Installation of PgBouncer" section.

Apart from using external tools, if you want to connect your application using pooling internally, use the documentation mentioned in the following list. Explaining the connection of each application is beyond the scope of this book, so we provide Azure documentation that includes step-by-step procedures with sample codes and that makes it easy to implement your applications.

- Use Python to connect and query data: `https://docs.microsoft.com/en-us/azure/postgresql/connect-python`

- Use Node.js to connect and query data: `https://docs.microsoft.com/en-us/azure/postgresql/connect-nodejs`

- Use Java to connect and query data: `https://docs.microsoft.com/cn-us/azure/postgresql/connect-java`

- Use Ruby to connect and query data: `https://docs.microsoft.com/cn-us/azure/postgresql/connect-ruby`

- Use PHP to connect and query data: `https://docs.microsoft.com/en-us/azure/postgresql/connect-php`

- Use .NET (C#) to connect and query data: `https://docs.microsoft.com/en-us/azure/postgresql/connect-csharp`

- Use the Go language to connect and query data: `https://docs.microsoft.com/en-us/azure/postgresql/connect-go`

- If you are using applications based on Java, the most widely used and advanced connection poolers, like C3P0 or DBCP are recommended for production use. See `http://www.mchange.com/projects/c3p0/` and `http://commons.apache.org/proper/commons-dbcp/`.

Summary

The chapter talked about the need for connection pooling and how it saves connection timing during new connections. It covered external connection pooling tools, like PgBouncer and DBCP, and other options for connection pooling, like setting up poolers in application code. In the next chapter, we are going to talk about monitoring. We will cover default monitoring provided by each cloud vendor for cloud servers/virtual machines and PostgreSQL services.

CHAPTER 12

Monitoring Cloud Databases

This chapter covers an introduction to monitoring, including why it is needed and how it helps in a real-time environment. This chapter also covers the monitoring that is included by default with each cloud vendor. The cloud vendors provide different types of monitoring, so you just need to differentiate among them when choosing the right monitoring. This chapter includes virtual machines and PostgreSQL services for each vendor.

Monitoring with Amazon Cloud

Amazon Cloud offers several services that let you build your databases, applications, or your entire infrastructure ecosystem. It is very important to have one service that lets you monitor the ecosystem built using AWS. As we are mainly concerned about PostgreSQL on AWS in this book, we need a service that helps us monitor instances. As you probably guessed, Amazon offers a service called CloudWatch that helps you monitor your RDS and EC2 instances. One of the important features needed in an infrastructure is historic data. CloudWatch Service helps you look into historic data and analyze the resource utilization so you can rightsize your AWS instances. All the data collected by monitoring will be retained for 15 months, even if the instance was terminated. This helps you look back at a certain point in history.

© Baji Shaik, Avinash Vallarapu 2018
B. Shaik and A. Vallarapu, *Beginning PostgreSQL on the Cloud*,
https://doi.org/10.1007/978-1-4842-3447-1_12

Monitoring an RDS or an EC2 Instance

Monitoring is enabled for all the RDS and EC2 instances by default. Statistics or diagnostic data about every RDS Instance is collected every minute or every five minutes as subscribed and made available for CloudWatch.

You may want to enable enhanced monitoring when creating your RDS instance or EC2 instance the first time. See Figure 12-1.

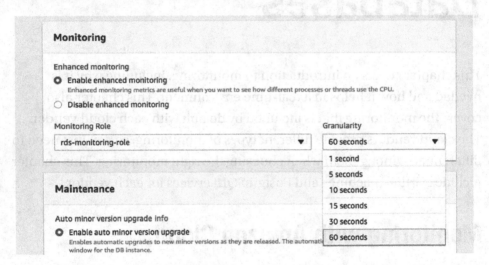

Figure 12-1. *Enabling monitoring*

To access CloudWatch, search for CloudWatch under Services, as shown in Figure 12-2. You can click on CloudWatch once it appears.

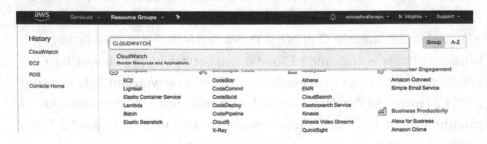

Figure 12-2. *Searching for CloudWatch*

There are two types of monitoring possible using CloudWatch.

- **Basic Monitoring:** This is free. You get seven metrics that are collected every five minutes free of charge. You also get three status check metrics for free.

- **Detailed Monitoring:** Collects the same metrics as the Basic Monitoring option, but at a frequency of every minute.

Here are the steps involved in enabling alarms or alerts for EC2 or RDS instances that are being monitored so that we are notified about service outage.

1. After logging in to the AWS Console, search for EC2 Under Services and click on it.

2. Now click on Instances to see the list of running EC2 instances on your account, as shown in Figure 12-3.

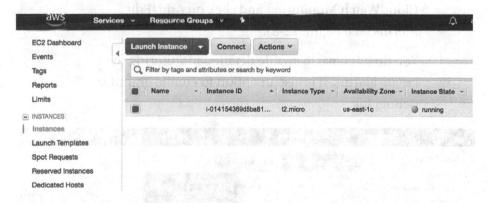

Figure 12-3. *List of running EC2 instances on the account*

3. Choose the instance for which you need to enable detailed monitoring. Click on Actions. Under the Actions dropdown, click on CloudWatch Monitoring and Enable Detailed Monitoring, as shown in Figure 12-4.

337

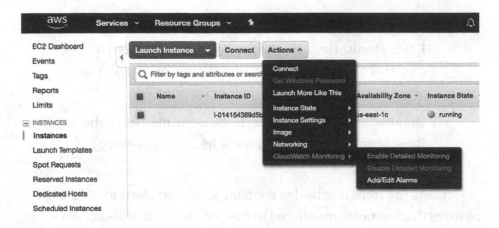

Figure 12-4. *Enable detailed monitoring*

4.   You have now enabled detailed monitoring, so let's see how you can create alarms.

Choose the instance for which you need to create alarms and click on the Actions dropdown. Choose CloudWatch Monitoring and click on Add/Edit Alarms (see Figure 12-5).

You do not have to enable detailed monitoring to create alarms. It is just an option to enable granular debugging.

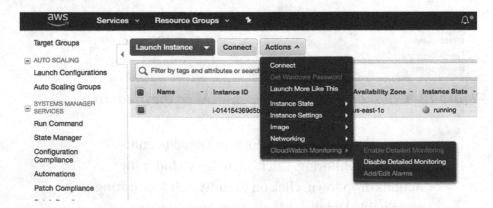

Figure 12-5. *Creating an alarm*

5. Once you click on Add/Edit Alarms, you get an
    option to Create Alarm, as shown in Figure 12-6.
    Click on it to proceed.

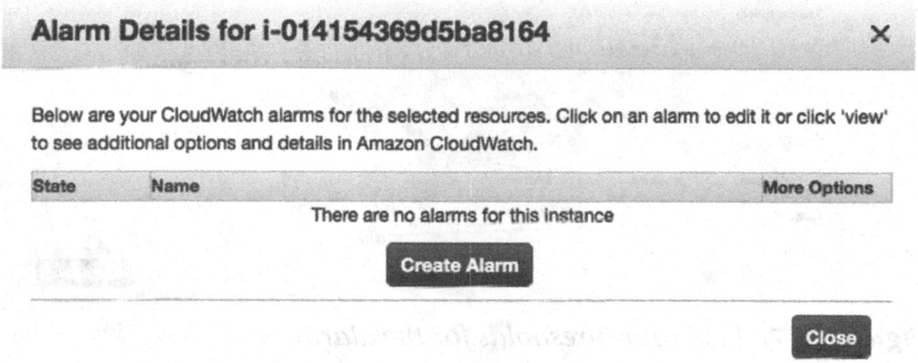

Figure 12-6. *Create an alarm by clicking the button*

6. Now you can choose a title for your alarm and pick
    the recipients who should be notified about it. You
    can choose the metric for which you need an alarm
    or notification to be sent. Alarms are not free. There
    is a charge involved, depending on the alarms you
    create. Choose the threshold at which you should be
    notified and then click on Create Alarm, as shown in
    Figure 12-7.

Create Alarm   ×

You can use CloudWatch alarms to be notified automatically whenever metric data reaches a level you define.

To edit an alarm, first choose whom to notify and then define when the notification should be sent.

☑ **Send a notification to:** CPU_Utilsation   cancel   **CPU Utilization** Percent

   With these recipients: avinash.vallarapu@openscg.com

   ☐ **Take the action:** ○ Recover this instance ⓘ
                           ○ Stop this instance ⓘ
                           ○ Terminate this instance ⓘ
                           ○ Reboot this instance ⓘ

          Whenever: Average ⬍ of CPU Utilization ⬍

                is: >= ⬍ 80   Percent

      For at least: 1   consecutive period(s) of 5 Minutes ⬍

Name of alarm: awsec2-i-014154369d5ba8164-CPU-Utilizatic

                                                    Cancel   **Create Alarm**

Figure 12-7. *Pick your thresholds for the alarm*

7. Here is a list of alarms that you can create
    (see Figure 12-8).

    • CPU Utilization

    • Disk Reads

    • Disk Read Operations

    • Disk Writes

    • Disk Write Operations

    • Network In

    • Network Out

    • Status Check Failed (Any)

    • Status Check Failed (Instance)

    • Status Check Failed (System)

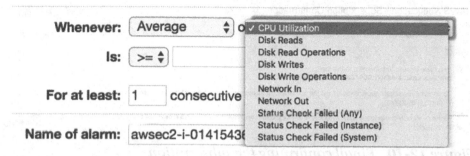

Figure 12-8. *The dropdown list of alarms that you can create*

8.   Once you have created your alarm, you should
     get a popup that says that you need to confirm
     your subscription within three days, as shown in
     Figure 12-9.

Alarm created successfully   ✕

Click the alarm to view additional details and options in Amazon CloudWatch (opens in a new window)
   awsec2-i-014154369d5ba8164-CPU-Utilization

Note: If you created a new SNS topic or added a new email address, each new address will
receive a subscription email that must be confirmed within three days. Notifications will only be
sent to confirmed addresses.

                                                                    Close

Figure 12-9. *Alarm created successfully message*

You should also receive an email that asks you to
confirm the subscription, as shown in Figure 12-10.
Click on Confirm Subscription.

Figure 12-10. Email confirming the subscription

9. If you need to add more alarms, you can search for
    CloudWatch Service and click on Alarms. You'll see
    an option to create an alarm (see Figure 12-11). You
    can then create an alarm for another metric.

*Figure 12-11. You can create more alarms through the CloudWatch
service*

10. There are several metrics available for creating
     alarms. These alarms are not restricted to an EC2
     instance (see Figure 12-12).

You can have alarms created for:

- EBS volumes

- EC2 instances (per-instance and across all instances)

- Logs metrics

- RDS instances (per-database and across all databases)

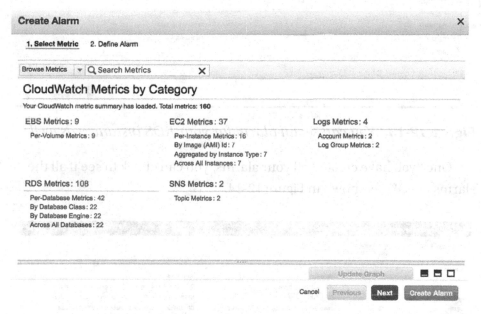

Figure 12-12. *Metrics by category*

As you can see in Figure 12-13, we can set an alarm for your RDS instances as well.

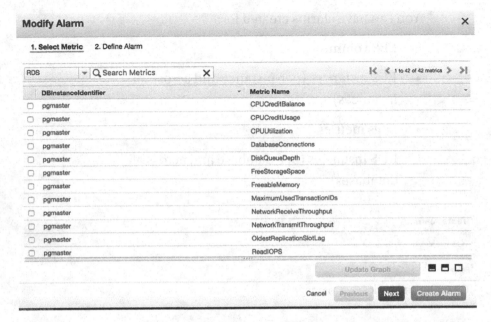

Figure 12-13. *You can set an alarm for your RDS instances as well*

Once you have created all your alarms, you can check to see if all the alarms are OK, as shown in Figure 12-14.

Figure 12-14. *Checking the state of the alarms*

AWS CloudWatch Dashboard

The Amazon Dashboard enables you to view all the resource utilization in a graphical view. These dashboards can be created or customized as you like.

To get a dashboard for your RDS instance, search for RDS service in the AWS Console. Then choose the instance that you need to see in the dashboard. Click on Instance Actions and then click on See Details, as shown in Figure 12-15.

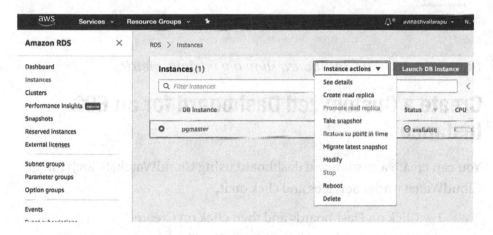

Figure 12-15. *Looking at the instances*

You should see a dashboard that gives you a graphical representation of CPU, disk IO, etc. (see Figure 12-16). You can click on an individual metric and go back to a point in time captured by CloudWatch. Similar information is available for an EC2 instance too.

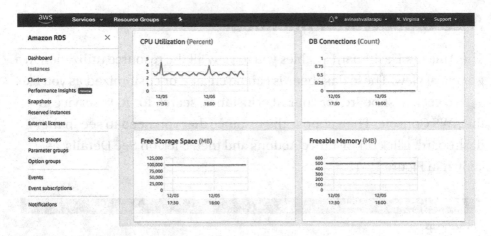

Figure 12-16. *The dashboard showing various metrics*

Create a Customized Dashboard for an EC2 Instance

You can create a customized dashboard using CloudWatch. Search for CloudWatch under Services and click on it.

1. Click on Dashboards and then click on Create Dashboards (see Figure 12-17). You'll see a popup where you choose a dashboard name. Click Next to proceed.

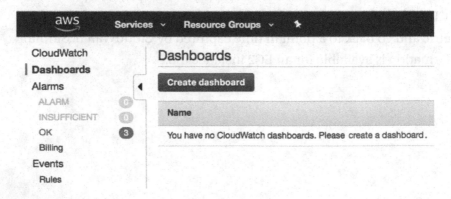

Figure 12-17. *Name the dashboard*

2. You can choose a widget type of your choice, as shown in Figure 12-18. Choose a widget type and click on Configure.

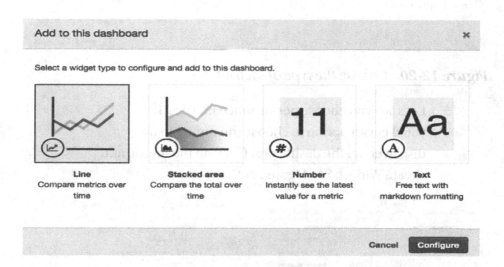

Figure 12-18.   *Choose a widget type for your dashboard*

3. Choose the service for which you need to create a dashboard, as shown in Figure 12-19.

Figure 12-19.   *Choose a service for the dashboard*

4. If you selected EC2, you can select Per-Instance Metrics or Metrics for All, as shown in Figure 12-20.

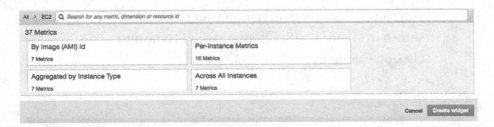

Figure 12-20. *Choose the type of metrics*

> 5. Let's say you choose per-instance metrics. If so, you'll get an option to choose the metric to be displayed on the dashboard. Click on the metric and Create Widget. See Figure 12-21.

Figure 12-21. *Creating the widget*

> 6. Proceed to create as many widgets as you need. You may finally see a dashboard. This dashboard shown in Figure 12-22 includes RDS and EC2 instances. However, it is wise to have multiple dashboards for each instance or instance type.

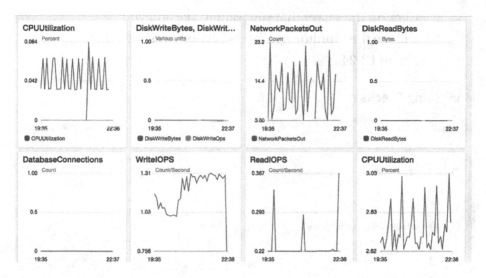

Figure 12-22. *Dashboard with RDS and EC2 instances*

Monitoring for Rackspace Cloud Servers

As all other venders, Rackspace provides monitoring for Rackspace Cloud servers by default. Let's look at the metrics it provides as part of the default monitoring service.

1. On the Rackspace portal, you can see your server created (see Figure 12-23). The Monitoring column shows green dots, which indicates monitoring of each metric.

Figure 12-23. *The Rackspace portal, with monitoring shown*

2. Click on the server that you want to see and you
    will see the Monitoring Checks section, as shown in
    Figure 12-24.

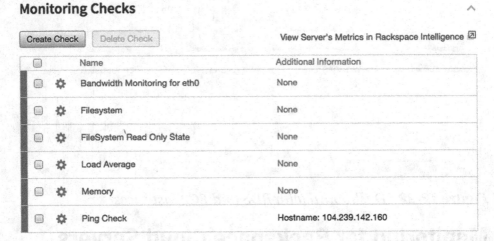

Figure 12-24. *Monitoring checks section*

3. If you click on each metric, you will see details with
    graphs. See Figure 12-25.

Bandwidth Monitoring for eth0

Check Details

Status	**Available** Check is working and reporting data
Parent Entity	Server-01
Check Type	Network
Parameters	Period: 60 Seconds ✐
	Timeout after: 30 Seconds

Network Activity View Check's Metrics in Rackspace Intelligence 🖾

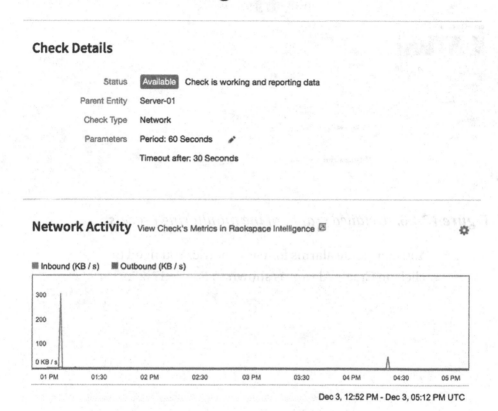

Dec 3, 12:52 PM - Dec 3, 05:12 PM UTC

Figure 12-25. *Graphs of the monitoring process*

4. If you click on View Check's Metrics in Rackspace Intelligence, you can some detailed graphs if you scroll down. See Figure 12-26.

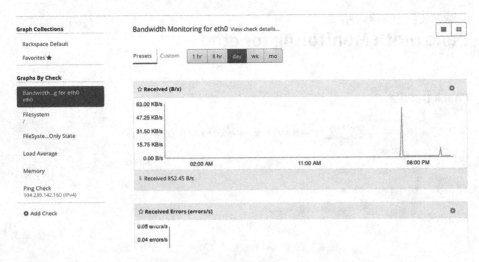

Figure 12-26. *Detailed graphs of the monitoring process*

5. You can create alarms for each metric. You need to
    click on Create Alarm, as shown in Figure 12-27.

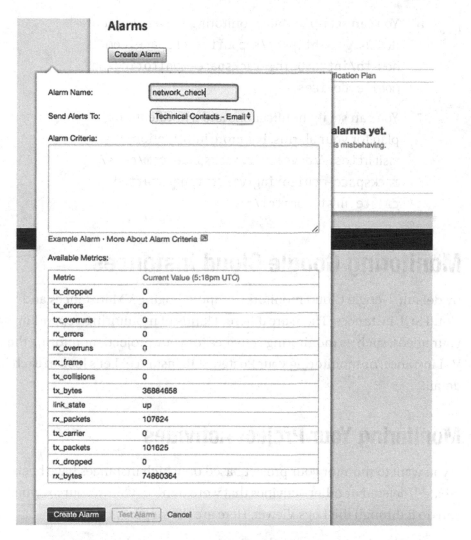

Figure 12-27. *You can create alarms for each metric*

You can find more about alarms at `https://`
`developer.rackspace.com/docs/rackspace-`
`monitoring/v1/tech-ref-info/alert-triggers-`
`and-alarms`.

6. You can set up mobile monitoring as well. For more details, go to `https://support.rackspace.com/how-to/introducing-rackspace-monitoring-on-mobile-devices`.

7. You can set up notifications and a notifications plan for your alarms. For more information, visit `https://developer.rackspace.com/docs/rackspace-monitoring/v1/getting-started/create-first-monitor/`.

Monitoring Google Cloud Instances

By default, Google Cloud monitors Compute Engine VM instances and cloud SQL instances. There are different kinds of monitoring depending on your needs, such as monitoring activities for your project, monitoring the VM instance, or monitoring your PostgreSQL instance. Let's look at each in detail.

Monitoring Your Project Activities

If you want to monitor your project based on which instances have been created/deleted or other activities that were done to your resources, you can do it through the Logs Viewer. Here are the steps:

1. Log in to your console using your credentials. `https://console.cloud.google.com`

2. Select Logging from the StackDriver section on the left panel, as shown in Figure 12-28.

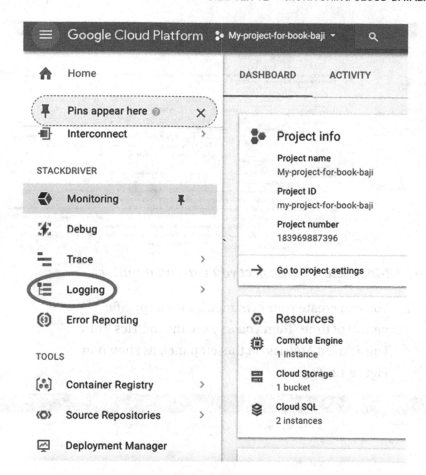

Figure 12-28. *Choose Logging*

3. Select the project that you want to monitor. You will
   see the activities performed under that project. See
   Figure 12-29.

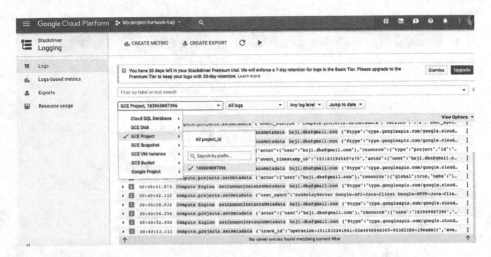

Figure 12-29. *Select the project you want to monitor*

4. You can create your own metrics for a specific period of time. Then you can see the metrics from Logs-Based Metrics on the left panel, as shown in Figure 12-30.

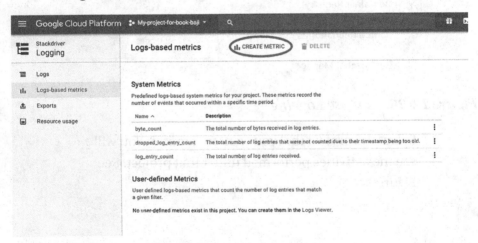

Figure 12-30. *Create your own metrics here*

5. Logging usage can be viewed from the Resource Usage tab on left panel of the same page.

Monitoring VM Instances

You can see hardware monitoring of VM instances, which is provided by default.

1. Log in to the console at `https://console.cloud.google.com`.

2. Select VM Instances from Compute Engine on the left panel.

3. Click on the instance that you want to monitor. You will see nice graphs of monitoring, as shown in Figure 12-31.

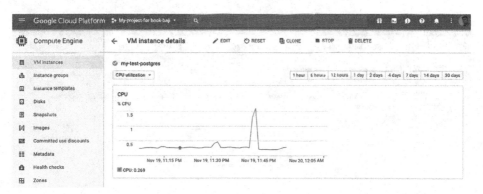

Figure 12-31. *Monitoring graphs*

4. You can see these metrics in the monitoring report:

   - CPU utilization

   - Disk bytes

   - Disk operations

   - Network bytes

   - Network packets

5. You can see graphs captured for 30 days.

Monitoring PostgreSQL Instances

You do not need to configure monitoring for PostgreSQL instances on Google Cloud, as it provides monitoring of some metrics by default. Let's look at the monitoring it provides.

1. Log in to the console at `https://console.cloud.google.com`.

2. Select SQL from the left panel.

3. Select the instance that you want to see monitoring and you will see the monitoring graphs in the Overview tab, as shown in Figure 12-32.

Figure 12-32. *The monitoring graphs in the Overview tab*

4. This provides operating system and database metrics. Figure 12-33 shows the metrics captured for the PostgreSQL instance.

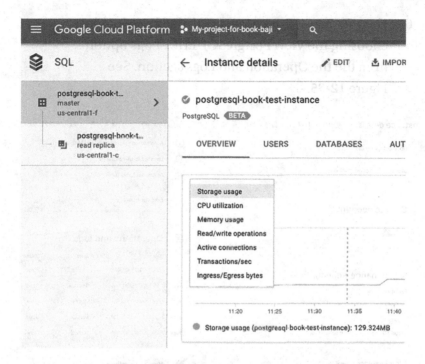

Figure 12-33. *Metrics captured for the PostgreSQL instance*

5. If you click on the Operations tab on the same page, you can see the operations performed for particular instances, such as shown in Figure 12-34.

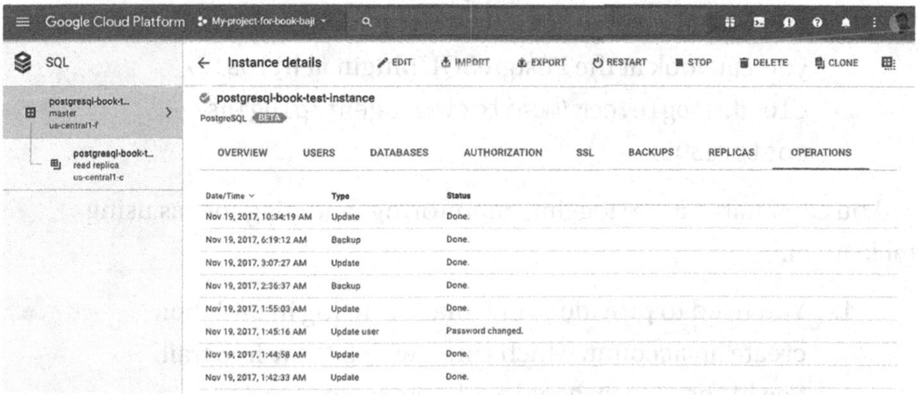

Figure 12-34. *Operations for particular instances*

6. You can also see the PostgreSQL database logs by choosing the View PostgreSQL Error Logs option from the the Operation and Logs section. See Figure 12-35.

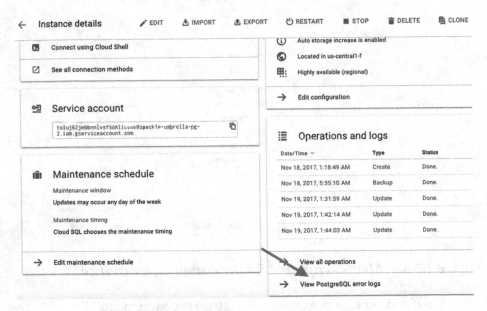

Figure 12-35. *Viewing the PostgreSQL database logs*

7. If you want to monitor more metrics of PostgreSQL apart from the metrics that are provided by default, you can look at the PostgreSQL plugin at `https://cloud.google.com/monitoring/agent/plugins/postgreSQL`.

You can enable more logging, monitoring, and diagnostics using StackDriver.

1. You need to provide your Gmail ID to log in and then create an account, which come with 30-day free trail. See `https://app.google.stackdriver.com/`.

2. Add a project that you want to monitor.

3. A typical StackDriver window is shown in Figure 12-36.

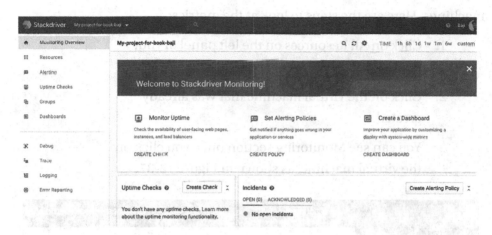

Figure 12-36. *Typical StackDriver window*

4. You can set up alerting policies, monitor uptime of applications and instances, and more.

Monitoring Azure Cloud Instances

As with all other venders, Microsoft Azure provides monitoring by default. This section looks at how monitoring works on these services.

- Virtual machines

- Azure Database for PostgreSQL

Virtual Machines

Let's look at the monitoring that's provided by default for Azure virtual machines. Here are the steps to look at the metrics:

1. Click on All Resources on the left panel of your Azure Portal.

2. Click on the virtual machine that was already created.

3. You can see Monitoring section once you click on the virtual machine, as shown in Figure 12-37.

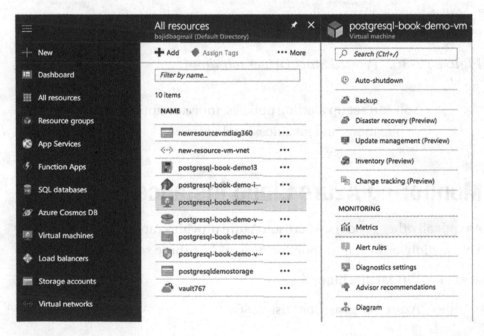

Figure 12-37. *Monitoring section of the Azure Portal*

4. If you click on Metrics under the Monitoring section, you can see the list of metrics that you can monitor, as shown in Figure 12-38.

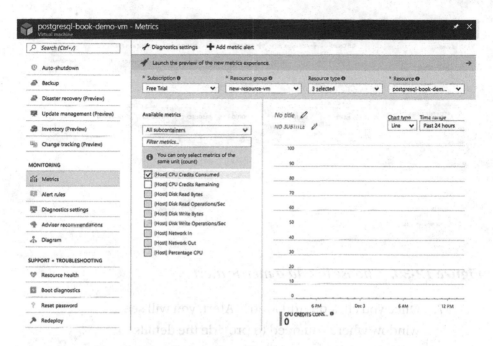

Figure 12-38. *Metrics that you can monitor*

5. You can select the metric that you want to monitor.
    Be sure to select the metric of same unit.

6. You can create alerts on each metric. For that, you
    need to click on Alert Rules on the same page.
    Then click on Add Metric Alert, as highlighted in
    Figure 12-39.

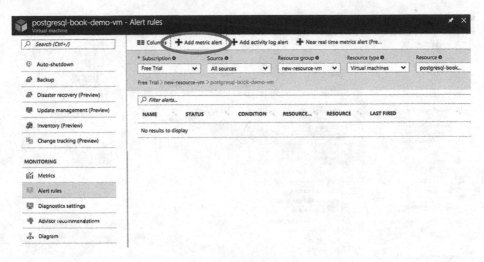

Figure 12-39. Choose to add a metric alert

7.   Once you click on Add Metric Alert, you will see a
      window where you need to provide the details to
      create an alert on a metric. See Figures 12-40
      and 12-41.

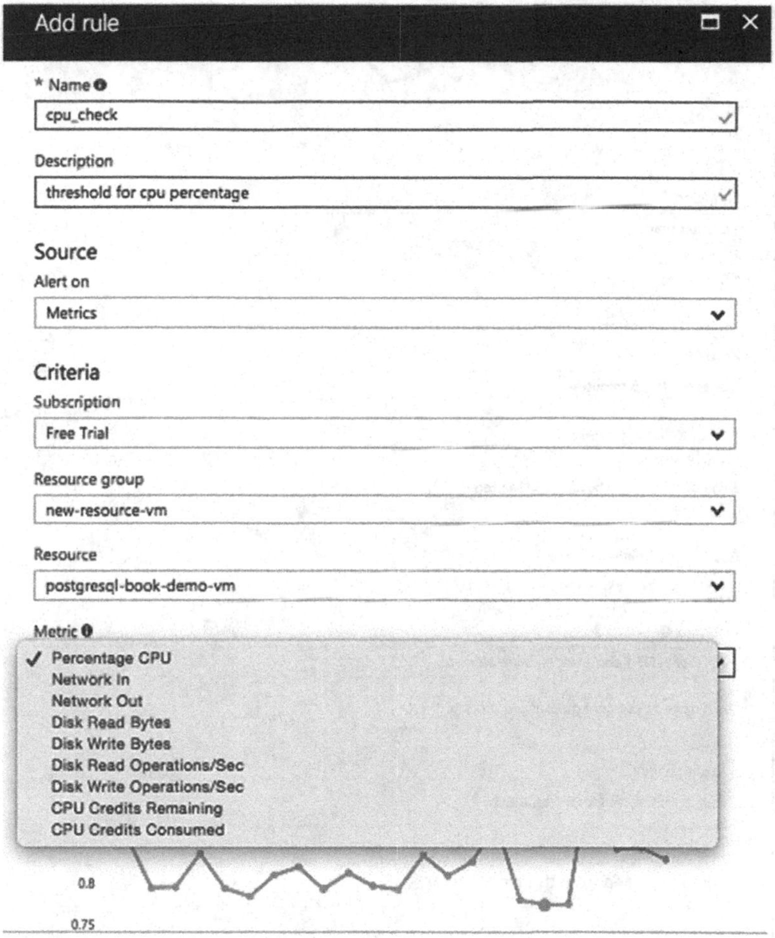

Figure 12-40. *Provide details to create the alert on a metric*

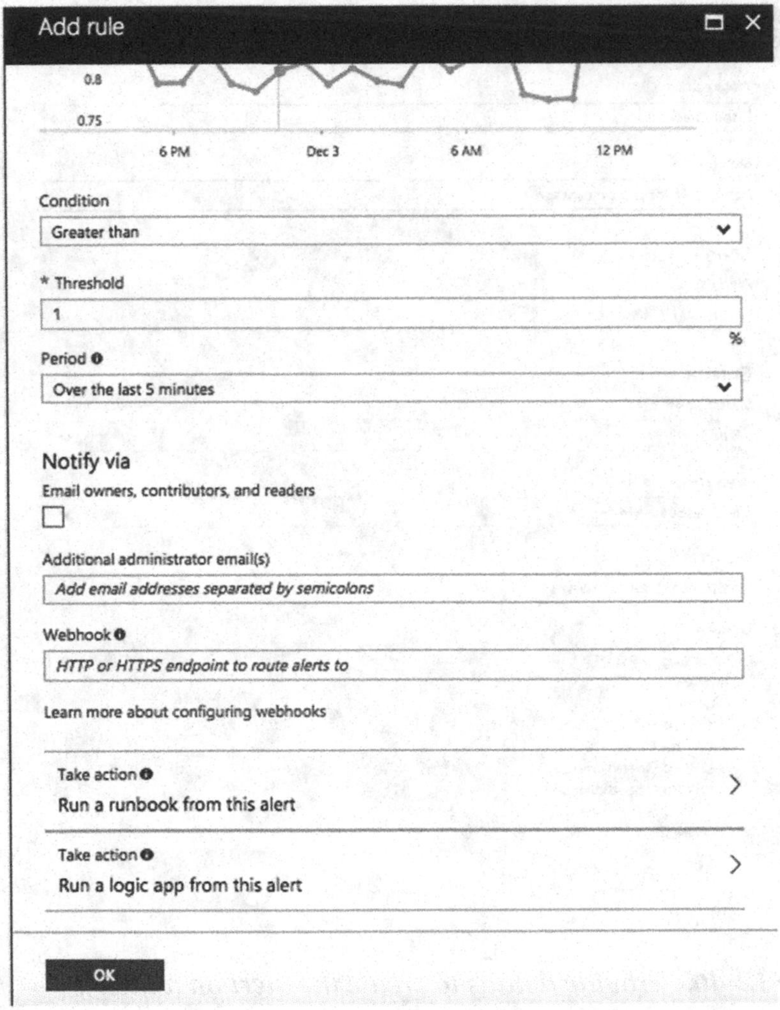

Add rule ☐ ✕

0.8			
0.75			
6 PM	Dec 3	6 AM	12 PM

Condition

> Greater than   ⌄

* Threshold

> 1

                                                            %

Period ❶

> Over the last 5 minutes   ⌄

Notify via

Email owners, contributors, and readers

☐

Additional administrator email(s)

> *Add email addresses separated by semicolons*

Webhook ❶

> *HTTP or HTTPS endpoint to route alerts to*

Learn more about configuring webhooks

Take action ❶   >
Run a runbook from this alert

Take action ❶   >
Run a logic app from this alert

OK

Figure 12-41. *Set up the alert*

Name: Specify a name to identify this rule

Description: Describe the rule

Subscription: Select the subscription

Resource group: Select the resource group that you want to create an alert on

Resource: Select the resource for creating the alert

Metric: Select the metric that you want this alert rule to monitor

Condition: Condition for the alert

Threshold: Threshold to send the alert

Period: Select a time span during which to monitor the metric data specified by this alert rule

Webhook: Choose the HTTP or HTTPs endpoint that will route the Azure alerts to other notification channels

Take action: Select an automation runbook to run each time the alert is triggered (see Figure 12-42)

Figure 12-42. *Select an automation runbook*

8. You can also look at advisor recommendations from Azure to set up metrics and alerts, as shown in Figure 12-43.

Figure 12-43. *Advisor recommendations from Azure*

Azure Database for PostgreSQL

Azure provides default monitoring for Azure database for PostgreSQL as well. Here are the steps:

1. Select the PostgreSQL instance and select Metrics from the Monitoring section. You will see the OS metrics, as shown in Figure 12-44.

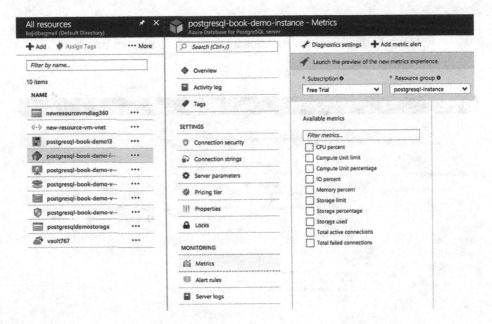

Figure 12-44. *Viewing the OS metrics*

2. You can also look at the Activity Log, where
    you'll see Log Analytics and Operation Logs. See
    Figure 12-45.

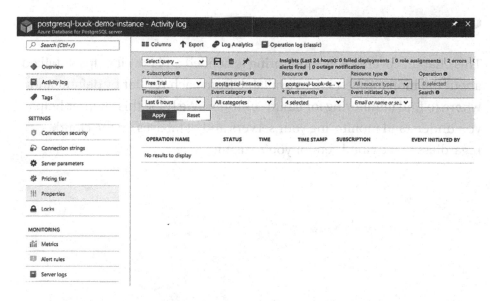

Figure 12-45. *The Activity Log shows log analytics and operation logs*

    3.   Check the PostgreSQL database logs from the Server
        Log option, as shown in Figure 12-46.

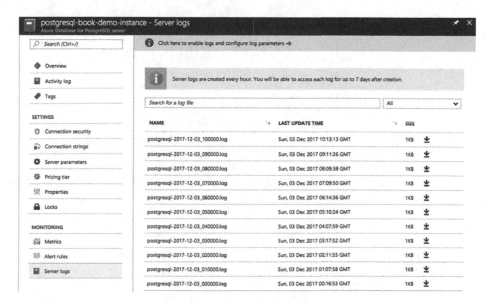

Figure 12-46. *PostgreSQL database logs*

Summary

This chapter covered why monitoring is needed and how it helps. It talked about the monitoring services available from each vendor by default and where to find monitoring for cloud solutions. We hope this chapter helps you understand monitoring your servers and databases on the cloud, regardless of the cloud vendor you're using.

Index

A

Accelerated computing instances
F1, 91
G3, 91
P3 and P2, 89–91
Amazon
AWS (*see* Amazon Web Services
(AWS))
EC2, 17–18
network security, 18
RDS, 16–17
Amazon Cloud
CloudWatch, 335
master key creation, Servers
admin user, choosing, 296
alias and description, 296
AWS Services Console, 294
create Key button, 295
encryption keys, 295
IAM users and roles, 297
monitoring RDS/EC2 instance
basic monitoring, 337
detailed monitoring, 337
enable enhanced
monitoring, 336
enabling alarms/alerts, 337,
339, 341–344
search for CloudWatch, 336

Amazon Web Services (AWS)
availability zones, 63–64
backing up
EC2 instance, 239–244
RDS instance, 236–238
CloudWatch dashboard,
345–346
connection pooling, 328–329
create account, 65–67
defined, 16
EC2 (*see* Elastic Compute Cloud
(EC2), Amazon)
read replicas, 274–278
RDS (*see* Relational Database
Service (RDS))
ANSI C, 33
AUTOVACUUM launcher process,
41
Autovacuum settings, 61
Availability zones (AZ), 63–64
AWS, *see* Amazon Web Services
(AWS)
Azure
connection pooling, 332–333
Database, 22
offers, 22
PostgreSQL (*see* PostgreSQL
software)

Azure (*cont.*)
  storage, 188
  subscription, 22
  virtual machine (*see* Virtual
    machines)
Azure Cloud Services, 305–307

B

Background writer settings, 60
Binary installation, 47
Blob storage, 264
  add new storage, 266–268
  add to create storage, 265
Buckets, 254–257
Burstable performance instances,
  82

C

CHECKPOINTER process, 40
Cloud
  -based cost model, 15
  computing
    pros and cons, 12–13
    vs. on-premise computing,
      12–14
    migrating to, 24–28
Cloud block storage
  Attach Volume option, 129–132
  block storage volume, 125, 128
  volume details and actions, 128
Cloud security
  Compute Engine, 220

Microsoft Azure Security,
  227–228
SQL Database, 232–234
SSH Keys, 226–227
VM instances, 220, 226
VM machines, 228, 230–232
Cloud SQL encryption
  cloud proxy, 305
  SSL, 304
CloudWatch, 335–337, 345–346
Commit LOG (CLOG)
  buffers, 39
Compute Engine
  adding a member, 221–222
  available roles, 223–224
  creation, 140
  dashboard, 139
  features, 138, 225
  Google data centers, 137
  IAM console, 221
  OS, 143
  PostgreSQL installation,
    148–150
  SSH keys, 148
  virtual machine, 141–142,
    145–146
  VM security options, 144
Compute Optimized instances,
  84–86
Connection pooling
  AWS (*see* Amazon Web Services
    (AWS)
  Azure, 332–333
  cost and time consuming, 311

external connection poolers,
312
forking, 310–311
Google Cloud, 330, 332
PgBouncer (*see* PgBouncer)
Rackspace, 330

D

Data at rest, 293
Databases as a service (DBaaS)
in business, 2–3
deliver production, 2
enabling, 1–2
features
administration, 9
high availability, 10
monitoring tools, 10
provisioning
mechanisms, 7–9
scalability, 11
security, 11
limitations, 8
organization
cloud vendors, 6
collaboration with other
team, 6
durable database, 4
fast-performing database, 4
high availability features, 6
horizontal scaling, 5
no single point of failures, 6
redundant, 4
reliability, 4

secured database
environment, 3–4
testing, 2
Data security model, 22
Deployment model, 266

E

Elastic Compute Cloud (EC2),
Amazon, 278–281
backup instance, 239–244
create customized dashboard,
346–348
create instance
Add Storage option, 97–98
add tag, 98
choose AMI, 95
choose instance type, 96
configure instance
details, 97
configuring security
groups, 99
create key pair, 100
EC2 dashboard, 94
.pem file, 101–102
create PostgreSQL instance,
102–104
dedicated hosts, 81
dedicated instance, 81
elastic GPUs
accelerated computing,
89–91
compute optimized, 84–86
M3 instances, 83

Elastic Compute Cloud (EC2),
    Amazon (*cont.*)
    M4 instances, 83
    R3 instances, 89
    R4 instances, 88
    storage optimized instances,
      92–94
    T2 instances, 82
    X1e instances, 86
    X1 instances, 87
  instances, 79
  IOPS, 17
  RIs, 80
  spot instances, 79
Encryption
  Amazon Cloud Servers
    EC2 instances, 299–300
    enabling, RDS instance,
      297–299
    master key creation, 294
  Azure Cloud Services, 305–307
  cloud SQL, 304–305
  Google cloud storage, 304
  rackspace cloud servers, 301–303

F

Fast-performing database, 4
Forking, 310–311

G

General purpose (SSD) storage
    (gp2), 70
Google Cloud

connection pooling, 330, 332
  failover, 285
  features, 19
  Google Compute
    Engine, 19–20
  high availability, 283–284
  load balancing, 21
  monitoring instances
    PostgreSQL, 358–361
    project activities, 354–356
    VM, 357
  platform services, 20–21
  read replica, 286–288
  security model, 19
  SQL, 153
  using snapshot option,
    persistent disk, 250–251,
    253–254
  virtual machine, 20
Google Cloud Storage (GCS)
  Cloud SQL, 153
  create buckets and upload files,
    255–257
  features, 152
  PostgreSQL, 153–156
  storage classes, 151–152
Google Compute Engine, 19
Google Could Platforms (GCP)
  application servers/web
    servers, 133
  database servers, 134
  Google Cloud Console, 135–136
  project deletion, 136–137
  project quota, 134

H

High availability cloud, *see* Replication
High availability features, 6

I, J

IaaS, *see* Infrastructure as a Service (IaaS)
Identity and access management (IAM)
    access-level privileges, 200
    AWS, 201–203, 205
    multi-factor
        authentication, 200
    policy document, 201
    types of access, 200
    user management, 199
Infrastructure as a Service (IaaS)
    cloud vendors, 23
    in organizations, 23
    subscribe, 24

K

Key Management Services (KMS), 294

L

Live Migration, Google, 20
Logical replication, 272

M

Memory optimized instances
    R3, 89
    R4, 88
    X1, 87
    X1e, 86–87
Microsoft Azure
    add new storage, 266–268
    add to create storage, 265
    blob storage, 264
    database, 22
    database for PostgreSQL, 269
    data security model, 22
    monitoring instances
        database for PostgreSQL, 369–371
        VM, 362–364, 367, 369
    offers, 22
    subscription, 22
    virtual machines, backup on
        backup policy, 262, 264
        Backup tab, 260–261
        options for backing up, 261
        vaults, 261
Microsoft Azure Security, 227–228
Multi-regional storage classes, 151
Multi-Version Concurrency Control (MVCC), 35

N

Nearline and Coldline storage classes, 151

O

One-click installers, 49
On-premise computing
    cost model, 15
    pros and cons, 13–14

P

PgBouncer
    configuration, 321–322, 324–326
    high availability, 327
    installation
        file creation, 318–320
        PostgreSQL 9.6, 316–318
    memory, 314
    session pooling, 313
    statement pooling, 314
    transaction pooling, 313
pgPulse tools, 29
plProfiler Console, 150
Point-in-time recovery (PITR), 154
PostgreSQL service instance
    advantages, 153–154
    authorizing networks, 165–166
    choose, database engine, 160
    client-server protocol, 155
    Cloud SQL flags, 166
    configuration options,
        161–162, 164
    creation, 157–159
    enabling auto backups, 164
    features, 154
    Google Cloud Console, 157

    Google Cloud Dashboard, 157
    Google Cloud SQL, 155
    Quickstart for Cloud SQL, 159
    set maintenance mode, 167
    types, 155
PostgreSQL software, 4, 288–289
    Amazon (*see* Amazon)
    architecture, 37
    ARCHIVER process, 41
    AUTOVACUUM launcher
        process, 41
    autovacuum settings, 61
    availability, 35
    Azure database, 189–190,
        369–371
    background writer settings, 60
    back up Cloud SQL, 258–259
    CHECKPOINTER process, 40
    cluster, 46
    configuration file, 53
    connection settings, 54
    creation, 190–192, 194–196
    environment variables, 49
    extensions, 30
    Google Cloud (*see* Google
        Cloud)
    installation
        binary, 47
        one-click installers, 49
        RPM, 48
        source, 44–46
    limitations, 36
    log, 57–59
    LOGGING COLLECTOR, 41

memory settings, 55

Microsoft Azure (*see* Microsoft Azure)

migrating to cloud, 24–28

monitoring instances on Google Cloud, 358–361

MVCC, 35

parameters, 4

PGDATA, 42–44

portability, 33

query planner settings, 56

Rackspace (*see* Rackspace)

reliability, 34

scalability, 34

secure, 34–35

security and authentication settings, 55

service startup on Linux, 50–51, 53

shared memory
    CLOG buffers, 39
    lock space, 39
    shared_buffers, 39
    temp buffers, 39
    WAL buffers, 39

SLRU, 40

STATS COLLECTOR process, 41

supports, 35

tools, 29–30

vacuum cost settings, 60

WAL, 36

WAL WRITER process, 41

write ahead log settings, 56–57

WRITER process, 40

Provisioned IOPS (SSD) Storage, 70

Q

Query planner settings, 56

R

Rackspace
  backups on cloud
    check backup details, 249
    check box, 245
    choose folder, 249
    Configure Backup page, 247–248
    create/restore/delete, 245
    manage backups, 245
    schedule, 246–247
  cloud block storage (*see* Cloud block storage)
  cloud servers, 301–303, 349, 351–354
  connection pooling, 330
  Managed Cloud, 107
  Managed Hosting
    dedicated server, 111, 113–117
    portal dashboard, 108
    PostgreSQL, 121–124
    profile settings, 108–109
    virtual server, 117–120
    VMWare, 110

Rackspace (*cont.*)
  offers, 18
  replication and high
      availability, 281
  supports, 18
Rackspace cloud security
  Rackspace account
      barcode, 216
      identity provider, 218
      mobile app, 214
      My Profile & Settings, 213
      security settings, 213
      user management, 217
      user permissions, 217
  VM, 218–219
Regional storage classes, 151
Relational Database Service (RDS)
  backing up instance, 236–238
  create PostgreSQL instance
      advanced settings
          page, 75, 77
      backups, 77–79
      choose database name and
          port, 77
      correct range for entry, 74
      launch DB instance, 71
      maintenance, 78–79
      monitoring, 77, 79
      select engine, 72
      select use case, 72–73
      settings, 75
  enables, 68
  gp2, 70
  offers, 68

Provisioned IOPS (SSD)
      Storage, 70
  subnet groups, 207–211
  VPC, 206
Replication
  AWS (*see* Amazon Web
      Services (AWS))
  Azure services (*see* Azure)
  Google Cloud (*see* Google
      Cloud)
  logical, 272
  PostgreSQL, 272
  Rackspace cloud, 281
  streaming, 272
Reserved Instances (RIs), 80
RPM installation, 48

S

sar tools, 29
Session pooling, 313
Single sign-on (SSO), 200
SLRU system, 40
Snapshot option, 250–251,
      253–254
Statement
      pooling, 314
STATS COLLECTOR
      process, 41
Storage optimized instances
      dense-storage (D2), 94
      high I/O (I3), 92–93
Streaming replication, 272
Subnet, 206

T, U

Transaction pooling, 313

V

Vacuum cost settings, 60
Virtual machines, 289–290
  account creation, 171
  backup on
    backup policy, 262, 264
    Backup tab, 260–261
    options for backing
     up, 261
    vaults, 261
  creation
    configuration settings,
     175–176
    data and metrics, 183–184
    deployment process,
     182–183

    extensions section, 181–182
    features, 179–180
    locations, 177
    operating systems, 174
    size, 178
  Linux, 184–185
  PostgreSQL, 185–187
  Start Free, 171
Virtual Private Cloud (VPC), 206

W

WAL WRITER process, 41
Write Ahead Logging (WAL), 36
Write ahead log settings, 56–57
WRITER process, 40

X, Y, Z

X1e instances, 86

Get the eBook for only $5!

Why limit yourself?

With most of our titles available in both PDF and ePUB format, you can access your content wherever and however you wish—on your PC, phone, tablet, or reader.

Since you've purchased this print book, we are happy to offer you the eBook for just $5.

To learn more, go to http://www.apress.com/companion or contact support@apress.com.

Apress®

Printed in the United States
By Bookmasters